The smart *Scene*

Written by Julie Saltmarsh and Tom Crawford
Photography by Tom Crawford
Design and layout by Julie Saltmarsh

Smart – *adj.* 1 well groomed, neat.
2 brightly coloured, newly painted, etc.
3 stylish, fashionable. 4 clever, ingenious,
quickwitted. 5 quick, brisk.

The Pocket Oxford Dictionary

Contents

First published 2007

Tempus Publishing Ltd
The Mill, Brimscombe Port
Stroud, Gloucestershire GL5 2QG
www.tempus-publishing.com

British Library Cataloguing in Publication Data.
A catalogue record for this book is available from the British Library.

ISBN 978 0 7524 4218 1

Typesetting, design and origination by Tempus Publishing.
Printed in Great Britain

1 Introduction

Adorable...that seems a good way in which to start, because to us, that is what **smart** cars are...completely adorable. That might sound rather peculiar as it isn't something that cars are normally categorised as. Racy, sexy, testosterone-enhancing maybe, but not adorable! There is something about their cute, compact design that just appeals to our paternal nature, as they are very adept at beguiling us into caring for them as if they were a child or a pet. How many cars make you feel like that! They hypnotise you into wanting to lavish time and hard earned cash on them, in an effort to enhance their already individual appeal. They cajole you into wanting to meet other owners so that they can preen and pose like shiny jewels in a grey old world. They persuade you to drive long distances together with other **smarts** in order to show the world how cute they are...and they are! They definitely have an inherent herding gene that is for sure. Contrary to popular myth, up until 2005 when the electric version was produced, **smarts** DID NOT need to be plugged in at the mains, which must have been the most frequently asked question from middle-aged gentlemen one met at petrol stations. Nor do **smarts** come as a 'flat-pack' from a certain brand of Swedish furniture store or require elastic bands for propulsion! In general, the **smart**, to the untrained eye, must seem a rather confusing vehicle. Outside it is small, but inside it is so roomy and airy, one could be mistaken for sitting inside a car of twice the length. It looks like it should be wound up by a key, but in fact it masks a powerful, efficient engine, no bigger than a generously sized handbag, which *Miss Polkadot* has in plenty, and only *s2trash* would admit owning in the privacy of his own cave! Some **smarts**, of course, can confuse the onlooker even more so, the **wolf-in-sheep's-clothing** variety. These little cuties have had some serious modifications done, including big re-maps and specialist exhaust systems. The look of total surprise by serious sports car owners when the **w-i-s-c** goes hurtling past them is something to behold!

We decided to write this book, because we are both passionate about these cars, and we wanted to share with you just how much this bijou box of tricks on wheels can cause so many people to have so much fun. Not since the VW Beetle craze of the sixties in the USA, or the Mini in the UK, has a car stirred such emotions. We hope to give you an insight as owners, into the world of **smarts.** The events, the modifying, the club scene and all that has happened since the tiny French car first hit our green and pleasant land in 1998.

Throughout this book, which contains photographs of the cars from one of the largest personal collections in the UK, many that have never been shown before, we will often refer to individuals by the users-names that they adopt on the website based **smart** clubs. Very often, as with their cars, they are just plain bizarre, amusing and very unique – a bit like ours really!

So, pour yourself a drop of your favourite poison and sit back and read, and see why there are just so many of us buzzing the highways of the UK.

Owning a **smart** has certainly changed our lives, we hope our book brightens yours.

2 All about us

We are Tom Crawford (*s2trash*) and Julie Saltmarsh (*Miss Polkadot*). Our first meeting was on the London to Brighton **smart** Car Run in September 2003, organised by thesmartclub, which at the time, was the largest website based **smart** car club around. Tom was taking pictures for Smartimes magazine and Jules had her car entered in the 'Zaniest Smart' competition, which she happened to win. It wasn't until early the following year when Jules tried to track Tom down, knowing that he had taken some photographs of her at the L2B, that we got chatting on the Funkysmart chat room, and discovered Tom had been a professional photographer and Jules a graphic designer. Tom had done work for the likes of the Times, British Airways, and had exhibited in and around London. Jules had done work for such clients as Marks & Spencer's and Britvic, as well as being a highly talented bespoke glass painter, sculptor and member of The Guild of Essex Craftsmen. With this amount of talent between us, it lead us to hit on the idea of producing a Smart Car Calendar for 2005. No one else had attempted one previously and with both of us having the perfect credentials for the job we went for it. The work had us attending many meets together and so we decided to form Spotty Badger Productions. We also started to write articles, as well as taking photographs for Smartimes, which took us to even more events. We then went on to start organising our own, including the amazingly daft annual M25 Run.

This book only came about due to another chance meeting on the Funkysmart chat room with *Messerschmitt_owner* (Campbell McCutcheon), himself the owner of a yellow roadster light.

Campbell works for the book publishers **Tempus Publishing** and approached us with the mad idea of producing this book. As the saying goes – the rest is spotty history!

Tom – s2trash

My history with cars was unremarkable, and a tad boring, until I brought a **smart**. The first car I ever owned was a 1968 Mini, which managed to keep working for five whole minutes before dying on me after leaving the house where I bought it. Although they tended to be a tad unreliable, I still loved Minis and treated myself to an 8 month old 'Mayfair'. Hours of fun were spent acting out scenes from the 'Italian Job' in and around London before such things as speed cameras and congestion charges were ever thought of. Like most good things, this came to and end with the news that there was going be the patter of tiny feet very soon (webbed if they were my genes), and the road to four-wheel blandness and fatherhood loomed. Now, after the birth of my son and several mundane cars later, **smarts** suddenly appeared on the scene, and naturally they grabbed my attention instantly. The first one I ever saw was on a TV programme, which could have been 'London Tonight', and there was this funny looking French car in a garage just up from Swiss Cottage. The gentleman being interviewed was extolling the virtues of these wonderful little cars, and how there were not any official UK importers yet. He went on to explain that a small batch had faulty rear screens caused by the rear window heaters, which made them go bang. Time-wise this must have been the latter part of 1998. The second sighting was Christmas Eve 2000 in Rye, East Sussex.

Tools of the trade

...pretending to be a hearse

s2trash

There, parked on a cobbled lane, in black with blue panels, sat a left hand drive **smart**. My family, wanting more urgent things like hot drinks and food, dragged me away screaming like a four year old because having seen one in the flesh I now wanted one, and they thought I'd finally lost the plot. The third sighting was during the Summer of 2001, at an event called 'The Bexhill 100', a locally organised car show. Walking along the promenade with 99 ice cream cornet in my hand, I saw two **smarts** parked up with their doors open. Wondering over, trying to look semi-uninterested around the sales man, I stuck my head in a yellow and black pulse. "Get in sir, look around". Rats he had spotted me, but the invitation was too good to miss and the wife and I jumped in. That was it, I *really* wanted one now. He explained about the cars and that he had imported seven into the UK. As I sat there day dreaming about being the next proud owner of one, I got brought back to reality with a crash, something I find women most adept at. "How would we manage with a two seater car?" came the most obvious remark. My first answer of "well you can always walk" was greeted with a swift slap round the chops, and I had to admit that having a second car as a plaything wasn't really on the list of must haves at that precise moment in time.

Now once in a while the god you pray to will smile sweetly on you and allow dreams to come true. The wife gave up her job in London and needed her own car for her new job closer to home. The moment she told me I must admit I couldn't help but think **smart**, **smart**, **smart**…

Like a message from the heavens, I just happened to be driving past Mercedes of Eastbourne and low and behold, there were **smarts** on the forecourt! The sun sent heavenly rays of light onto them showing me the way to motoring utopia. Ok, it was cold, overcast and raining, but with a swing of the wheel and one mega u-turn, I was standing in the show room like a kid in a sweetshop. Having old clothes on at the time, I was viewed up and down with suspicion, a normal occurrence some say, but I wasn't about to rob the till or nick a car, indeed I wanted to purchase one of their fine cars. When I explained it was the **smart** I was after and not a Mercedes, they relaxed and moved me out of view of their more upmarket customers. I think the test drive was to humour me, but I managed to scare the poor sales girl half to death with gear changes at 5000 rpm and doing 45mph in a 30mph zone, with a grin on my face like a man possessed by demons. Back at the dealership and allowing time for the sales girl to regain composure, she said "I take it Sir liked the car?" "Not arf – I'll have one". And all without telling the wife! I am not gong to bore you with the trials and tribulations of ordering my **smart**, but the dealership at Eastbourne only had cars on loan from Smart of Gatwick and couldn't tell me what options were available and so I was unable to place my order. They were also waiting to see if they would become a **smart** dealer themselves. I shall now skip the really boring and long winded bit and move on two weeks. It is a Monday morning and I am at the Southeast Smart Centre, Sevenoaks, Kent. After another test drive it was time to sit down over a coffee and place that order. I had made up my mind that I did not want the glass roof, as I have never been a fan of air-conditioning and it would be a furnace in the summer. It had to be an all black car as well. The salesman told me that in that case it had to be a pure. That sounded ok to me, as it was the cheapest in the range and what I saved now could be spent later if I wanted any extras. He also informed me that if I was prepared to wait, there was a new mark coming soon. So, with a smidgeon of persuasion I decided to wait for the newer model.

The time sped past and on a hot sunny summer's day in August 2002 I took ownership of what may well be the first registered Mk 6 pure in the UK. It was at this very moment that the fun started. While waiting for the delivery of the car, I had spent my time surfing the net for anything **smart** related I could find. It was at this time I found Funkysmart, and was taken aback by how many members this website based club had. I immediately joined under the user-name *Tom.c*. Little did the site admin know at the time, that they would have to treble their moderators once I joined! It was whilst searching the meetings section that I read about the 'Badgers Mount' meet in Kent, and despite getting horrendously lost, I drove to my first one that August. This was to become a momentous occasion and the cause of requiring very deep pockets. I encountered my first modified cars, and I got the bug big time! If I had been told at the time how the **smart** would become such a major part of my existence in so many ways, good, bad, and just plan bizarre, I would never have believed them. This has become a 600cc journey of wonder and discovery along the tarmacadam highway of life.

Jules – Miss Polkadot

I first fell in love with a **smart** when Wally, the landlord of my local pub bought a brand new **smart** that he had imported from France in February 1999. It was one of the very first cars that appeared in the UK, hot off the press so to speak. It was a left hand drive, hello yellow pulse, with a black Tridion and bright twister blue interior. It wasn't the look of the outside of the car so much that really pulled my heartstrings, but the irresistible little 'face' on the dashboard, with those bug eyed pods. I had never seen anything quite like it, and if a car can 'pull', it sure pulled me on that first glimpse. That little car got so many ooohs and aghhhs, and not just from me. The **smart** was a real conversation starter for the publican, who conveniently parked it right outside the front of the pub. Trips to the pub became twice as enjoyable, as I got to see that irresistible little **smart** every time. When Wally decided to change his car, my heart skipped a beat – what no more drooling on Saturday lunchtime? – oh woe is me! He teased me by saying he was getting a mundane car with four seats and a nodding dog, but I didn't believe him. On my next visit there stood a vision from heaven – an aqua orange passion with a silver Tridion and upholstered in red. Pavlov would have been proud of me! Wow! What a showstopper of a car! Oh! How I longed to own one myself…and so the dribbling continued.

Not until late in 2002 was I in a position to be able to own a **smart** myself, when I began an intensive search for just the right one. It sadly began to dawn on me that a brand new **smart** was out of my price range, and the choice of second hand **smarts** at that time was rather limited. An overdue trip to the pub was therefore called for, to drown my sorrow and gloat at the aqua orange sitting perkily in the car park, looking just like a pet waiting for attention. Pulling up outside, just before Christmas, I did a double take, for there keeping the orange **smart** company was another, very shiny, silver and black **smart**! My overdue trip to the pub had obviously been very overdue, for in the preceding few months since my last visit Wally had acquired this nice little number for himself and given the aqua orange to his partner. This silver and black passion was nice to see in order to do a comparison, but somehow, for me, didn't have that extra 'wow' factor that the orange one did. A few weeks later, still in the market for a **smart**, I made my annual Christmas Day visit to the pub for a festive drink with Wally. Sideling up to me with a wink, Wally asked me if I wanted to buy a **smart**! 'The orange one?' I asked excitely. 'Not likely!' Wally replied, 'Ann won't part with it, but one of them has to go, so the black one is yours if you want it'. Thinking on my feet, I decided to accept, for although it lacked the special 'wow' factor I craved, I could give it its own 'wow' factor some how or other, I am a designer after all.   What an expensive Christmas drink that turned out to be, still, bet there are not many people who can claim to have bought their **smart** on Christmas Day!

The day before Valentine's Day, with an appropriately pulsating heart, Wally handed me the keys and the car became mine. MINE! ALL MINE! With a grin on my face stretched taut as elastic, a fate that befalls most **smart** owners, I took charge of my new acquisition and proudly drove her home, a dream come true and a moment etched in my mind forever. Proudly sitting on my driveway, I made a decision to leave the gleaming little car exactly as it was, exactly as it had left the factory, plain, unadorned and beautiful! I took a million photos of it, from every angle, every weather condition and bored my friends silly with the results. I'm sure I overheard someone say it was a mid-life crisis! Ah, so what! I was having a great time.

For those of you who already know me and my car, you will appreciate that the 'keeping the car completely plain and unadorned' line didn't last five minutes! It actually lasted about 2 months before my son *Microdot* had the bright idea to cover it in spots! My eyebrows disappeared up under my hairline. 'SPOTS?' I laughed, wondering why this cool teenage child would ever suggest such a thing. I had never seen a car with spots on it. 'Exactly my point,' my son quipped.

'SPOTS!'...mmmm...now there's a thing...but what sort of spots? Round, coloured, chocolate candy spots were too obvious, and I pre-empted the fact that they had probably already been inflicted on a **smart** or two. Nah! This called for something completely different! Something far more modern or indeed retro as it turned out. The spot theme inspired me to design some 60/70's style spots and circles for the panels, and migrated to the interior with Dalmatian style spotty fabric. (I shall bore you about that considerably more, later, dear reader, when you will find my car in the 'Customised smarts' section listing all of the additions and changes made to my car). It now had its 'wow' factor, and whether onlookers love it or hate it, it causes a reaction wherever it goes, and you can be sure that there is not another one like it on the whole of this planet! (Thank God some say!)

Miss Polkadot

Polkadot

I am a little smarty, my name is Polkadot
I have a dotty body and I look real hot

Whenever that I go out, the people stand and smile
For I am bright and beautiful and just stand out a mile

My seat covers are dotty, were made special' for me
By my very special owner and I'm happy as can be

And now I've had a re-map, a Brabus up-grade kit
With twin pipes that are shiny, I'll go faster.....just a bit!

I'm a black & silver smarty and when you see me out
My little dots will make you laugh, of that there is no doubt!

© Miss Polkadot 2003

...longing to fly

The Designer Dalmatian look

3 The smart Timeline

The history of this wonderful iconic vehicle is long, very complicated and at times bordering on the tedious. As all of this information is readily available on the internet and has been documented in nano detail in previous publications, at the risk of being accused of 'dumbing down' we have decided to present you with just a general idea of what happened, when and by whom – in other words a timeline.

The last thing we want is you getting bored and abandoning this book so soon after you have picked it up!

The first big name you will hear about when discussing the history of the **smart** is Nicolas Hayek. Born in 1928 he was no youngster but he certainly had a young outlook on life and design. He is credited with the title of being the brain child behind the concept of the **smart** car, which was so called due to the collaboration between the two companies Swatch and Mercedes making 'MCC Swatch-Mercedes Art', and a little artistic licence turning it into '**smart**'. He was, at that time, better known as the CEO of Swatch, the iconic Swiss watch company. His idea was to try and create a small economical car combining the attributes of his famous watches; in other words, a 'Swatchmobile', fun, cheap, simple and environmentally friendly. His original idea was for an electric or hybrid powered car. Although this never materialised at the start of the venture, it has since come to fruition with the production of the fortwo EV edition in 2006. Mr Hayek's first steps were to take his ideas to Volkswagen, with whom he joined forces with in 1991. Unfortunately, Volkswagen decided to not take the project further after completing some market research that revealed unfavourable results combined with managerial changes at the company. Undeterred, Mr Hayek kept his ideas simmering and waited for his big break. The other big name associated with the birth of the **smart** is of course Johann Tomforde, a talented car designer working for Mercedes who had specialised in designing two seater concept cars on and off for the previous twenty years and who was to end up leading the whole **smart** development along with Christoph Baubin, financial director and Jürg Schär the marketing director. These three founder directors had the unenviable task of not only designing the car, but the entire factory and where it was to be sited, the manufacturing process, the structure of the organisation, the financing, retail and marketing, the whole shebang. It was Tomforde who came up with the revolutionary method of modular construction of the car, with the factory being fed partially constructed components on site by the system partners only when required, and constructing one of the most environmentally friendly factories in Europe.

1993

January 1993 - Mercedes-Benz do a feasibility study to develop a small car, soon after which Nicolas Hayak gets his big break as talks begin concerning the collaboration between Swatch and Mercedes-Benz.

1994

4th of March 1994 - A press conference is held announcing a joint venture between Mercedes-Benz and Swatch. The waiting was over and the first steps towards creating the crazy little car that has become a cult had begun.

April 1994 - The newly formed company MCC (Micro Compact Car) is established in Biel, Switzerland.

20th of December 1994 - Hambach, France is chosen as the site location for the factory to build the new cars, which many an owner has since toured, and is officially christened Smartville. The factory is situated only 10 miles from the French and German border and only a two hour drive to Mercedes headquarters at Stuttgart.

1995

September 1995 - Sees a concept study of the car at the IAA (Intenationale Autmobil-Ausstellung) in Frankfurt, Germany.

14th of October 1995 - The foundation stone is laid at the factory site in Hambach, and building work commences to the 'plus' shaped factory, designed to make delivery more accessible by award winning architects.

1997

12th of June 1997 - work starts on the engine plant in the then Daimler-Benz AG in Germany

September 1997 - sees the world premiere of the **smart** city coupé at the IAA in Frankfurt.

October 1997 - The notorious 'Elk' test on an 'A' class Mercedes that caused the vehicle to flip over, causes huge disruption to **smart** production, as the same test on the **smart** produces similar results. Production postponed for six months for more critical testing.

27th of October 1997 - The factory building work at Smartville is completed. (We will cover the factory in more depth further in the book).

December 1997 - Johan Tomforde is re-assigned to other duties within Daimler-Benz as the company is now called, and finance director Christoph Baubin moves on too. Dr Gerhard Fritz takes over the position from Johan Tomforde.

1998

1st of July 1998 - Production finally starts on the **smart** city coupé at Smartville, Hambach. The original hybrid Swatchmobile engine was not reliable, so the car makes its debut with a more conventional three cylinder petrol engine. Nicholas Hayak parts company with MCC.

10th of July 1998 - Advanced sales are taken in **smart** centres in 9 European countries (but not the United Kingdom at this point).

September 1998 - *Lil.smartie's* car (Mk 1) is registered in Belgium, and is the oldest known running car in the UK.

October 1998 - The launch of the **smart** city coupé begins in 9 European countries: Belgium, Germany, France, Italy, Luxemburg, Austria, Switzerland, Spain, and Holland.

1st of November 1998 - Daimler-Benz AG takes 100% control of MCC.

November 1998 - Stirling Moss imports a **smart**. Initial sales were well down on those expected. 20,000 were sold in 1998 against a prediction from Nicolas Hayek of 200,000...oops!

The first range of cars comprised of four models: pure, pulse, passion and Limited Edition 1. The passion came with two types of specifications; the sports or the comfort package. The colour options included mad red with twister blue or orange interior, and the Limited Edition 1 had an expensive option of colour coded leather trim, including the gear knob, seats and door pockets. The dashboard displays a small plate bearing the car's manufacture number. There have been various rumours going around that some of the very early cars had Mitsubishi engines fitted rather than the Daimler-Benz units. We have not been able to confirm this information ourselves but certainly others in the trade have heard of this being the case also.

Now at this point we need to explain that **smart** do not use the term Mark 1, 2, 3, 4 etc. It is a reference term that has originated and been used by folks in website clubs as an easier way of keeping tabs on the myriad versions of cars that appear over the years. **Smart** themselves only ever use the term first generation **smart** (SG1) and as from March 2003, second generation **smart** (SG2). We will continue to use the term Mark (or Mk as it is abbreviated) as it is easier to cover a break down of changes and for anyone who reads **smart** club website forums you will know where we are coming from.

1999

1st of January 1999 - The business side of **smart** is transferred from Biel to Renniger in Germany, and is renamed Micro Compact Car **smart** GmbH.

March/February 1999 – Smartechnique, the first UK independent trader imports cars to the UK and opens in Wellesley Road, Chiswick, London.

May 1999 - The Mk2 version is quickly launched due to very hard ride and suspension problems with the first cars. The wonderful Mk 1 is dropped, as are the mad red coloured panels. At last the Brabus development with **smart** is complete.

November 1999 - The Mk3 version now has an internal boot release catch; new panel colours are added including bay grey and the jazzy numeric blue.

December 1999 - The **smart** cdi (diesel version) is launched in the nine original European countries and **smart** becomes the first car manufacturer to sell cars via the internet. The 100,000[th] car rolls of the production line.

2000

May 2000 - The **smart** cabrio is launched in the 9 European countries.

October 2000 - The Mk4 city coupé is launched at the Birmingham International Motor Show for the UK market. A new ECU is fitted with trust PLUS in place of trust. The fuel cap is now locked by a solenoid in place of the original key; the key itself is changed to a 3 button operation.

2001

February 2001 - The **smart** concept crossblade, based on a **smart** cabrio is unleashed to the world's press at the Geneva Motor Show.

April 2001 - The **smart** cabrio is launched in the UK in the left hand drive version only

Now we are on to the Mk 5 cars and the range is toned down. Suspension is changed to MacPherson struts at the front. New interior and exterior colours are added with some removed. Options such as heated seats, electric door mirrors and silver mirror covers etc are now available. The pulse is re-developed to 62bhp.

October 2001 - The right hand drive version of the **smart** cabrio comes to the UK at last! **November 2001 -** Japan receives its first batch of **smart** cars.

2002

January 2002 - Sees some minor specification enhancements and slight change to body design of the **smart** city coupé.

March 2002 - Presentation of the **smart** crossblade as a production car at the International Motor Show in Geneva causes a big stir.

June 2002 - The **smart** crossblade is launched Austria, Belgium, Czech Republic, France, Germany, Holland, Hungary, Italy, Japan, Luxembourg, Slovak Republic, Spain, Sweden, Switzerland, Taiwan and the UK as a limited edition run of only 2000 cars.

July 2002 - The Mk 6 right hand drive **smart** city coupé arrives for the UK market. The range is upgraded with new front styling and the distinctive peanut shaped front lights. The rear valance has a face lift (or should that be a rear lift?), and the turbo is up-graded with a stronger unit. The pure now comes with dash board pods as standard and **smart** stop supplying left hand drive cars to the UK.

September 2002 - The new roadster production line gets underway in Hambach.

October 2002 - Smartville celebrates its 5th anniversary and 430,000 cars have been produced since their launch.

2003

March 2003 – Sees the launch of the second generation G2 **smart** (Mk7 to us). The pure is now available with a 61bhp engine as well as the standard 50bhp version, with the other models now having 698 cc engines. A striking Metal C> badge is now fitted (comically known as the chicken head logo) instead of the word **smart** on front panel. ESP light appears on the dash when activated, the car now has hill start assist (HAS), a service level indicator, softer suspension, and an OBD diagnostics port next to the driver's storage tray.

April 2003 - The launch of the **smart** roadster and roadster coupé as a production car. Brabus cars become available throughout mainland Europe in **smart** city coupé and cabrio versions.

May 2003 - The international press test drives the **smart** Brabus city coupé and cabrio in Bottrop, France

26th of June 2003 - The **smart** forfour is presented to the international media in Zurich Switzerland .The event is called forfour day and but they are only allowed to scrutinise a static car. Also this month the **smart** city coupé and cabrio and are launched in Finland.

August 2003 - Mexico sees the launch of the **smart** city coupé, cabrio and roadster coupé.

September 2003 - The roadster is launched in the UK, although one was seen at an event here in the August. Press launch of forfour at the IAA in Frankfurt.

October 2003 - Turkey gets the roadster, **smart** city coupé and cabrio.

December 2003 - Cyprus and the Lebanon get the roadster, roadster coupé, **smart** city coupé and cabrio.

lil.smartie – the oldest known smart in the UK

2004

January 2004 - The **smart** city-coupé and cabrio get re-branded and are now known as the fortwo coupé and fortwo cabrio. An automatic rear wiper is added, this comes into play when reversing, providing the front wipers are on too.

February 2004 - The International Press test drive the forfour in Rome, Italy.

March 2004 - The International Press get to test drive the Brabus roadster and roadster coupé in Nice, France (alright for some!). This is also the month that the Brabus roadsters are launched in both versions.

April 2004 - The **smart** forfour is launched for the European market.

26th of April 2004 - The newly formed **smart**-Brabus (GmbH) opens its headquarters in Bottrop, Germany.

May 2004 - A limited edition of 70 models of the white **smart** fortwo i-move, based on a fortwo cabrio which comes complete with an Apple iPod and MP3 connection, is launched.

20th of May 2004 - A **smart** car creates a world stunt record by climbing a television tower on a high wire in Stuttgart, Germany. Wonder if it got a parking ticket?

June 2004 - International Press test drives the **smart** forfour cdi in Stuttgart, Germany.

September 2004 - The left hand drive forfour cdi is launched at the Paris Motor Show for the European markets and as the right hand drive version for Japan. Canada also gets the forfour cdi.

October 2004 - The **smart** brand is launched in Norway, Malta and Romania.

November 2004 - The **smart** brand is launched in Malaysia and the International Press test drive the sportstyle forfour edition at Mallorca, Spain.

2005

January 2005 - The **smart** brand premieres at the North American International Auto Show (NAIAS) in Detroit.

February 2005 - World premiere of the Brabus forfour at the Geneva Motor Show, and the International Press get to test drive the car in Nice, France.

April 2005 - Work commences on a clay model of the new **smart** crosstown concept car.

August 2005 - The crosstown show car is ready. Rumours abound about the end of the roadster. The nightrun and truestyle fortwo editions are launched together.

4th of November 2005 - The rumours were true and the last roadster rolls off the production line.

December 2005 - The fortwo edition pink is launched and received with great enthusiasm by lovers of all things pink; so much so that the numbers of models produced are drastically increased to meet demands.

Petrol engine block

2006

January 2006 - The British Motoring Press try out the fortwo hybrid which has a 27bhp electric motor running in tandem with a 800cc, 40bhp diesel unit.

April 2006 - The Grandstyle fortwo edition is launched with a gorgeous cream leather interior. News appears that the Smartville factory will close for 18 weeks this coming year to re-tool for the new fortwo; this will be spread over the year.

July 2006 - The full electric version of the fortwo makes its debut at the British Motor Show and the forfour range stops production due to poor sales figures.

August 2006 - The Project Kimber consortium – which plans to build restyled and rebadged **smart** roadsters and coupés and sell them for less than the Germans could – expects to set up its factory in Wales thanks to a £3m subsidy from the Welsh Assembly.

September 2006 - The Brabus Limited Edition red is launched in both fortwo coupé and fortwo cabrio versions in the UK, having only been previously available in Germany. Lots of spy shots of the new **smart** car appear all over the internet to very mixed reactions.

November 2006 – The first blue chip corporate partners take delivery of the electric EV edition **smart** for trials. **Smart** finally release the press pack on the new fortwo or model 451 as the factory will call it. The very first C7 Kit Car is built and registered for a UK customer.

20th of November – The last of the 450 model **smarts** are built.

A grand total of **770,256** (450 model) cars were produced, and the very last one was a cdi with ruby red metallic panels.

2007

January 2007 – At Smartville, Hambach, production of the new SG3 **smart** fortwo gets off to a successful start. The first vehicle produced in the pure equipment line has white body panels and a black tridion safety cell. The new **smart** can do everything that the previous model could do – but even better. This means that it is even more comfortable, more agile, safer and more environmentally friendly than its predecessor. Available to order from 15 January 2007, with prices no higher than for previous models. The new edition will arrive on the market in April and will be available as both a coupé and a cabrio. There will be two naturally aspirated petrol engine versions to choose from, delivering 45 or 52 kW (61 / 71 bhp) respectively, and one turbo engine rated at 62 kW (84 bhp). The diesel version, the **smart** fortwo cdi, has a power output of 33 kW (45 PS). With CO2 emissions of just 90 grams per kilometre, the **smart** fortwo cdi achieves "three litre" status, having the lowest CO2 emissions of any car on the market at that moment in time.

Crosstown Prototype – Photo courtesy of
DaimlerChrysler Media Archive

4 The smart Range

The fortwo

We will start this chapter with the **smart** city coupé, or fortwo as it is now known. We still think city coupé has a nicer ring to it and fits better with the cars style and image. There is always something exotic about the word 'coupé' that conjures up images of driving in warm climates with the wind in your hair and not a care in the world. For many of us, normality is driving on motorways and in traffic clogged cities or maybe just the dreaded school run. However, from now on we shall refer to it as the **fortwo**, (and not 'Fort Wo' as some wag jested with us recently!). The fortwo, the original **smart**, started with 4 models: pure, pulse, passion and Limited 1. Other limited editions will be listed later along with cabrio, Brabus cars and diesels. Before we continue however, we need to explain that when ordering a vehicle from new, the specifications on **smarts**, particularly the fortwos, have a habit of changing like the wind. One moment something is classed as a standard part, and then it suddenly becomes an optional extra, so things can get very confusing. For this very reason and the fact that there are so many variants, we have not compiled an options listing but just noted major differences. Something else to be aware of is the fact that the SG2 **smarts** can turn up from the factory fitted with SG1 parts and vice versa, much to the amusement and confusion of many independent **smart** dealers and mechanics. You may also notice on your travels in the UK that there are some right hand drive fortwos, built pre July 2002 that have the old style oval headlights. Ulrike Bianchi, Head of Communications and our guide round the factory at Hambach, filled us in as to why there is this anomaly. Apparently, along with the narrower 'K' car model of the **smart** built especially for the Japanese market, some standard ones were built for them too. However, these standard models cost far more to import and tax than the special 'K' car and Japanese public were not prepared to pay the extra for them, consequently many of them were left sitting at the factory. Some UK dealers managed to acquire some of these vehicles and sell them in the UK before the official release of the right hand drive SG2 with the new peanut shaped headlights. *Captain Pugwash*, a Bexhill Beach Party veteran has one of these Japanese rarities.

The pure

This is the basic model in the **smart** range and the one that *s2trash* owns, although his car is not in its original form. The pure until 2003 was restricted to 44 bhp, when it became available with two engine options, 50 bhp or 62 bhp. The 44 bhp version is the hardest of the **smart** range to re-map. The most notable feature of the pure is its hard roof. The glass roof was, however, available for the 62 bhp car. The tridion on the pure is black and the range of panel colours were limited. Another notable feature of the pure is that it didn't come with fog lights as standard, but could be ordered as an optional extra. The pure has a black grille with plugs that can be removed if fog lights are to be fitted at a later stage because on the Mk 6 onwards the wiring loom is in place, allowing the option for retro fitting.

Hogster's pure

Limited Edition pure spotted in France during the trip to Hambach

A picnicking pulse belonging to importedsam_123

The pure and pulse have the temperature censor pre-fitted to the front, although getting it activated is not an easy task and *s2trash* has yet to have his done. Keeping with the external part of the car, the pure comes with steel wheels as standard with either a full or centre hub cap as a factory option. Something else that is different with the pure is that its rear lights that have orange glass on the centre lights. The pure comes with the softip-automated, sequential 6 speed transmission, and has a golf ball looking gear knob in grey, but the softouch-automatic gear programme with kick-down was an available option. The interior of the pure has always been only the one choice in colour: scordic grey upholstery with matt grey contrast components and storage boxes in the doors. One big change to the interior was the fitting of the clock and rev counter (pods) to the Mk 6 cars as standard, which for a lot of us, are one of the **smart** cars main features. All of the pures from Mk1 to Mk5 only had the pods fitted as a customer option. For some strange reason, the Mk 6 had them fitted as standard, then, in 2004, they reverted them back to an option-only fitting. This was all very confusing. From the Mk 7 onwards, air-conditioning was added as an option, but only on the 62 bhp version. One piece of information that has eluded us is the weight of the pure. In its standard form, without softouch transmission and air conditioning and the lack of a glass roof, we know the car is lighter but by how much we have yet to ascertain. If you ever get the chance to drive a standard pure and then a passion, it is noticeable just how light the pure feels on the road, the passion having all the extras.

The pulse

The pulse is often referred to as the sporty version of the standard fortwo range. The pulse has a black tridion, but with silver as an option. It comes with a glass roof and sunscreen, with the option of a solid roof. The pulse has no air conditioning as standard fitting, which a little odd considering how hot it can get in the summer with the glass roof. As with the pure, the censor for the exterior temperature indicator and frost warning is already behind the grille, although it is not activated. The pulse has a silver front grille and fog lights fitted as standard. Prior to 2004 the cars came with Sportline alloy wheels, before being changed to Coreline alloy wheels which run wider tyres than the pure and passion. These are 175/55 R 15 on the front and 195/50 R 15 at the rear, compared to the other models that sport 145/65 R 15 on the front and 175/55 R 15 at the rear. The Sportline ran the same size tyres as the pure and passion. Mk 5 cars were re-developed to 62 bhp. Standard transmission is the same as the pure with the softouch factory fitted option. From 2004 the steering wheel gearshift (paddleshift) became available as standard, instead of a very pricey aftermarket option. The steering wheel is leather, as is gear knob; the interior cloth comes in a choice of twister blue or twister green, with storage nets in the doors.

The passion

As owned by *Miss Polkadot*, this is the top of the standard range of fortwos, and, unlike the other two models, has a silver tridion and silver wing mirrors. It had a glass roof and sunscreen as does the pulse. The solid roof is an optional extra. This solid roof can be retro-fitted but the bonding requires two days to set. Starline alloy wheels were standard until 2004 when Styleline alloys replaced them. The passion has a leather steering wheel and gear knob. Again, as with the pulse, the front grille is silver, with fog lights as standard. Air conditioning and air-bags on the passion also come as standard, as does the external temperature and frost warning indicator, although both the other models have the censor in place, as previously mentioned. The upholstery cloth comes in a choice of bungee red or bungee

Littlerou's passion

A lovely cabrio at Southeast Smart Centre

Roadrage's black Brabus cabrio

grey, with storage nets in the doors, and unlike the other models, comes with the luggage compartment cover. The centre consol pods and the rev counter became a factory fitted option only as from 2004, just like the pure.

The cabrio

The cabrio version of the **smart** was introduced to the UK in April 2001, only as a left hand drive car. It appeared as a right hand drive option in October 2001, being the first of the models to actually do so. Initially, the cabrio option was only available for the pulse and the passion models. Not until 2003 did the pure have the soft–top version. The cabrio specification is dependant on which model is purchased, i.e. pure spec on a pure cabrio. The self-folding, electric Tritop roof, works at the touch of a single button. Made from durable fabric, the roof can be stopped in three different positions. These are, amusingly called by **smart**: Tritop L, Tritop XL and Tritop XXL, one assumes referring to the size of the hole in the roof. The roof bars are easily removed and neatly stored in the tailgate, allowing an even larger XXXXL space! Most of the exterior rear end of the cabrio is different from the other models, with the tail light cluster; wheel arches and tailgate having a different design to incorporate the folding roof.

The diesel (cdi)

The diesel (cdi) has to date, never been officially imported to the UK. However, that hasn't stopped people privately importing them here, although they are very scarce. *Daggie12* from The Essex Smarties Smart Car Club has one of them, a lovely all silver cabrio that she brought over from Germany. Previously owned by her brother who works for DaimlerChrysler, this nippy little diesel that commands around 80-90mph, is economy personified, and well suited for those with less than deep pockets when it comes to fuel bills! The engine is rated at 799cc and shares the technology used in the Mercedes-Benz E 320's inline-6 diesel engine, although this is a 3 cylinder, inline cdi turbo diesel engine, with rear mounted air cooling. An interesting fact is that the fuel tank carries only 22 litres as with pre Mk 6 cars. The range of models is the same as normal fortwos i.e. pure, pulse, and passion. With sales of more than 140,000 cars by Nov 2005, the **smart** fortwo cdi is by far the most successful "three litre" car worldwide i.e. consuming just 3.4 litres per 100 kilometers. At **smart**, environmental issues and economic reality go hand in hand, the sales figures being the proof of the pudding.

The roadster and roadster coupé

The original idea behind the roadster was to create a nippy two-seater car, similar to the British sports cars of the past, but with all the modern, up-to-date technology and engineering of today. This could explain why the UK has been its biggest market, as there hasn't really been much in the way of new small sports car production here since the demise of the MG's and Triumph's. Although launched in April 2003, the roadster was never officially imported to the UK until the September of the same year,

cdi fortwo spotted in France

cdi engine

Standard roadster at Newark 2006

and it had many potential owners chomping at the bit in anticipation. There are two models, the **smart** roadster and the **smart** roadster coupé, the coupé having the fully glazed fastback. Both of these models come as Brabus versions. There is a choice of several different roofs for all the models, including a fully automatic electrically operated soft top made of fabric, a 2-piece solid removable hard top with a matt finish and a glass roof. The two roof bars are easily removed and are then very neatly stored in the front luggage compartment. The roadster has a robust tridion safety shell, which puts an end to the potential twist and shakes that more vintage sports cars suffered from in the past, and more importantly provides a very high level of safety in an accidental collision situation. This sleek and curvy car is fitted with a mid-mounted 3-cylinder Surprex turbo engine, which only weighs around 60kg, and is rated at 698 cc/80 bhp/60 kW. The Brabus models, having the same size engine, have been tweaked to produce a power output of 101 bhp/74 kW. Kerb weights vary from 790 kg for the roadster, 810 kg for the coupe, 832 kg for the Brabus and 852 kg for the Brabus coupé. The lightweight design of both the engine and the bodywork, coupled with the fact that the car is only 1.2 meters high, positively ensures a very low centre of gravity. Along with wide tyres, rear wheel drive and good weight distribution, the roadster produces fantastic handling performance, that is certainly comparable to more expensive makes on the road today. The roadster was never going to be a drag strip racer but that was never the aim, but it certainly delivers a healthy acceleration of 0-6.25mph (0-100km/h) in 10.9 seconds, and the Brabus versions a wee bit faster at 9.8 seconds. Having paddle-shift gear change on the steering wheel, makes for some nifty driving too, and comes as standard on both the Brabus models. The roadster also has the option to turn off its traction control, and testing the cars capabilities in a controlled environment is a very tantalising thought. We have seen many a roadster owner having fun on a damp field, performing doughnuts and pirouettes with ease! Unfortunately, the roadsters have suffered from some leaking problems around the door seals which were rectified fairly promptly after the problem was detected. New rubber door seals are now fitted with a much courser surface, which apparently stops the leaks in most but not all of the problematical vehicles. In days gone by a leaky car was part and parcel of owning a soft top car, it came with the territory so to speak. These days perfection is required in every walk of life, but not unfortunately always attained. Some roadsters have also suffered leaking wing mirrors but again these problems were quickly rectified.

Vermaak's roadster coupé

Black Brabus roadster at Billing 2004

Al Young's roadster after competing in the Monte Carlo Rally ~ complete with dirt

The forfour

In April 2003 the world got the first glimpse of the new concept car to join the **smart** family; at 3.75 meters long, a **smart** big enough to accommodate four people and consequently christened the forfour. In September that year it was officially revealed to the press at the IAA in Frankfurt, and launched at the Paris Motor Show in September 2004. In terms of the reaction to this car by seasoned fortwo owners, it was rather mixed. Based on a Mitsubishi Colt, the designers did try to keep to the cute **smart** formula in terms of looks, but never quite pulled it off. It had the removable plastic panels and those iconic pods inside the car, the very items that make **smart** cars **smart**, but there was something about them that just kept them apart from the other **smart** family members. As a functional car, they are excellent, they just lacked that spark of character that folks found endearing in the fortwo and roadster.

As with the **smart** fortwo coupé, cabrio, roadster and roadster-coupé, a choice of different design and equipment options are available for the **smart** forfour. Models available are purestyle, black edition, coolstyle, pulse, passion. The pulse offers a full range of high-quality, sporty features. The passion caters to the highest comfort requirements whilst offering an attractive price-performance ratio. Air conditioning, leather steering wheel, alloy wheels and fog lamps are just some of the comfort features included in the passion. The forfour comes with a choice of three petrol (1.1 litre, 1.3 litre & 1.5 litre) and two 1.5 litre diesel engine variants with power outputs of 68 bhp and 95 bhp. In addition audio, navigation, telecommunication, comfort and safety equipment, including ESP as standard and disc brakes both front and rear, courtesy of the affiliation with DaimlerChrysler and the Mercedes Car Group, add up to a premium product. Weighing in at less than 1,000 kilogrammes, the forfour offers a power/weight ratio of up to 12.2 kilogrammes per kilowatt (9 kg per bhp), which is comparable with the attractive ratio of the

smart roadster and roadster-coupé. The forfour also comes with a conventional five-speed manual transmission as standard (the first manual gearbox in a **smart**). The newly developed, automated "softouch plus" six-speed transmission is available as an option. The lounge concept forfour, another model option, which *lil.smartie* owns custom painted in sparkly pink, lends the interior of the **smart** forfour a veritable living room feel. The backrests of the two front seats can be folded down so that they are almost level with the rear seats to create a large horizontal seat surface. As with the **smart** fortwo, **smart** forfour customers can choose between a plastic roof, a panoramic glass roof and an electric glass sunroof. The tridion safety cell of the forfour is available in three colours: Silver, black and titanium. These three colours can be combined with the body panels which are available in ten typical **smart** colours for all trim lines: jack black, phat red, graphite blue, ice white, melon green metallic, starlight silver metallic, bay grey metallic, star blue metallic, flame red metallic and deep green metallic. June 2005 saw the launch of the most powerful production **smart** yet, the BRABUS forfour. It is powered by a turbocharged Mitsubishi 4G15 engine, developing 130 kW (177 PS), 27 PS more than its "brother", the Mitsubishi Colt CZT. It can reach a maximum speed of 221 km/h (137mph) and accelerate up to 100Km/h (60mph) in 6.9 seconds. The forfour was actually produced at the Netherlands Car B.V. factory in Born in the Netherlands, in conjunction with Mitsubishi Motors as previously mentioned. This is the same factory that produced Volvo 340 cars in 1970's and 1980's and the Volvo v40's in the 1990's. To save production costs, the forfour shares most of it's components with the 2003 Mitsubishi Colt which includes the chassis, suspension and a new generation of MIVEC petrol engines. **Smart** however, specifies different springs and suspension bushings for the forfour, making it handle better than the Colt. The 1.5 L cdi diesel engine on the contrary, is a three-cylinder Mercedes-Benz engine derived from the four-cylinder of the Mercedes-Benz A Class, which is available with either 68 PS or 95 PS.

However, because of disappointingly slow sales and high production costs, DaimlerChrysler decided to phase out the forfour and stopped production in the summer of 2006.

Besty's black Brabus forfour at Whatlington

Flame red forfour passion at the L2B 2005

Bay grey forfour passion at Brighton racecourse 2005

The first forfour customised by S-mann at Billing 2005

Silver and black forfour pulse on Lindisfarne Causeway

Limited Edition smarts

There have been quite a few of these appear over the years, and all in what appears a rather haphazard timeframe. There are several occasions where two new edition models have been launched together.

Limited Edition Mk 1 fortwo

The very first of these was the Limited Edition Mk1, produced in 1998. As far as we know they all had black tridions and white panels. Specification wise, they were very close to the passion but had a blue cloth interior along with blue plastic components. The seats were trimmed in tan leather which co-ordinated with the blue custom mats trimmed in matching tan leather piping. The gear knob was also finished in tan leather. Another nice touch was the Special Edition identification plate, positioned on the dashboard just under the windscreen, showing the car model and limited production number, and a Limited 1 emblem under the wing mirror. Another early model we were first told about by *jonboy* was a pure with a glass roof as standard. As far as we have been able to ascertain, none of these particular models ever made it over to the UK, but we did see one for ourselves in France by *pure* luck!

Jamiebeveridge's early Mk 1 Limited Edition

Crossblade posing for Smartball Charity promotion at Biggin Hill

1:18 Crossblade model

The Crossblade

Originally based around the fortwo cabrio, **smart** magically conjured up this totally wacky car and presented it to the world at the Geneva Motor Show in early 2001. Its totally outrageous design made the jaw of every car journalist in the world hit the tarmac at 100mph! Although this vehicle has no roof, doors, nor a conventional windscreen, it's very unconventionality had those that saw it smile with appreciation. Appreciation, that a car company had the guts to promote something so radical; and promise that it would put this maverick, quirky car into production within a year. And it did. In June 2002, **smart** unleashed into the sea of mundane vehicles a squad of 2000 hand-built crossblades, each with their own limited production number. With such a small production the number of vehicles destined for the UK was limited to 40 cars only and which appeared here in the July.

Dr. Helmut Wawra, Development & Design director at MCC Smart says that: "The Smart crossblade deliberately does without all protections against wind and weather. This car with its reduction to essentials focuses on blue skies and high spirits. It's like a motorcycle on four wheels"

The crossblade is five inches longer and three inches wider than the fortwo cabrio and is equipped with a 599cc, three-cylinder, six-valve, petrol, SUPREX turbo engine as used in the fortwo range. It has a power output of 70bhp at 5,470rpm, 80lb ft of torque from 2,200-3,500rpm, a six-speed sequential automatic gearbox and is rear-wheel drive with 16" three spoke Spikeline alloy wheels. It also has, due to the limiter, a standard top speed of about 84mph, although unless the driver is wearing a full protective motorbike helmet, driving at that sort of speed is pretty exhausting. Drivers are fully exposed to the elements with nothing but a minimalist transparent wind deflector for a windscreen, and steel safety bars at the side for doors. The tridion is reinforced with numerous high-strength panels in the floor, the A and B pillars are also reinforced and along with the integrated roll bar, this gives the car the desired flexural strength and torsional rigidity and the ensures occupant protection. The crossblade has the standard **smart** airbags for both driver and passenger, seat belt tensioners and belt force limiters making this vehicle command the same demanding safety engineering as the fortwo. Unlike the fortwo range, the crossblade only comes in the one model and one colour – black. The tridion is clad with matt titanium plastic components in the area of the roll bar, the B-pillar and the door sills. The body panels are supplied in jet black. The creature comforts in this car are all pretty sparse, but that presumably is part of the reason this motorized skateboard is such a hoot. The dashboard and seats, which like all fortwo seats are very comfortable, are covered in a water-repellent, fire-red neoprene-type plastic making it well prepared for the effects of the elements and makes a visually distinctive feature in the interior. The central fascia houses the waterproof stereo and the basic heater controls. The steering wheel and gearshift knob are finished in black leather. Sadly, because engineers could not waterproof it effectively there is no rev counter pod, but there is a cup holder. How effective this would actually be in keeping a can of sugary fizz or a boiling cup of coffee in place whilst being buffered about in a motorway crosswind is highly debatable. Just like a motorbike, the whole car is waterproof. A single-piece plastic tray lines the floor of the interior and four water drainage channels ensure that rainwater drains through the floor of the tridion thus protecting the electric cables against moisture. The seat surfaces each have two water drainage channels in the rear side seams. The driver's airbag is protected against rain water by a hood made of black, waterproof material. The crossblade even has a nylon tonneau cover hidden in the tiny boot, which is supplied as standard, for when the car is parked up. As previously mentioned, instead of conventional doors, the crossblade is equipped with steel safety bars at passenger shoulder height. They swing upwards with the help of a gas-operated strut. The bars have a matt black plastic cladding and cushioned pads provide a comfortable armrest. Although undoubtedly safe, the ability of being able to see the road rushing past your feet can take a while to get accustomed to! With its silver tridion; jet black panels, front, rear and over the back wheels; the prominent, matt black front and rear spoilers and the front meshed grilles; this amazing little car certainly comes big on charisma and visually is utterly unique. Robbie Williams, the international entertainer formerly from the UK boy-band 'Take That', was the first official owner of a **smart** crossblade. At the official handover on 18 April 2002 in Hamburg, he received the car with the production number 0008, as specially requested by him. The crossblade with production number 0001 was later auctioned by *MCC smart GmbH* with the proceeds going to Robbie Williams' charity "Give It Sum!" *Miss Polkadot* has driven a crossblade and was amazed, despite the appearance of how many bits are 'missing' compared to a standard fortwo, at just how sturdy and solid the car feels. Although having owned several different convertible cars over the years, driving the blade was a whole new experience for her. 'At just over 40mph the wind noise drowns out the sound of the engine and with no rev counter strict attention is required on the gear change front. With no encapsulating protection to speak of, the wind pressure on the drivers face can cause eyeballs to vibrate in a rather disturbing manner, and so protective eyewear is a complete must; plain old sunglasses are just not man enough for the job. In fact, a full motorbike helmet is best for both driver and passenger, protecting them from low flying bumblebees, stones and fast food wrappers inconsiderately thrown from other vehicles, and of course rain that ends up feeling like rods of steel at any speed. You can see why **smart** brought out a specific range of protective crossblade clothes and accessories; it wasn't just as a fashion statement'. Despite being likened to a 'bumper car' at a fairground, it drives like a dream. Despite it looking like half a **smart**, it is incredibly safe. Despite it being a clone, like 2000 peas in a pod, it is a real head turner. Despite these little quirky idiosyncrasies, which, to be fair is all part of the experience of owning such a wacky vehicle; the blade is a real barrel of fun and is surely one of those all time classic cars.

The fortwo Edition i-move

In May 2004 **smart** brought out 70 models of this innovative i-move Edition for sale in the UK. The white fortwo cabrio passion with a silver tridion safety cell has a matching 20Gb iPod engraved with the **smart** logo as standard, and a **smart** 'iPod Car Kit' consisting of a special mount with an iPod connection. Additional exclusive specifications include Brabus 16" alloy wheels, dashboard mounted clock and rev counter with white dials, interior accent parts finished in white, heated leather seats, leather interior including door trims and dashboard, and an upgraded sound system. The iPod car kit can be bought as an accessory for the fortwo and the roadster models for aft market fitting.

The fortwo Editions nightrun and truestyle

Both of these Limited Editions were released at the same time in August 2005. The nightrun, was based on the pure but came with a three spoke leather steering wheel incorporating the paddle shift gear change system, Brabus sports exhaust and heat shield, Brabus Monoblock VI wheels, ESP, hill and brake assist, ABS, radio/cd player with sound package, glass roof with sun blind and air-conditioning and fog lamps. This also comes with its easily identifiable nightrun edition emblem under the wing mirror. The 3 cylinder Brabus Suprex petrol engine on this model is 698cc and rated at 74bhp. Supplied only with jack black panels and a black tridion, this all-black model certainly looks stunning. The truestyle was released in both the coupé and cabrio option, based on a 61bhp SUPREX turbo engine but with the pure trim and Jetline alloy wheels. The high standard spec included an exclusive ruby red metallic paint finish with the choice to go for a bay grey or star blue metallic paint option and also included the truestyle edition emblem.

The fortwo Edition grandstyle

The fortwo grandstyle is a special edition sporting body panels in an exclusive dark green metallic paint finish with a silver tridion safety cell. This special model was introduced in April 2006 and was an instant hit, except with photographers. This particular paint colour is extremely difficult to capture and reproduce accurately, as it tends to appear black in colour. Years ago, Jaguar had the same problem when they painted their racing team's cars in a similar colour. After much debate they had their cars resprayed several shades lighter so that any camera equipment could reproduce their corporate colour more convincingly to the public.

The grandstyle is available as a fortwo coupé or a fortwo cabrio, with a 45 kW (61 bhp) petrol engine or a 30 kW (41 bhp) diesel engine fitted with a diesel particle filter as standard. Available with an option of very classy beige leather upholstery comprising of heated leather seats, interior door trim and storage pockets in beige leather and a black leather-effect instrument panel, how could you not take up the offer. The audio package has option of incorporating an MP3 interface (for the connection of external audio devices), a clock and a rev counter. The special flow silver painted contrast components give the vehicles interior a strikingly high-quality feel.

The fortwo Edition pink

There were rather a few raised eyebrows when this little number appeared in December 2005, but it has proved to be so popular that the original limited edition of 50 cars was increased to 150. With groovy Candy Pink body panels, silver tridion and radiator grille it definitely appeals to the **smart** owner's feminine side. The car comes with Styleline alloy wheels, air conditioning, glass roof, driver and passenger airbags, leather steering wheel and gear knob. It is based on a 61bhp 698cc turbo charged petrol engine, with ESP, ABS, hill and brake assist and acceleration skid control. The pink theme continues inside with the dashboard instrument pods and stalk ends accented in more candy pink paint. Sadly, the leather seats, steering wheel and gear knob are not upholstered in pink leather, just grey material to match the bungee grey interior. Still, it really is pretty in pink.

White i-move Limited Edition pods

Limited Edition nightrun – photo courtesy of Daimler Chrysler Media archive

David Robinson's gorgeous green grandstyle cabrio at Dungeness Estate

The fortwo Brabus Edition red

Available as a coupé and a cabrio, this latest special edition launched in the UK in September 2006 is fitted with a 74 bhp Brabus-tuned petrol engine. It is equipped with exclusive intense red body panels and has matching intense red paintwork on the tridion, front spoiler, side skirt and door mirrors. In addition to its powerful engine and striking good looks, the fortwo Brabus Edition red comes with an impressive list of standard equipment, including softouch transmission, exclusive leather/ Alcantara seats, dashboard and door trims with red contrast stitching, 3-spoke leather sports steering wheel with gearshift paddles, air conditioning, front fog lights, cockpit clock and rev counter, Brabus twin sports exhaust with heat shield, Brabus aluminium pedals, gear knob and handbrake lever, Brabus velour floor mats, audio package and 16" Brabus Monoblock VI alloy wheels. Dermot Kelly, Managing Director, Mercedes Car Group said: 'There's never been a **smart** fortwo quite like it. This distinctive and exclusive special edition will appeal to customers who want to stand out from the crowd and enjoy the fun-packed performance that a Brabus-tuned engine can offer'. Funnily enough, *Justrules* who can be spotted in our Customised chapter modified his car prior to this edition coming out and it looks extremely similar, all red with added body kits. The only difference is that *Justrules* car can probably beat this version at the lights for sure!

The fortwo Edition ev (Electric smart)

In 2006 the UK was selected to run a market trial for the introduction of a fully electric version of the fortwo. Making its debut at the British Motor Show in July this environmentally friendly vehicle has for the time being, only been made available on a lease arrangement to selected UK corporate customers starting in November. Once the trials have been successfully completed the ev will be available to the general public. The **smart** ev sets a new benchmark in the electric vehicle sector; it has 30kW output and a top speed of 70mph using a powerful Zytek electric motor. It offers even better in-town performance than its petrol powered stable mate, with 0-30mph in 6.5 seconds. Powered solely by electricity, this car can achieve the equivalent of 300mpg which amounts to a saving of 80% in fuel costs compared to a standard fortwo. The **smart** ev is also exempt from vehicle excise duty and congestion charge and with a range of up to 72 miles between charges, which takes 5 hours; it really will only be suitable for very short hops around the city. Some folks living in high rise apartments however may find it a bit of a drag trailing an extension lead the length of two football pitches down the side of their building and along the road to their car every night, and wondering if the cable will still be there in the morning or wake up to find the kids abseiling down it before breakfast! DaimlerChrysler UK is also working on a plan to eliminate all carbon dioxide (CO_2) emissions generated through the production process of this car. Measurements will be taken at every step of the process, reduced where possible and the remaining unavoidable emissions offset through a mixture of renewable energy, energy efficiency and forestry projects which will save and absorb 1 tonne of CO_2 for every tonne the **smart** ev produces. These measurements or 'carbon footprint' as it is known, will be undertaken prior to the first blue chip corporate partner deliveries in November 2006. The offset projects will be located around the world, with one based in France, where the **smart** ev starts its life, and in the UK, where the final drive train assembly is undertaken by technology partner, Zytek Group. The CarbonNeutral Company and DaimlerChrysler UK expect the **smart** ev will be confirmed as the world's first CarbonNeutral car, as well as being powered by green electricity and having zero emissions.

In a world where we have to act now rather than just think about reducing greenhouse gasses, **smart** have to be admired for doing just that, even though acting now costs money.

Pink Limited Edition at Belford, Northumberland

Brabus red Edition at Mercedes-Benz World, Brooklands

Electric ev smart taken at the L2B 2006

Brabus roadster Bi-Turbo V6 prototypes

In 2003 Brabus created a prototype version of the roadster coupé with two merged 3-cylinder engines. This was produced to celebrate the 100th anniversary of the Solituderennen, a former German race track that held motor sports events up until 1965 on a 11.4km circuit near Stuttgart, named after the nearby Castle Solitude. This V6 bi-turbo powerplant had a maximum power of 218 bhp for a weight of only 840 kg. Astonishingly, this gave it the same power-to-weight ratio as a Porsche 911 Carrera 4S. **Smart** claimed the car could accelerate to 100 Km/h in under six seconds. Since the twin-turbo V-6 occupies almost as much space as two three-cylinder engines, the fuel tank which comes in the form of a Formula 1-type foam rubber fuel bladder had to be relocated to the nose of the car, where the luggage compartment used to be. The bigger engine also forced a change from separate coil springs and dampers to concentric units to support the de Dion rear suspension. Only ten cars were built and presented at the Castle Solitude Memorial Day. Unfortunately, they are not available for sale and are not even allowed to be driven on the public roads in Germany. Several of Mercedes' own race drivers however, like Markus Winkelhock, were allowed to drive guests around the event's race track on the day. However, the UK was privileged indeed when **smart** allowed one of the roadsters to be shipped over here and used as the lead car for the start of the London to Brighton Run in 2003 and in 2004. A really super car, but with a supposed price tag of around £350,000 each if it ever went on sale, and with all the extra and rearranged hardware allowing only enough shopping room for designer shoes and handbags, perhaps it is best to stick to the standard versions and leave this one to a moment of fantasy.

The roadster Editions Bluewave and Brabus

There have been several limited editions, with the 'Bluewave' being one of the early ones, appearing in November 2003. This edition had colour coded body trim, blue carbon internal trim, leather seats and Brabus accessories. Early in 2004, a full spec Brabus roadster was launched, costing considerably less than the 'Bluewave' edition. This rather riled some 'Bluewave' owners, as they had paid much more for a car with far less performance. Once they had been confronted by several miffed customers, **smart** offered 'Bluewave' owners the choice of cash-back, an SB2 engine re-map or part exchange for a Brabus roadster at a lower cost. This was a nice touch in the customer relations department. The Brabus roadster and roadster coupé came with their power increased to 74 kW (101 PS). The Brabus versions have a different twin sports exhaust, lower suspension, polished six-spoke Monoblock VI 17" alloy wheels, front spoiler, side skirts and radiator grille. The exclusive Brabus interior includes a leather trimmed dashboard, alloy-effect accent parts, instrument graphics, leather and aluminium gearknob, aluminium handbrake handle, aluminium pedals and Brabus labeled floor mats.

The roadster Edition light

The roadster light is basically the same spec as the standard roadster but without a few of the extraneous fripperies, an economy version in plain English. Just 400 right hand drive versions were produced and put on the market in March 2004. One of the main differences is the roof. The roadster light has a matt hard top in place of a soft top that can be retracted at the touch of a button. Unfortunately, this means when a rain cloud suddenly appears and releases its contents the driver has to pull over and physically get out and manually replace the hard top, instead of impressing his passenger by coolly pressing a digit on the roof switch. The interior is decked out in Uni black cloth as apposed to leather and although wired for sound, audio equipment is an option, which actually gives the owner a better choice as often this is upgraded by discerning ears anyway. There is a choice of six body panel colours but only a black tridion is available in this edition. This model sports a three-cylinder turbocharged 698cc engine, the same as is found in the fortwo coupé, although in this instance it has been boosted to produce 80bhp. With the addition of steel wheels instead of alloys this car weighs just 790kg and can accelerate to 60mph in 10.7 seconds, topping out at 109mph.

The roadster Edition speed silver

This sporty, elegant roadster sprayed in the exclusive speed silver metallic paint that is normally reserved exclusively for the **smart** roadster Brabus and roadster-coupé Brabus, was launched in May 2004 as a limited edition of 755 cars. Based on the standard roadster with an 82bhp petrol engine, it is equipped with all the standard roadster features and with a soft top that can be electrically opened and closed when the car is in motion, even when driving at top speed. The one main thing that makes this limited edition special is the paintwork.

The roadster Edition RCR

Another really nice model is the roadster coupé racing edition, or RCR, which we were lucky to encounter whilst at a meeting at the DCUK headquarters in Milton Keynes. The RCR is a great looking car and was produced with the intention of paying homage to the Brabus V6 bi-turbo, which **smart** were inundated with requests to buy even though the car was never officially on sale. Launched in June 2005 for the UK market, this model has a top speed of 115mph and is fitted with the SB2 re-map. Other features include racing red body panels and colour coded front and rear grille, spoiler and trim. The car comes complete with a Brabus twin sports exhaust and 17" Brabus Monoblock VI alloy wheels. The interior has more tasteful touches with Brabus Alcantara and leather seats with red quilted stitching, a Brabus aluminium gear knob, foot pedal pads and hand brake handle, a three spoke steering wheel with paddle shift and a badge stating what production number the car is, as there has only been a limited edition of 50 made.

The roadster Edition finale

With the sad demise in production of roadsters full stop, it was a welcome sight to potential buyers that **smart** launched the finale edition in April 2006. This edition came in both roadster and roadster-coupé models. Specifically for the European market, the edition launched at the Geneva Motor show was a limited collector's edition of only 50 cars. It was based on the top model, the Brabus Xclusive with 101 bhp and came with satin brown metallic painted body panels. The interior was unusually upholstered in brown leather. It also had the new Runline alloy wheels and Brabus exhaust, frontspoiler and side skirts. In addition to this, a UK-only 'Finale Edition' was also unveiled at the same time, with a higher limited edtition of 200 cars available. This commemorative special edition has an 80 bhp engine and boasts an impressive level of specification, including 17" Runline alloy wheels, metallic paint, air conditioning, cockpit clock and rev counter, starter switch integrated in the gear shift lever, sound package, interior contrast components in 'flow silver' and an exclusive colour combination on the roadster of speed silver body panels, colour coded front and rear grille with a black tridion. It also features leather door and cockpit trim and a central arm rest. As **smart** have obviously intended, this will surely become a classic. However, with the future production now hopefully secure by another leading car manufacturer, this will not, we hope, be the last we see of these terrific sports cars, even if they will be slightly in disguise.

V6 Bi Turbo roadster at the start of the L2B 2005

Brabusmatt's Limited Edition Bluewave roadster

Messerschmitt_owner's Limited Edition roadster light

RCR Limited Edition photographed at DCUK headquarters, Milton Keynes

Roadster Edition Xclusive finale owned by RacingSnake

5 The Events

There have been some great events held in the UK since the clubs started forming, back in early 1999. Some are just one day affairs, while others have lasted up to 5 days, and several have been held for charity. What the events and meetings all share in common, is the gathering together of like-minded people with an abundance of pride and enthusiasm for **smarts**. Both of us have now been to many events and have even organised a few ourselves, one of them being the incredibly daft *M25 Run*, but more on that later. The sizes of the events can vary from just 10 cars to 2000! The biggest is *The London to Brighton Run*, which is where we shall kick this chapter off.

London to Brighton – The History

This is by far the single, biggest event in the UK. It attracts people and **smarts** from all over the UK and abroad. It was here, as previously mentioned, the authors of this book first met, or rather nearly collided! Fate seems to have played a part in this near miss, as this book would never have materialised had *s2trash* not been in such a hurry to keep up with *Vermaak*, the mullet wearing moderator who used to patrol the posts on the Smartmaniacs website and cut up *Miss Polkadot* at a roundabout! *The London to Brighton Run* has to be the one event that all **smart** owners should try to do at least once. The site of so many **smarts** all gathered in one place, is a fantastic sight to behold. From here on in, *The London to Brighton Run* will be referred to as the **L2B** , as it is far too long-winded giving it its full title every time, plus, it is handy to know what the short version means when you see it mentioned on a website.

The Very First Smart L2B – 2001

The s2crew, the **smart** modifying club from Sussex, decided just for a bit of fun to emulate a long standing Mini Club event by staging a London to Brighton run, just for **smarts**, starting from Hyde Park in central London', said *siman91,* an early participator in **smart** related events.

'We only just made it to the start just as everybody was setting off, so we missed out on the at-the-start photos, which was a bit of a shame, as it was the beginning of **smart** history really. We also got very lost coming out of London, eventually passing through Victoria Station taxi rank! My excuse is that those were the days before satellite navigation was popular and we relied on good old paper maps, the ability to point a finger and shout at your navigator! ~ Note to self...don't let my wife read this!' Approximately 90 cars attended this very first event, with no involvement from any **smart** traders, just **smart** owners. Stopping off at Pease Pottage Services on the M23 on the way to Brighton, the s2crew decided it was a convenient place to re-group, have a pint and a chin wag, before setting off for Madeira Drive. 'We had a fantastic day out, which we rounded off with a mini cruise through Brighton itself before heading off home, smiling all the way'.

The First L2B organised by thesmartclub – 2002

The first **L2B** that thesmartclub organised, with help from DCUK, was held on the 21st July 2002. Every year since then, it has been held in September. It was an idea that thesmartclub admit they copied from the s2crew, but with the help, influence and organisational skills provided by DCUK, it was inevitable that their event would snowball into the massive meeting it has now become. The very first starting venue was Alexandra Palace, attracting approximately 500 cars, which was a fine turnout indeed. It was a beautiful hot sunny day, which initially was so pleasant, but which turned to near cases of heatstroke when the **smarts** got caught in traffic jams throughout the city. An incident in Brixton, South London involving the Police had caused a major backlog of traffic, which left many drivers stranded for two hours plus – an unforgettable experience indeed for some! It was partly due to this that the event was forwarded on to September and an out-of-city starting venue sought.

This event was featured on *Top Gear* later on in the year, and naturally showed the wackier side to **smart** owners by showing the mad, mad, grass-covered **smart**! It was the watching of this very programme that convinced *Miss Polkadot* that the **smart** was definitely the car for her, although not being an owner of a sheep; she decided that maybe the acquisition of something a little less pastural looking was required. The finishing point was Madeira Drive, the famous road that sweeps along the seafront in Brighton. For anybody who has done the London to Brighton Bike Ride, or seen the Vintage Car Rally on television, it is a road you would be familiar with.

2003

Billing Aquadrome

Billing was the brainchild of Dave Kaye (*Mr. Funkysmart*), who founded the internet-based **smart** Club, Funkysmart. Along with his ever trusty, raffle ticket selling sidekick, *Tangerine Teal*, they set about organizing the first ever international **smart** camping weekend in the UK.

Looking back, little did we know that Billing was to become the **smart** version of Woodstock and the VW Bugjam, all rolled into one. How does one best describe Billing the place? Billing Aquadrome is actually an enormous camping venue located in Northampton, the heart of England, which is easily accessible from all parts of the country. The campsite has an extensive range of leisure facilities, including a jet-ski lake, fishing, licensed bars offering tempting meals and a variety of entertainment. Rather like a mini Milton Keynes, with mobile homes instead of brick-built houses, Billing is very self contained, with its own funfair, shops, restaurants and a pub. There is an excellent fish and chip shop and an Indian restaurant, which was frequented several times. It is a very pleasant place with lots of surrounding lakes, trees, grassy paddocks with even a canal meandering through the site. *Mr. Funkysmart* and *Tangerine Teal* organized this first foray as a two day affair over the weekend of the 28/29 June 2003. They invited **smart** related traders to attend, of which there were only a few at that early stage, including Smarts R us, the independent **smart** specialists, who brought quite a few second hand cars down with them for sale, along with a selection of their unusual custom parts. Smarts R us must have sold out of nearly everything on the first day, judging by the queues of owners at the door to their marquee. Smart of Hertford brought their promotional wagon and sold oodles of **smart** scale models and **smart** merchandise. *Miss Polkadot's* son *Microdot* became a very proud owner of a 1:12 scale radio-controlled roadster at this event and proudly showed off his skills at performing doughnuts on the grass. S-mann from the Netherlands and Michalak from Germany also had representatives, with both having brought show and concept cars with them for all to drool over.

S2trash attended the whole weekend event, leaving East Sussex at 6am on the Saturday to join up with other **smarts** from Brighton on route. The weather forecast for the weekend was hot and sunny, a perfect arrangement for a weekend of **smart** camping. Arriving at around 10.30 am-ish after the long drive up, *s2trash* was greeted by *Mr. Funkysmart* who he had chatted to on-line before, but never in person. He never did suss out how Dave knew it was him getting out of his car, but he got a handshake and a "Hello, you must be *tom.c*". One suspected that *s2trash's* reputation preceded him! ('*tom.c*' was the username that *s2trash* had way back in the early days of joining the website clubs, but far too tame a name now, for those in the know!) The first cars had been arriving since 10am, and by lunchtime over 100 cars had appeared and were very busy erecting a **smart** corral of tents. One of the modification crazes at the time was the vertically parked wiper blades. *Vermaak* and *Manic* performed the wiper blade 'surgery' to six cars completely free of charge, doing it just for the fun of helping out.

The late afternoon proved to the world that the British cannot BBQ to save their lives as Billing started to smell like a cremation site for burgers, sausages and sad looking chicken pieces. Not having taken any utensils or a BBQ, *s2trash* played safe, cheated and bought a curry, and sat with the very strange 'Karrot Krunchers' club from Peterborough. Well, how many folks do you know that go camping sporting curly orange clown wigs?

A small selection of the 700 cars at the show

The Karrot Krunchers causing a fire hazard

Smarts R us trading area complete with trailer

After smugly watching the said burnt offerings been eaten, *s2trash* became privy to one of the best games of rounders in the history of the universe, which started up between the 's2crew' club and the 'Karrot Krunchers'. This game became a free-for-all, with water pistols and assorted light armaments being used to gain advantages. The game only ended when the s2crew got hungry and walked off the field of battle in search of sustenance and refreshment. The actual outcome of the game never was recorded, just melting away into myth. It was one of those – you had to be there – moments. As the sun started to set, 138 owners had set up camp, and the night time activities started with many an owner getting extremely jolly from the falling down water brought along purely for medicinal purposes, don't you know! The s2crew, now known as the 'Combustible Kings', burnt every thing they could lay their hands on as the night got colder on their BBQ fire, and it was rather tempting to singe a few of those orange wigs...

Now, *s2trash* had never done camping, as in sleeping outside, before. All he had taken with him for the weekend was a borrowed sleeping bag. No tent, no provisions, no sense. In a strange sort of way, this hapless appearance gained him the sympathy vote from all and sundry, and he was allowed to park himself and his car in the Funkysmart marquee. Trying to nod off in a sleeping bag placed directly on bare ground, all alone inside a large marquee, doesn't make for the best of sleeping arrangements, but at least he wasn't exposed to the elements, or the rest of the campers! He finally drifted off to sleep at around 2am, only to be woken with a sudden tug on the bottom of his sleeping bag by *s2stealth* and *mccsmartarse*. They had thought he was a rubbish sack and had had plans to add him to their funeral pyre! Some might say that that was a particularly tempting idea, but trying to balance a cold 6'4" carcass on a wobbly disposable BBQ, defies even the ingenuity of Heath Robinson, so they left him to carry on snoring.

Sunday morning arrived far too soon, and although the sky was blue and the sun shone, heralding a very hot day ahead, *s2trash* woke at 6 am, very, very cold, and stiff as a stick of rock. Sleeping directly on grass, even if it was inside a marquee, was not at all comfy! The best thing to do was to get his old ticker and his achy joints moving by walking around taking some photos of other disheveled campers, and promising them it wouldn't cost them too much money to have the negatives destroyed! Lo and behold, out in a field, he found another mad camper without equipment. *Massive*, aka Steve Goddard, founder of fabulous Smartimes magazine, was fast asleep in his car, looking decidedly the worse for wear – another first time camper by the look of things. *S2trash* felt so much better as that now made two mad fools instead of just the one! Amid that special fragrant aroma of bacon cooking on a campfire, some of the cars that had traveled from afar started to pack up camp and head off for home, even before the gates opened at 10am, mindful of the very hot temperatures forecast, over 30°c! It certainly had been a fabulous first camping weekend for **smart** owners, young and old, with over 500 cars attending, and many long lasting friendships were formed because of it.

For *Miss Polkadot*, this was her very first foray into **smart** gatherings. She had purchased her car in the February of this year and due to her inquisitive nature, and fortitude, found all the car clubs on the internet and made a point of joining in everything that was going. She was only able to make it to Billing on the Sunday, and so had missed out on all of the high jinks that occurred on the Saturday. Her car made an impressive appearance at the campsite though, certainly proving that individualism was certainly alive and kicking. No-one had seen spots quite like those on her car. With a retro 60's feel in black and white, her **smart** was fun, hip, modern and to pardon the pun, spot-on! She had made friends with *Zippy*, from the Walton club, after contacting him on the Funkysmart website, and joined him and several other owners in a convoy all the way to Billing. Little did she know that this would be the start of one BIG **smart** adventure, and the first of many such convoys. She hadn't actually met *s2trash* at this stage in the proceedings and so, momentarily, was spared...well until September and the London to Brighton!

Bexhill Beach Party 2003

The first of these was held in August 2003, one of the hottest weekends since the summer of '76 as it turned out. The idea was to meet up on a very long, beautiful stretch of beach just outside Bexhill called Cooden Beach, where you could comfortably park your **smart** on the shingle, albeit with some caution. Here, it was planned for everyone to soak up some rays, have some fun, games and a BBQ, followed by an overnight stay at a local campsite. This was the very first event *s2trash* had organised and he didn't think there was much that could really go wrong – which as always was a mistake to think. At 6am that morning, *s2trash* drove up to **smart** of Brentford to collect his vehicle, which had had a new roof fitted. With his car back on the road, *s2trash* made off to a roadside café just outside Battle on the A21, where he had arranged to meet up with some of the folks heading down for the Beach Party. There he sat in a miniscule patch of shade, and waited, and waited and waited. Worrying that he had somehow got the day wrong, which has been known before, *s2trash* continued to melt in the blistering heat. After what seemed an eternity, a red roadster pulled in at 2pm, much to *s2trash*'s relief. Driven by a young chap called *Jason*, his car was one of the earliest roadsters registered in the UK. He was shortly followed by *s2herman* in a silver fortwo; with news that there had been a bad accident and getting onto the A21 had been almost impossible. It also came to light later on in the day that someone with sat nav, had led one convoy of **smarts** down a dead end country lane, in an attempt to evade the traffic jams, and thus missed the café rendezvous. And so it was that only a very small tube of **smarts** hit the beach. It wasn't long though before the others started to arrive, which was amazing as some had come from as far as Manchester!

Now, as mentioned before, it was dam hot. In fact it hit 35 degrees making the sea feel like a warm bath. *Vladaria*, the mistress of the smartmaniacs website, made the absolute most of it and stood in the sea like Botticelli's Venus (but without the oversized seashell), champagne glass in hand, but with what turned out to be coca-cola. Well, she was driving after all, but she certainly has style!

Vermaak, later on that afternoon fitted a new CD head unit to *Vladaria's* car, although leaning over watching him work like she did, may have been the reason it took so long to fit and not the sweltering heat like he suggested! It was around this time that the long suffering wife of *s2trash* and his son finally turned up with the much sort after food and drink, and he was able to get on with the BBQ. Mind you, it was so hot, if the food had been left on some stones there would have been no need for a BBQ!

Now how could one best describe Bexhill-on-Sea? In a nutshell, Costa del Geriatric would be one of the kinder phrases to portray the place. To be fair it is a very pleasant seaside town, with a goodly amount of affluent properties, and of course a fantastic beach. One cannot be sure that Bexhill was quite ready however for the influx of **smart** cars and their owners, because by mid-afternoon, 25 **smarts** had accumulated on the beach and they were starting to draw attention from everyone in the area, including that of the local press. Naturally, despite the owners beginning to wilt, they posed for the cameras. Any photo opportunity is a good photo opportunity, so they say, and once it was over it was barbeque time. The poor people relaxing in the beach huts near by unfortunately received more than their fair share of fumes as the smoke from the barbeques wafted their way, as well across half one side of Bexhill. The heat of the day had put everyone in go-slow mode and with the planned leisurely convoy to Eastbourne not setting off till later, there was a lot of sitting around doing as little as possible. It was a enjoyable afternoon despite the extraordinary heat and it wasn't long before *s2trash* started a water fight with some kids, and came off worst, not that he would admit it. Once the searing sunshine began to dim, and the first breath of an onshore breeze began to arrive, cars began to be packed up in preparation for the trip to Eastbourne. The first part of the drive was through a place called Little Common. Much to the complete shock of the drinkers at a pub called 'The Wheatsheaf', seeing one **smart** back then was rare, but 25 all at once! – they must have thought their ale was spiked. The convoy of **smarts** then headed west along the main coastal road towards Eastbourne, taking in Norman's and Pevensey Bay.

As the **smart** convoy hit town, the normal finger pointing and looks of disbelief started. Despite all of the sets of traffic lights and pedestrian crossings along the beach road, the convoy cleverly managed to stay together as it pulled up outside 'The Grand Hotel', a pre-planned place to re-group should the convoy have got split up. Now *s2trash* does admit that the group made a lot of noise outside this grandiose establishment, but swears it wasn't that but the sight of the cars that brought so many people out onto their balconies to look at this unique assembly of cute cars. That particular snapshot in time, taken on that warm barmy summer's night will forever be a vivid lasting memory for *s2trash*, (memory being something he isn't blessed with in great abundance!). With the posing over, folks scrambled back into their cars to resume the trip. It is always handy to have a set of two-way radios if attempting a convoy and there had been two sets kindly available for the drive, courtesy of *Tangerine Teal* and *Massive*. One radio was lent to *s2trash's* son and navigator and the other was given to the last car in the convoy. *Massive*, who was heading home straight from 'The Grand Hotel' experience, naturally took his radio set with him. This left the convoy up the street without full communication, which would have been fine if *Vermaak* had not thought that it would be fun to take the convoy via the night club and bar section of Eastbourne. Confident in his knowledge of the area, the lead was handed over to him.

Twenty-four cars did a mass u-turn in the wide road outside the hotel. Please remember, dear reader, that they now had only one radio set, and needless to say within five minutes the cars started to get lost! The next 30 minutes were spent trying to find every one of them. Ten cars, with *Vermaak* leading, had managed to stay together and as they pulled over to try to figure out how to find the lost cars, *Vermaak* got an earful from *Tangerine Teal* via her mobile phone, so at least everyone knew where she was! Finally, a decision was made to head back to Bexhill and hope that the remaining lost **smarts** got picked up en route, which, in a ramshackle sort of way, was actually managed with exclamations of "Oh, there's another one" every now and then. With all the cars, minus *Massive*, back at the beach, a fire was lit which took on

Botticcelli's Venus

Smart beach invasion

36°C at 5.30pm!

the size of a funeral pyre. After the stifling heat of the day, the cooling evening breeze was just wonderful, and reluctantly, just like all good things, it had to come to an end. Many **smart** owners had arranged to camp at local campsites and so they meandered off along with the rest who went directly home, including *s2trash* and his very sleepy navigator/radio operator. The following morning the folks that camped decide to head for the beach again, where *s2trash* met up with them for a couple of hours to say thank you for coming down and making the day such a success and say goodbye to a terrific bunch of people. No one could have guessed at the time how much everyone enjoyed themselves and that this chilled out event would turn into an annual pilgrimage to the south coast, and grow from a one day outing to five day, extra long weekend!

The London to Brighton 2003

On 27th September 2003, the starting venue for the second *L2B* organised by thesmartclub was changed to Kempton Park Race Course. This was both *Miss Polkadot's* and *s2trash's* first *L2B,* and they were both taken aback by the amazing amount of cars appearing at the start! 800 to be precise! Neither of them had ever seen that many **smarts** all in one place before. Not only that, the lengths some folks had gone to customise their cars, and themselves, was truly amazing. There was Noddy and Big Ears in one car, accompanied by Mr Plod the policeman in another. There was a fortwo completely disguised as an orange carp with fins and eyelashes. There were cars in England football colours, cars covered in skulls, tomatoes and of course spots. The brand new V6 Bi turbo roadster, one of only ten ever made, was flown over from Germany especially for this event, and was given the honour of having pole position. With minutes to go before the off, the air was electric and the noise of hundreds of revving engines and tooting horns certainly stirred the emotions.

Sunday 27th September was definitely a fateful and memorable day. After the cutting-up incident at the entrance to Kempton Park, *Miss Polkadot* and *s2trash* coincidentally found themselves parked right behind one another on the staring grid; just as well they found the funny side of things and refrained from giving each other a bunch of fives! Being right at the front of one of the 18 lines of **smarts**, and sixth in line to depart, meant that they were able to leave fairly soon after the 10am start. Those at the back of the pack had to wait nearly an hour before they managed to get going. The journey took them via Hampton Court, Esher High Street, then onto the M25, before joining the M23 to Brighton.

Never officially a mid-way stop, Pease Pottage Services on the M23 has become the mid-way point for a lot of **smarts** on the L2B run; an excuse for essential sustenance, chat, oh and of course some fuel. Driving into Brighton was great fun, as **smart** cars were still a fairly rare site back then. Just to see peoples faces light up, or look bewildered, as they all whizzed round tooting horns for any reason they could find, was such fun. Groups of people gathered on bridges waving ecstatically, thankfully throwing beaming smiles and not bricks! The finish point, as with the first *L2B*, was again at Madeira Drive and the authors' first introduction to independent traders selling custom-made parts. Coincidentally, they both bought thesmartclub air scoops for their cars that day; the latest modification sweeping across the website clubs at that time, and they both have them still.

During the course of the afternoon three car competition categories: Most Modified, Best Concourse (unmodified and production class) and Zaniest **smart**, entered by a total of 75 pre-selected cars, were judged by representatives of DCUK and thesmartclub. As if you didn't already know, *Miss Polkadot's* **smart** which is covered in retro 70's circles and dots on the outside and is upholstered with spotty Dalmatian style fabric on the inside, was, not surprisingly, entered into the Zaniest category. *Miss P* and her son *Microdot*, had both been dared by a friend to dress matching the car, a challenge they took on board rather readily. Naturally, a lady must have a co-ordinating handbag, so *Miss P* customised one to match. (An item *s2trash* has since *often* been on the receiving end of!).

Start of the rally with the V6 Bi Turbo roadster

Surely this is a car rally, not a carp show!

Peas release me - let me go!

Entering into the spirit of the day, *Miss P* and *Microdot*, wearing co-ordinating clothes and accessories, wowed the judges to win the Zaniest Smart Car competition! When presented with the glass trophy by Al Young, head honcho of thesmartclub, it was commented that the very high standard of modifications to her car and the attention to detail with regard to having a 'matching son and handbag', had swayed the judges in their direction, over and above the other entries, who *Miss P* had thought were far more deserving than her. "I could not believe that we had won, we entered just for the fun of it, and fun we certainly had, not thinking for one moment that we would actually win, it was just fantastic!" The Concourse section was won by a lovely lady with a Numeric Blue 4/2 in pristine condition, who had gone to incredible lengths to dye her hair the same colour turquoise as the panels on her car. The Best Modified group was won by the king of the LED's – *T1NY W*. Historically speaking, this was the beginning *of T1NY W*'s **smart** modifying bug, with his car sporting only half of Blackpool's illuminations at this stage. One look at the interior of his car made one's jaw drop 3 floors down! He had ripped out the dashboard, re-modelled it, beautifully covered it in mushroom coloured Alcantara and installed a flat screen computer monitor within it that rose up majestically at the press of a button so that all the onlookers could watch a DVD. He had also added amazing new speakers the size of dinner plates, a whopping great amp that filled the boot space and pushed the envelope with his 19" replacement wheels! It was literally just awesome, so unique and so beautifully done. A well deserved winner, but this was only the start of his **smart** transformation.

We will be looking at 'Tiny the Transformer' in detail later on.

The L2B 2003

It's dark outside, time to get up and get our outfits on; for it's a very special day, today's the BRIGHTON RUN!

The polish and the cloths are packed, the car inside is tidy; for hours we have worked on her, our Smart is VERY shiny!

5.45 ~ its time to go, speed off onto the night; we meet a Smartie on the way, it's starting to get light.

At Clacket Lane we meet more Smarties heading for the meet; we race along the motorway, our Smartie 'Tube' complete.

We arrive at Kempton Park at last, the atmosphere's electric; with Smarts all colours, mods and tweeks and some drivers, quite eccentric!

We've never seen so many smarts all gathered in one spot; there are 14 hundred little dears including 'Polkadot'!

There's lots of happy people here, taking photos, chatting, preening; there's not a grubby smart in sight, they've been so busy cleaning!

We're getting nervous and excited just preparing to depart; red Roadster '6' will lead off, followed by a shoal of smarts.

Its 10am and time to go, the klaxon is a sounding; a thousand Smartie hooters peep, my heart it sure is pounding!

We're OFF! We blast off through THE START, we wave, flash, toot and shout; what a marvellous sight to see, we're crazy there's no doubt!

For the ordinary motorists, amazing it must be; to spot the jolly Smarties a-racing to the sea!

Along the streets, on bridges, the people wave and cheer; as we rush along to Brighton, in time for ice-cold beer!

In Brighton, slowly travelling, in traffic stuck, we're fine; then cruising down Madeira Drive, to cross the FINISH LINE!

There was a bit of trouble, at Black Rock to park the cars; and the surface under little wheels, was like the stuff on Mars!

But never mind, we did it, and boy did we have fun; so we'll all be looking forward to next years Smartie Run!

© Miss Polkadot 2003

The first crossblade s2trash ever spotted with a re-spray

Flower Power!

Winners of the Zaniest smart

Beaulieu 2003

This has now become known as the last big **smart** event of the year, but it had humble beginnings way back on a cold November day in 2003. This first event was organised by *s2trash* all on his lonesome and without adult supervision! As always with him there was an ulterior motive, to get into Beaulieu for free. Beaulieu is the stately home of Lord Montagu and home to the National Motor Museum. It is famous for hosting large car events and its amazing collection of vintage cars, motorbikes, commercial vehicles, motoring eccentricities and memorabilia, including the world famous Bluebird car, housed in the purpose built museum. Set in the picturesque New Forest it is a superb place to hold a **smart** meet. When *s2trash* called Beaulieu to ask permission to arrange a **smart** meet the staff thought that it was a great idea and were more than happy to organise the day and bent over backwards to help all they could. It was decided that the **smarts** should be situated in their hard court arena which is positioned right next to the Motor Museum itself. As the event was being planned for November, hard standing was far preferable to getting stuck in muddy grass and on the plus side it meant that the event would be next to the museum and the general public would be able to admire the **smarts** on show. Feeling rather pleased with himself, *s2trash* posted details of the event on all the web site forums and there seemed to be a good response to it.

Tangerine Teal had phoned *s2trash* to say that she would come down the night before to help him set up ~ keep an adult eye on him more like.

Sunday the 9th of November – the day of the event dawned and *s2trash* needed to leave home at 6am to allow plenty of time to make the 137 mile journey from Battle to Beaulieu. Rolling in to Lord Montagu's estate at 9.45am to see that the Beaulieu organisers had gone to the trouble of making special 'Funkysmart' signs for the event, *s2trash* was most impressed.

Shortly after arriving, a member of the Beaulieu staff came along and asked if *s2trash* had any idea of the number of cars that would be turning up. Unable to give a definitive answer, he said that he had hoped for at least thirty cars or more, which put a smile on the staff members face. It wasn't long before *Tangerine Teal* suddenly appeared standing next to *s2trash* like a fairy godmother on speed, grinning and keeping him under her watchful eye and between them both devised a plan to arrange the cars as they arrived. *Nino Nick* had volunteered along with *Mad Dan,* to help with the parking and they too arrived bright eyed and bushy tailed – well *Mad Dan* especially, as legend has it that he is half man, half squirrel! Digging deep into the recesses of *s2trash's* low capacity memory storage facilities, he thinks that Smarts R us arrived next in two separate cars, having driven 187 miles from Nottingham.

The official opening time for the event was 10am. At 10am it was all quiet. Apart from the odd car that had arrived there were hardly any **smarts** to be seen and *s2trash* began to wonder if he had a flop on his hands and if this had been such a good idea after all. He started to make his escape plans while *Tangerine Teal* made plans to keep *s2trash* right where he was. With both of them standing at the entrance with one member of Beaulieu's staff, trying to decide who felt the most doom and gloom in percentage terms, they became shaken to the core when suddenly what seemed like a zillion **smarts** appeared all at once! The rotters had all meet up at a service station and driven down to Beaulieu on mass. This left *s2trash*, *Tangerine Teal* and the Beaulieu staff having to run round like mad taking money left right and centre.

After a few manic minutes the staff member received a call on his 2-way radio that said "We are sending you help, there are **smart** cars backing out onto main road – the damn things are everywhere!". Not wanting to keep the incoming **smarts** waiting in a queue for too long, the cars were rushed through in two lines with money flying everywhere. Ten exhausting minutes later all of the cars were in and neatly parked up, all credit to *Nino Nick* and *Mad Dan* who between them, managed to do a sterling job.

Looking rather 'Fagin-like' *s2trash* had a coat full of bank notes that had to removed and counted. *Tangerine Teal* relieved him of his monetary burden and took it

Smart *funky sign*

Some of the attending cars on parade

NinoNick gives smart a hug

off to a safe place to be counted. The Beaulieu staff could not believe that 55 **smart** cars plus their passengers had turned up for the day, making a very good turn out. With the fear of the event being a flop disappearing within minutes, *s2trash* was told that even the Rolls Royce Owners Club sometimes attracted only 20 cars, so to have that many **smart** cars arrive on a cold winter's day was for them a huge success, as it resulted in more people visiting the Motor Museum. Everyone was happy all round. *Tangerine Teal* had some commemorative car stickers of event made up, every one of which sold and so she went on to busy herself selling raffle tickets. A force to be reckoned with! *Massive* from Smartimes magazine was there, chatting to one and all about the latest modifications that they had done to their cars and discussing the popularity of his **smart** publication. With so many cars to choose from, *s2trash* photographed every thing he could like a kid in a sweet shop. From his point of view the light was awful for car photography, low and bright with long hard shadows...... oh, how he suffered for his art!

The morning just slipped away with folk chatting **smart** talk all over the place, when the thought of food started to come into play. Trotting off to the cafeteria to get some sustenance, *s2trash* was invited by the s2crew to join them and the Sussex Branch at their table. He should have known better, but he joined them all the same, and ended up in the middle of a food fight started by *s2stealth*. Never one to shy away from offered food, *s2trash* was quite happy to polish off a well aimed chip that landed in his ear, despite it having skimmed the floor before getting a coating of earwax! Smarts R us had brought with them an amazing fortwo that they had recently resprayed using an incredible flip paint, and which *s2trash* was allowed to borrow for a shoot after he turned on his charm. The paint turned from green to purple to gold, and back again, and it took much of his knowledge, experience and tricks to balance out the horrible hard light in order to get a half decent image. The end results were worth the effort, managing to capture the colours perfectly.

One of the initial reasons for staging this event, was for *s2trash*, who was the organiser, to get into the Motor Museum for free, a cheapskate idea that he freely admits to. Unfortunately for him, his cunning plan backfired because with so much to see and photograph and people to talk to, he never actually got anywhere near the place! Maybe he would have to arrange another one next year just so that he could try and get inside the museum. With the shadows now getting longer and the temperature dropping fast, people started saying their farewells and made tracks to leave. The Beaulieu staff came over to thank *s2trash* for an amazing show of cars and asked if he would like to bring them back again next year. Trying not to look too excited he beamed from ear to ear and said "You are darn right, we would love to!" Standing around chatting with the last of the stragglers, they were suddenly aware that it was almost dark and *s2trash* decided that it was about time he hit the road for his long drive home. After collecting the cash from *Tangerine Teal's* safe deposit box, *s2trash* went and handed the money over to the Beaulieu staff. Once inside their offices he oversaw a recount of the takings. After a great deal of complicated calculations regarding a sliding scale for entry fees, it appeared that there was a small surplus to requirements.

As the event was not a money-making exercise *s2trash* decided to donate the proceeds to a charity of Beaulieu's choice. If his gold fish memory proved correct, £150 was handed over, much to the absolute delight of the staff. At least in having a good time they had helped others too, and *s2trash* felt a little less bad about getting in for free, even though he didn't get to see the vintage cars.

A calm moment before the food fight

The original Smartarse and s2Eagleye

Who is buying the coffee?

2004

M25 Run - The Dumball Rally

This initially started as a joke post on one of the **smart** club website forums. With nothing better to do, *s2trash* dreamt up this silly idea of getting together a few cars and driving clock-wise all the way around the M25, on a Saturday evening, just for the hell of it! Never in a million years did he think anyone would take him up on his ludicrous idea and be daft enough want to drive around the world's largest car park. For those unfamiliar with Britain's largest ring road, the M25 is a three lane motorway, 117 miles in circumference that encircles our capital city, London, and was built with the intention of alleviating traffic congestion, a situation that it just hasn't been able to fulfil somehow! As it became obvious people really wanted to do this run, some hastily made plans were cobbled together! Having met up with *Miss Polkadot* earlier in the year, she offered to help organise the event. The first thing to arrange had to be a starting point, and 'Bluewater' shopping complex in Kent was decided upon. So, on a May Bank Holiday Saturday, at 5pm *s2trash* and *Miss Polkadot* turned up at Bluewater to welcome any mad **smarts** arriving to join them in this crazy, fuel guzzling excursion. Having had around 30 replies on the website club forums from people wishing to take part, *s2trash* printed off copies of all the relevant information needed to help his fellow nutters complete their journey, including the service stations where everyone would be stopping on route. By the time the 7.30pm start time came around there a total of eleven cars that had made an appearance. Common sense must have got to a few over just how daft this trip going to be, but the fact that anyone turned up at all was a surprise. So, for the historical records and the naming and shaming the attendees were; *s2trash, Miss Polkadot* (who was travelling as Trashie's passenger), *Bubski, Mccsmart2002, Blackmagic, s2herman, Bluebottle* and her passenger, *Sprintmick* and his wife, *jim808, Putzie,* and *Claptnei.* With all drivers in possession of clearly printed details of who the lead car was, where they would be stopping etc., and armed with several sets of walkie-talkie radios, everyone set off. Well, the eleven cars managed to get as far as the third roundabout upon leaving Bluewater when dear *s2herman* took a wrong turning. The consensus of opinion was that that he must have seen a burger van, but luckily within a few seconds the group got back together and were soon rolling along the motorway. *Mccsmart2002* had decided to go as a passenger with *Bubski* so he could film the event more easily and not risk trying to drive and film at same time. His golden locks could be seen flowing in the breeze as he hung out of *Bubski's* car to get that 'perfect angle'. On the information sheet *s2trash* had handed out it had stated clearly *not* to follow *Bubski* if he moved out of the convoy. Due to having *Mccsmart2002* on board filming, you guessed it, *Bubski* moved out into another lane to allow his cinematographer passenger an alternative viewpoint and all followed. By the time the convoy had nearly reached the first service station there were three cars with radios at the front of the convoy, instead of being evenly spaced throughout the line. *Putzie* had realised what had happened and radioed through to say he would pull into the hard shoulder, the idea being he could get to the back and ride shotgun. But best laid plans don't always materialise...and what happened, the convoy followed him onto the hard shoulder. Watching the goings-on in the rear view mirror it did look amusing with **smarts** snaking all over the place like a huge multi-coloured python! Somehow, everyone eventually managed to pull into the first service station, Clacket Lane, as one whole convoy without anyone driving past the turning on the motorway. *S2trash* felt very happy he had got this far and parked his car with a smile on his face, only to get one hell of an ear blasting from *Miss Polkadot* for parking in a disabled bay. The sentence used was "you might not be disabled now, but if you don't move you could soon well be!" Such moral high ground from one so small!

It was a beautiful evening and had been the warmest day of the year so far. With nobody in the mood for rushing, most folks just sat and drank coffee while calmly contemplating the dippy drive they were embarked upon, whilst *Putzie, Mccsmart2002* and *s2Herman* stuffed their faces with their second round of fast food. As everyone meandered back to their trusty steeds, several people wandered up to talk about the cars. This would have been fine had it not meant the first stopover had lasted over an hour! A group of **smarts** will always attract interest, but it would have been very rude to say to them "bugger off, don't you know we have a cruise to finish?", now wouldn't it! Once all had made their escape from the adoring masses and anyone needing fuel had topped up, it was' tally ho' and off again, with radio cars in the front, middle and back. *S2trash* had made it absolutely clear from the start that speed limits would be adhered to, that it wasn't a race and that everyone was to stay in line. That was until *Bubski* radioed through to say "there's a stretched limo coming up behind you *Trashy,* in the middle lane!" What they wanted to do was capture on film *s2trash* sitting up the backside of the limo. Ever one to be helpful, the order was obeyed, and *s2trash* then proceeded to break every rule he had laid down on his information sheet! What a site that must have been, a 30 foot long, white limousine with humble little *s2trash* tailgating and *Bubski* under and overtaking, just so *Mccsmart2002* could get some film footage! The poor limo driver must have thought to himself what the heck was going on, being attacked by two **smarts** from all angles!

Now, at around the time of the limo baiting another **smart** fortwo, which appeared to just be travelling along our route, joined the convoy. As the cars pulled into

South Mimms Service Station, the second and last stop of the night, they also followed; even into the lorry park that *s2trash* led every one by mistake. Once parked up *s2trash* went to chat to the mysterious **smart**. As it turned out, *Jim808's* Mum and Dad had hired a **smart** and decided to come along for the last part of the cruise. They had hired the fortwo for the weekend prior to buying one, just to get the feel of it, and decided on a whim to join their son and his unhinged friends on this madcap escapade. Although glad to have another **smart** on board, the lorry park wasn't the best place to stop, and so the convoy made a mad dash for the safety of the correct car park, going the wrong way round of course. "What a 'No Exit' sign? I didn't see that!" said *s2trash* pleading innocence. Although it was only around ten o'clock in the evening, surprisingly most of the food facilities had shut up shop, a bit of a strange occurrence in a service station that is open all night! Despite this minor setback, everyone managed to sit around for an hour chatting about **smarts**. During a long conversation about travelling long distances, it came to light that *Blackmagic* had driven all the way down from Manchester to do the event and was by now, not surprisingly, feeling completely shattered! Time was getting on and so goodbyes, hugs and kisses were liberally spread around, as everyone prepared to drive the last leg of the M25 and depart off home in various directions.

On leaving South Mimms, most had said they wouldn't be going back to the finishing/starting point of Bluewater, as it would have taken them out of their way, which was a bit of a shame, but it was getting late. And so it was that only three **smarts** crossed the Dartford Bridge and completed the first 117 mile, M25 Run or 'Dumball Rally' as it will be forever called. As *s2trash* lay his weary head to sleep that night and counted the cars speeding around the M25, a wry smile spread across his face as he wondered if anyone would be daft to do it all again next year, but anti-clockwise!

...give us a lick!

Photographic evidence that they were indeed mad enough to turn up!

I want a burger THIS big!

Billing Aquadrome 2004

The second Billing 'Smartfest' became a 3 day event, which was held over the weekend of the 25th to 28th of June. Travelling in convoy with *Vermaak* and his girlfriend, *s2trash* went up to the Billing Aquadrome in Northampton on the Thursday, to help the Funkysmart crew out with the setting up of the site and to arrange a **smart** driving course, which, it was later found out, broke every rule in the health and safety book! Due to a mix up with the entry passes, the jobs-worth staff wouldn't let *s2trash* or the other helpers in, so they spent several hours hanging around the entrance waiting for a' big cheese' to sort out the problem. It took a persuasive phone call from *Tangerine Teal* in 'don't-mess-with-me' mode to gain them access, and get on with the job of sorting out the area ready for the next day opening. Typically, although the helpers had the most serious intentions of starting work, a game of Frisbee seemed much more important and took priority over even the serious task of setting up camp. The event organisers were delayed in getting to Billing, which left the trusty helpers to make more of their own childish entertainment. For the first time in his life, whilst under fire from Frisbees, *s2trash* had to erect a tent. Like a scene from an old 'Carry On' film, a strengthening wind had the tent moving around the field with *s2trash* looking on with bewilderment, until it was pointed out to him that the metal things called pegs where there to pin the tent to the ground! Eventually, Dave Kaye *Mr Funkysmart* himself, *Tangerine Teal* and *Wayneaucock* rolled into town, mustered the grown-up kids into shape and the marking out of the trade stands soon began.

This year's show had attracted many more traders than last year, including some new companies bitten by the **smart** bug. Up until now, a great deal of 'bling' buying had to be done via the internet or over the phone, as the companies were far and few between. Some of those that attended were S-mann, Smarts R us, Smartarse Design, NCT, Bantam Trailers, Tardis Trailers, Concept Tuning, Smartechnique, Smart of Hertford parts department, Neoquip, and Smartimes, the dedicated magazine for **smarts**. Once all the trade stands had their pitches marked out, there was a convoy to the nearest supermarket for the purchase of important alcoholic provisions, and hopefully they would remember to get some food and drink too. For one person, and it could only have been *s2trash*, the top priority was to buy a pair of long trousers due to the fact that he had only taken shorts and was now freezing his butt off in the biting wind – well, you would have thought that as it was late June winter woollies and thermals wouldn't actually be required – how wrong could one be! Northampton has the most confusing out-of-town superstore car park and it caused many a **smart** to go every which way but the right one, in this subterranean mini mall. There was much head scratching as to where to go but eventually everyone managed to park. Unbeknown to Tesco's, they were about to be invaded by an advanced party of **smart** owners out for a bit of fun. The shopping trolleys, which were not much smaller than the cars, could be handled with ease and some unscrupulous owners decided to do a few wheelies and burn ups along the aisles, scaring the living daylights out of staff stacking shelves! *S2trash* had gone as *Tangerine Teal's* passenger and being a southern wimp and feeling very cold, proceeded to undress in her car and change into the cheap pair of corduroy jeans he had just bought in Tesco's, with his backside on full view to all and sundry on forecourt of the petrol station! Back at the campsite the destruction of good food began with the ritual lighting of the BBQ's. *S2trash* would have written more about this pivotal moment but it appeared that alcohol may have played a part in his distinct loss of memory from this point in time, for the next several hours.

Friday

At 5am *Tangerine Teal* could be heard cursing the lout who had covered her tent in bread the previous night. As rapidly as it had gone *s2trash's* memory suddenly sparked into life. Ducks had come from all the neighbouring ponds to feast on the free offerings, and were pecking at *TT* through her tent. Meanwhile *s2trash* stood sniggering at *TT's* very appropriate user name (*Tangerine Teal* is a duck) and at the said crime he *may* have committed. A **smart** driving course was set up on one of the fields with *s2trash* using his car as a test vehicle to make sure it was driveable. Traders had been arriving since the previous day and by 10am **smarts** in all colours from all over the country, including county **smart** car clubs, began arriving at the site. Midday saw *Miss Polkadot* and the *Essex Smarties* roll in and pitch up all together down one side of the site. In an unbelievably contrived situation, *s2trash* completely managed to avoid lending a hand in the erection of *Miss P's* supersized tent – forever to be known as 'Polkadot Palace'. Strangely enough, the Friday night became another fog filled haze for *s2trash*, although he did have vague recollections of eating fish and chips and sitting around chatting for hours. Contrary to popular belief, *s2trash* is not used to alcoholic beverages and when consumed, they literally go straight to his head, disabling any sensible brain cells he may have had lurking around!

Saturday

Sporting a thick head, Saturday dawned early for *s2trash* with much picture taking being at the top of the agenda. Spotty Badger Productions were using this important gathering of **smarts** of all kinds, as an opportunity to get some cracking photographs for the calendar they were producing for the following year. By 10am the crowds had started to roll in thick and fast. It was a fantastic turn out! Sadly, several hours of torrential downpours marred the proceedings late morning and the commencement of the driving course looked dubious. The luck of the gods shone down in time and the weather brightened sufficiently for the afternoon driving course to commence. Feeling slightly on tender hooks, *s2trash* crossed everything he owned, including his tripod, and prayed the course would work. *Microdot* was the time keeper; *Miss Polkadot* the record keeper and *s2trash* the starter and marshal for part of the course. *Eric* a Funkysmart moderator and a few other volunteers, expertly marshalled the rest of course. The rain had made the course a little damp and greasy and there were some interesting slides to entertain the onlookers. The worst of the fortwo owners was *Fudge* who threw his new cabrio around the course with gusto, and some superb doughnuts were choreographed by a few roadster owners who had disabled their Trust plugs. Thankfully, the course itself worked and many owners had a go. The evening saw plenty of organised entertainment with bands and performances in a large marquee, followed by a party that overflowed outside and continued well into the night.

Miss Polkadot

Pink chic

Wayneaucock, Tangerine Teal and Dave Kaye, the event organisers

The Funky beer arrives

Jodrell and Scotty eye up the smart talent

Sunday

Sunday morning was a big contrast to the day before; it was beautifully sunny and warm. Having arisen from his coffin-like sleeping quarters, *s2trash* drove to the shower block with three other male **smart** owners for their daily ablutions. Two of them, including *s2trash*, finished their showers simultaneously, and since they could hear someone else still in the shower they took it to be the forth owner. *S2trash* and the other two, just for a laugh, decided to send large quantities of cold water over the cubicle door onto the fourth man. With the schoolboy prank over and sides aching from laughing, they went outside and noticed there were only three **smarts** and not four. As it began to dawn on them that if a car was missing the owner was too, the person they had dowsed in the shower cubicle probably wasn't the **smart** owner they had thought it was. As they stood there realizing their mistake, a young child walked out of the shower block looking pretty upset and bedraggled. The three embarrassed owners then made a very hasty retreat back to the campsite before they had a chance of being reported to the RSPCC. This was only the start of childish antics of the morning. In the vicinity of the Essex Smarties encampment, *Brettstar*, *Zigzag*, *s2trash* and *Microdot* proceeded to have a gentle kick about with a football. As with all games with boys, it all turned boisterous and the ball kicking became more testosterone fueled, resulting in the said ball ricocheting from tent to tent like a scud missile. This was all brought to an abrupt end by *Miss P* who gave them a school-marm scolding, after the ball had bounced off her car for the umpteenth time! Whilst this was going on the *s2crew* had a massive super-soaker water fight, the two main perpetrators being *s2stealth* and *mccsmartarse*.

After his telling off and with his tail between his legs *s2trash* sloped off to the driving course area to re-instate the numerous cones that had gone walkabout during alcohol fuelled antics the previous night. Armed with a stop watch, *Microdot* joined *Miss Polkadot* again to assist in the timekeeping for the duration of the competition. The driving course was very popular and got very competitive towards the end between *SmartsRcool* and a young man called *Dominic*. They competed round after round, with *Dominic* finally taking the winners' podium with the best overall times. The winner's prize was an extremely expensive, stunning flip watch donated by one of Billing's organizers. Elsewhere on the site, *Vermaak* set up a demonstration on how to fit bass bins and after market speakers on a fortwo using *NeilOs'* car, having used *s2trash's* car the day before for a similar display. After lunch all the cars that had entered the three car competitions, Best Modded, Best Paint Job and Best Vinyl, were requested to line up their cars in the main arena area ready for judging. *Miss Polkadot* decided, just for a laugh, to enter her spotty car in the Best Vinyl category, for entertainment value if nothing else, as she could see there was some stiff competition. The standard of entries was high and it was obvious that a lot of time and hard work had been put into the preparation of the cars.

Later in the afternoon *Miss P* and *s2trash* stole a few moments to have a look around at the trader's stands and were able to get their first close up look at one of the new forfours that a local **smart** dealer had brought along. At the time, neither of them were terribly impressed by the look of it, it just didn't have that cute factor, it looked a tad chunky. However, like all things, time is a great healer, and the forfour has grown on *Miss Polkadot*, with cantankerous *s2trash* just preferring the front and back view.

Massive had asked *s2trash* to photograph *s2Eagleye's* car for his next edition of the magazine, so he got Rob to take his car over to a quiet spot beside the canal running through the campsite. Never having seen this car before both he and *Miss P* were quite frankly amazed when they saw it and their jaws dropped when they saw in detail what this man had done to his car. Having previously been involved with motorbikes he had modified his car using numerous bike parts and had stripped his engine, painted it blue and red and made a Perspex cover so that it could be viewed like a work of art. For that was exactly what it was. (Check out this amazing car's credentials in the Customised **smarts** section). During the shoot, *Microdot* had wandered over to see what was going on and he too was mesmerized by this stunning **smart**. With the photography over, *s2Eagleye* kindly offered to give *Microdot* a ride back to the main campsite. Eager to show off the capabilities

Smart crime scene

NeilOs and Red Cookie

Vermaak installs new bass bins

40

of his car to his 12 year old passenger, *s2Eagleye* revved up the engine and for only a very short distance put his foot to the floor, in an area devoid of people. Minutes after dropping off *Microdot* grinning ear to ear, *s2Eagleye* was apprehended by Billing officials, who told him that he had broken site rules by speeding and dangerous driving and had him escorted off the entire Billing site by several men in four by fours. The entire incident was nonsense and badly handled by the officials, particularly at a later date when *s2Eagleye* found out that he had been 'reported' to the Billing security team by a group of over envious **smart** owners who didn't care for the way they thought *s2Eagleye* had been 'showing off'. Sadly, there are always a few that spoil the fun of the many, in whatever walk of life one frequents!

Over both days of the weekend various competitions were held. On the Saturday *Vermaak* and *s2trash* judged the ICE Sound Off competition, and were continually pestered to reveal who had won, but both remained tight-lipped. *Miss Polkadot,* who was oblivious to the winner's announcements as she was engrossed in packing up her tent, suddenly heard someone shouting at her from across the arena. She had only gone and won the Best Vinyl competition! She just couldn't believe it and immediately stopped with the packing and rushed over to collect her prize. She had won a £100 voucher from Smartarse Design and a small hip flask engraved with 'Billing 2004'. How fantastic was that!

The other winners who all received wonderful prizes were:

ICE Sound Off – Mark Williams
Best Modded – Richard Dukesbury
Best Paint Job – Sharon Woodmansey

It really had been a great weekend and many felt sad to have to pack up and go home. At least folks would go home and spread the word and tempt more people to go the event the following year – this was turning into The Best **smart** Rally in the UK.

Billing 2004

Billing, Billing, Billing, Bling, Bling, Bling; There were so many smarties my heart was in a spin.
They sparkled in the sunshine, all parked up on the grass; Like lots of little wine gums, their panels shone like glass.
The S2Crew were there you know, the Essex Smarties too; The KK's came from Cambridge, and the S-mann boys, woo-hoo!
Jim B he came from Sweden, from Wales Lacroix he came; Alsmart flew in from Florida, just having fun their aim.
The Funky stand was there with Dave, a-selling pints of beer; In special smartie glasses, each one a pint of cheer!
There were some wacky cars there; daisies, pansies, fluff; And some highly moddied beasties, those guys sure know their stuff!
We spent a pretty penny buying smartie bling; Neons, shiny handles, and of course the re-mapping!
Big wheels, spoilers, side skirts, dump valves, de-lips, tints; You name it, filters, air scoops, the owners now are skint.
We had car comps at Billing, Vinyl, Moddied, Ice; And Susie at the Funky stand selling Funky merchandise.
The weather wasn't brilliant but in their droves they came; For fun was had at Billing despite torrential rain!
Tom.c set out a drive course, Miss P took down the times; And penalties, retirements, were on the smartie's minds!
The Roadsters stopped their ESP and spun around the course; Showed-off their doughnuts, handbrake turns, the grass it came off worse!
'Twas party night on Saturday, Paul did his party piece; Sung songs and played piano, was late when it did cease.
We all had such a good time; we'll do it then next year; And pray for decent weather and lots more Funky beer!
© Miss Polkadot 2004

Bexhill Beach Party 2004

After the previous years successful trip to the beach, *s2trash* got pestered to organise another one for 2004. Cobbs Hill Farm had been chosen as the camping venue, a small family run site with all the appropriate amenities but without the rowdy crowds, set down a lovely country lane just outside Bexhill. The length of the event, had been extended from a day trip to a long weekend event; well why not, everyone had such a great time the previous year.

Friday

Miss Polkadot and The Essex Smarties travelled down in a tube in afternoon and descended on *s2trash* at his old place of work. One particular member of staff *s2trash* had worked with cheekily wondered if *Miss Polkadot* wore spotty undies, and thought that here was an opportune moment to ask her about it. *S2trash* never did find out if he got an answer, but his work colleague had either started using make-up or *Miss P* had given him a black eye! With *s2trash* looking like 'Stig of the Dump' covered in bike oil and with the Essex Smarties in tow, they headed off to the campsite. Feeling in a helpful mood, *s2trash* stayed and helped *Miss P* erect her tent. Tent! This, he thought was being economical with the truth to say the least. She was only knee high to a grasshopper but she had brought along the infamous 'Polkadot Mansion'! After completing the mansion erection in 29°C heat, *s2trash* sluggishly crawled back home for a much welcome shower and change of clothes prior to returning for the evenings events. The first port of call was 'The Mermaid', a traditional sea-side pub on Bexhill sea front and home to the Bexhill Meet. It seemed a good place to chill out and have some dinner after all the exertion of the tent erecting. Enjoying the summer evening sun sat *Funkymonkey* and his side-kick *James*, *Mr T* and his wife *Mrs T*, *Daggie*, *ZigZag*, *Miss P* and *s2trash*. *Polkadot* bless her, managed get a heel stuck between some paving slabs causing her to lunge into the corner of a marble table, knocking it over and causing a cascade of drinks to go everywhere but down the owners throats. Once everyone had dripped dry in the evening breeze and *Miss P* had overcome her undignified fall, a trip to Hastings was decided on as a nice way to round the evening up.

By now *jamiebeveridge* had joined the group, having driven past the pub by chance with his trusty companion *Jeff* in his old Mk 1 fortwo. Taking things at a nice leisurely pace, the little convoy of cars drove along St Leonard's and then Hastings Sea front, causing lots of looks and grins, as is only to be expected. The convoy then headed off through Hastings Old Town, along a street full of cafés, bars and revellers. As always, the convoy caused a bit of a stir, with most of the folks pointing and grinning at these mad cars squeezing through the throngs that had spilled out onto the lane. After having scattered the locals, a quick stop-check was ordered to see if there was any damage. With only one car receiving a globule of alcohol-enhanced spittle, the foray into the lane had been a success and the convoy was able to sedately continue on its way back to the campsite, where the shaken but stirred Essex Smarties sat around chatting into the wee small hours.

Saturday

The forecast was 'hot, hot, hot' and so everyone was up bright and early. Someone needed to stake a claim on a large section of beach down at Herbrand Walk and so *Miss Polkadot* and *s2trash* lead the advance party down there. After a short detour via the local butchers for essential barbeque fodder, both *Miss P* and *s2trash* made it early enough onto the beach to grab a prime location for the party. It may have only been 10am but shorts were all that were required, and bikinis of course for the ladies! It was going to be a scorcher again, just like last year. Whilst standing reminiscing about last years do, *s2rash* was suddenly brought to his senses by the thundering sound of what he thought to be hooves of the four horsemen of the Apocalypse; but then spied a freshly brushed and tied mullet – it had to be *Vermaak* and the thundering sound of his house music! Next to arrive was *Zoë Patch* and her brother in her all-silver fortwo passion. Her car has to be one of the finest non-modified cars in the UK. A non-modified car can be categorised as such, providing any additional **smart** accessories have been fitted at the factory. Gradually the **smart** owners that finally managed to crawl out of their tents started to turn up and arrange themselves on the shingle beach along with some other **smart** day trippers. The tide was out so there was a bit of a trek to the sea but that didn't stop several brave souls going down for first dip of the day.

So what else went on? Well, the local press turned up again as they did the previous year and photographed everyone for a short 'exposé' in The Bexhill Observer. By mid-afternoon the infamous Sussex Branch and s2crew had members rolling into town, swelling the ranks of the beach invaders from planet **smart**. *S2gtmracing*, with his lovely wife *Kat*, had come in her Bluewave roadster. Under the pretext that he needed to go to the loo, *s2gtmracing* borrowed the keys to *Kat's* car and off he

Friday night outside The Mermaid

Smart owners getting cooked on the beach!

Bubski - The man from Atlantis!

went in search of the public conveniences. Everyone else, one presumes, made use of the natural facilities and just peed in the sea! At this stage *s2trash* was cooking on the barbeque and with 'Gordon Ramsey' style language was ordering his wife around, when running over the beach with gazelle like grace appeared *Jason*. "Tom! Gary (*s2gtmracing*) is stuck in a ditch, but don't tell *Kat*, can you help?" *S2trash* told *Jason* he would be there in a moment as his wife looked unimpressed that he might be leaving his post as head chef. Now, the bit about "don't tell *Kat*" would have been fine, if only she hadn't been sitting next to *s2trash* when *Jason* told him of the mishap. As *Jason* ran back off to *s2gtmracing's* aid, *Kat's* ears pricked up and she shouted "I'll kill him!"

Meanwhile, back at a ditch with a roadster stuck in it....

Upon seeing *s2gtmracing* go off-roading, a BMW driven by some very well built West Indians immediately pulled over to literally lend a hand. Having seen the predicament *s2gtmracing* found himself in, they very kindly and promptly just literally lifted the Bluewave out of the ditch, much to *s2gtmracing's* profound relief! Then, with a smile on their faces they handed him the roadster's side skirts that had become detached! When *s2gtmracing* returned to the beach, thinking he had got away without *Kat* knowing what he had just done, his face looked only slightly flushed. Within seconds of looking at his wife his face became ashen as she confronted him with his mishap. Luckily, it was just cosmetic damage to the car and a very large dent in *s2gtmracing's* ego! Back at the beach *jamiebeveridge* very cleverly turned his **smart** into a mobile cooker. With his tailgate in the open position, and the engine cover resting on it, *jamiebeveridge* placed his disposable BBQ on the cover and lit it, much to everyone's consternation! It was a humorous but slightly disturbing site to see flames flying out of the back end of the car, with a cool-as-a-cucumber student wondering what all the fuss was about. Amusingly *jamiebeveridge* was soon to start a University course entitled 'Danger Management'! His escapade will have certainly given him first hand experience with potential incendiary devices!

The beach party event is a very chilled out affair and apart from the convoy planned for the evening, everyone is free to come and go as they please. Some folks hadn't felt up to searing either themselves or their steaks on the beach, and several people used the opportunity to go exploring a little bit of Sussex. By the time they returned in the late afternoon, the beach bums had cleaned up and were raring to go out on the drive to Beachy Head. With all the cars lined up facing the right way and loads of hand-held radios they headed off onto Eastbourne sea front, and the shock of a life time! It became all too obvious that something was '*going down'* in Eastbourne and the convoy was heading straight for it! Tonnes of rubbish lay strewn everywhere, and this normally sleepy costal town was suddenly packed with hundreds of Nigerians on a day trip from London. Whether it was a special holiday or religious day, no one was quite sure, but the shear amount of these visitors all sporting their Sunday best outfits was a complete eye opener! To begin with, the drive along the seafront hadn't incurred any problems but as they got further along they started to get some uncomfortable looks.

Miss Polkadot who was at the back of the convoy and innocently flying a Union Jack flag from her car became a little uneasy that her flag may have become easily misconstrued, and felt a trifle apprehensive when she got stuck at some lights, as the huge influx of visitors were milling about all over the road in between the cars. Never has a set of traffic lights seemed to take so long to change! Finally on the move again, the convoy of little cars pulled out of Eastbourne and started the climb up onto Beachy Head. It wasn't long before The Beachy Head pub found its car park thronging with multicoloured **smarts** just in time to watch the sun set over The Seven Sisters. After admiring the fabulous view from the top of the Downs as the sun sank and sprinkled the sea with droplets of light, it was time to think about returning to Bexhill. *Vermaak* asked if the convoy could travel back via his mother's house, as she had just bought a new **smart** and he thought it would be a nice surprise for her to see everyone parked outside in the street. With *Vermaak* now playing the leader it was off to the leafy suburbs of Eastbourne. *Vermaak's* mum was indeed surprised and delighted to see the 25 **smart** cars outside her house, although what the neighbours had to say about it is another matter! After lots of hugs and waves goodbye, those people who had just come to the event for the day, made their way back homewards. The remainder of the convoy drove sedately back to the beach. *s2trash* then lead the way back to the Cobbs Hill Farm campsite, where everyone was in for a surprise welcome.

Innovative cooking style!!

Refreshment stop at Beachy Head pub

Cooling down late afternoon

Melissa, *Jonny Pants*, *ZigZag* and *Brettstar*, who had stayed at the campsite during the trip to Beachy Head, had brought along with them an enormous bag of tea lights. During the time the campsite was devoid of **smarts**, they had marked out parking bays, walkways and a driveway with hundreds of tea lights! What an amazing site that will forever be etched in everyone's memory! It could have been **smart** wonderland and certainly put everyone in a fantastic mood for an evening of fun. The happy campers sat around well into the early hours chatting and recalling the day's events. One amusing moment to treasure was watching *Bubski* attempting to single handedly erect his tent in the dark whilst smoking, drinking, having a pee and being mercilessly heckled – that dude has style!

Sunday

Sunday morning arrived sunny and bright, unlike the state of the campers. For them and the effects of the previously evenings revelry made for a slow start. *Bubski* and *s2trash* went off in search of bacon and cigarettes whilst the rest decided what they wanted to do for the day. Some went to Bodiam Castle while others de-camped and headed back home. The remaining few sat round most of the day chatting and just chilling, and those that had caught just a little too much sun the day before, hid in the shade. The last three cars finally departed the site around 5.30pm, making their long drive home a bit bearable once the sun began to go down. It had been a great weekend, the weather had been marvellous and those that had attended had already pleaded with *s2trash* to make plans for the next one. So what could he say but 'Yes'

The London to Brighton 2004

The third *L2B*, held on 26th September 2004, began at Sandown Park Race Course, just a few miles from Kempton. For the previous 18 months leading up to this, *Miss Polkadot* and *s2trash* had been writing articles and supplying photos for Smartimes magazine, and so they were allocated the job of covering the event. Both of them had brought their kids along with them, so they each had a mini-navigator/serial sweet muncher to keep them company on the journey. This year, the number of **smarts** that appeared at the start looked considerably higher than in 2003. The grand total of 1098 cars was counted this time! Now that is a lot of cars and people to say hello to! As they had now started to get known on the **smart** scene, lots of folks kept coming up to chat to them. It was really nice to eventually get to meet so many people from the websites, and actually put names to faces. For some strange reason they all seemed to know who they were, long before they recognised them...must be something to do with those ruddy spots! *Miss Polkadot* had the bright idea of swapping kids for the drive down to Brighton. It was now 10am, and time for the off! Everyone switched on their engines and started their horns tooting. Thank goodness they were near the front. With so many cars it would have taken ages to get going had they been stuck at the back! All the cameras were out, including theirs, ready for the driving shots. Automatic would have been handy in the car at this very moment, *s2trash* can steer with his knees, but changing gear with his hands full of camera gear he has yet to master! The gorgeous Limited Edition V6 Roadster, resplendent in red, graced the UK's shores yet again to take pole position from the off.

Within ten minutes they were on the M25, accompanied by some of *Miss Polkadot's* Essex Smarties. They had planned on stopping at Pease Pottage Services on the M23, as it had now become the unofficial halfway point, and a **smarts**-only service station! As with all the previous *L2B's* there is an elaborate display of fancy dress, but the ones that stuck in *s2trash's* mind this particular year, were two ladies dressed as surgeons, drinking tea from a flask and non **smart** owners looking in disbelief as they drove/walked past them. Anyone for a quick resuscitation? There was also a gentleman covered from head to toe, in shoe polish, and garnished with half a hundredweight of gold chains, a scary Mr.T from the 'A' Team. At the time nobody was quite sure if he was real or not, so they kept their distance just to be on the safe side. He sure looked like he shouldn't be messed with. There were two very memorable cars to appear this year; the first was a roadster in shark fancy dress. and was the cleverest piece of needlework anyone had ever seen. Totally brilliant and totally fun – one of the main constituents of the *L2B*. The second, and probably the cutest, was a fortwo cabrio covered in turquoise fur fabric in the likeness of Sully from the film 'Monster's Inc.' Every panel had been individually painstakingly covered, washed, blow dried and groomed to perfection. Aptly named 'Fluff', the passenger seat and boot space gave rise to a vast collection of 'Sullys', from key rings to four foot replicas of the cute and hairy loveable monster. Not to be outdone, *Miss Polkadot* allowed *s2trash* to temporarily sit in her passenger seat so she could make a similar claim, except the monster in her car wasn't quite so cute!

After finally getting fed and watered, they re-joined the A23 to Brighton. It was a fairly fast drive to the coast; until they hit their first jam about two miles from the racecourse. It was here, whilst stuck in a stationary line, *Miss Polkadot,* accompanied by *s2trash's* son *s2CricketBoy*, instigated a sweet fight. There were sweets flying all over the place, as they pathetically tried to aim them into *Sally Sweet Pea's* open top cabrio, and missed miserably. It seemed to take forever to travel the last few miles. It didn't help when *s2trash* sent their tube of cars the wrong way...Oops! After what seemed time eternal, crawling along in first gear towards Brighton Race Course, they finally made it. There seemed to be an awful lot more cars there, than had started back at Kempton and according to thesmartclub records, 1627 cars were counted through the finish line. Madeira Drive would have been a nicer point to finish, but the number of cars would have been too great to be accommodated as the previous year there had been parking problems with only half that number of cars.

At around 1.45 pm a call was made for all the entries in the fortwo competitions to make their way to the judging area, where the celebrity guest judge, Tiff Needell, former racing driver and TV presenter, would decide the winners. There were three categories, split into two groups, one for fortwos the other for roadsters. The outcome of the judging caused a sharp intake of breath in some quarters as several cars were disqualified for displaying Mercedes badges, no matter what size they were or how well they were hidden from view. Mr Needell, kindly pointed out to the amazed crowd that the actual make of the car was **smart** and not Mercedes, and therefore had no business sporting the incorrect logo, wherever it happened to be. Point taken, remarked some onlookers, but it would have been fair to have mentioned it to the competitors prior to the event. In the previous *L2B* competitions there had been no mention of this issue. Maybe it is time that ground rules are staked out, even when it is a light-hearted. Still, after such a public admonishment, everyone will know what to do next time for sure. Next up it was judgment time for the roadsters competition. Understandably, some of the entrants looked a little nervy as there was no time for any discreet badge removal!

The winners of the 3 categories were as follows:

Fortwo

Zaniest - Laura Lowe (more famously known as *Fluff*) • *Concourse* - Rebecca Webber • *Most Modified* - Vicky Rees

Roadster

Zaniest - Tina Hart • *Concourse* - Mike Baguley • *Most Modified* - Paul Mordell

Tiff Needell announced that 'this years *L2B* is indeed the biggest gathering of owned **smart** cars in the world, around 2000 cars', and the crowd roared with enthusiastic shouts and applause. We forgive him for overestimating by the numbers by 373, but it was still a huge number of **smarts**. *S2trash* was a bit miffed though, as he only had enough film in his camera for 200! Time he embraced the digital age with bigger chips! With the excitement of the competitions now over and loads of fab photos safely in the can, *s2trash* dashed off and had a picnic with some of the Essex Smarties mob. They know how to live it up that lot, smoked salmon sandwiches and white wine, but not a pair of white stilettos in sight. After gorging himself on picnic handouts, *s2trash* decided to have a walk around the trade stands and met up with the S-mann guys from Holland. They have made it to nearly every major **smart** event in the UK, and have become well known with their originally designed **smart** parts, and paint finishes.

As the event drew to a close some members of the Sussex branch s2crew and Essex Smarties decided to cruise down to Brighton seafront. There was plenty of messing around; posing for photos, chatting and standing up on the walkways, watching the sun go down over a line of **smarts** all parked (illegally) in a row, making it the perfect end to the day. The evening too ended on a very pleasant note with the quenching of thirsts at the famous Beachy Head Pub, a venue frequented by **smarts** at the end of the Bexhill Beach Party Cruise, another annual event held in the summer.

V6 Bi Turbo roadster starts the run for the second year running

Ready and waiting

The unlikely lads

L2B in re-Verse

Get up at crack of sparrows, outside it is still dark; The sun it hasn't risen yet, a lonesome fox does bark.

I open up the garage door, and inside quickly dart; For inside sleeps my precious one, my spotty, dotty smart.

All shiny from the day before, from water, chamois, wax; My little 'Dot' is gleaming, and blinged-up to the max.

Pressing buttons on the 'lolly' key, she's bathed inside in blue; For now the 'Dot' has LED's, it's such a groovy hue!

We pack the boot with sarnies, biscuits, drink and sweets; It's going to be a long day, and the biggest Smart car meet!

Gonna meet my Essex Smarties, at Brentwood on the way; There's nine of us in total, I'm leading, if I may...

At Clacket Lane we meet up, Kent crowd and a forfour; We all stop there for coffee; we've grown to thirty four!

So off we go to Sandown Park, new venue for the Start; Two hours before the starting gun, we're ushered to be parked.

He's making moddies to his car, Tom.c is on the ground; A little crowd now gathers, they think he's clowning round.

"Sticking summat on me pipes", his little voice it quivers; "Copied Miss P's end caps", then from underneath Tom slithers.

There's loads of cars to look at, not one of them the same; From neon green to Sully fluff, they are anything but plain.

There's a shark complete with tail and fin, Eyeore, Winnie-the-Pooh; There's pink fluff and blue tartan, and the rainbow colours too!

So now there's near 2000, all waiting eagerly; For the start of this year's rally, the famous L2B.

We're off at last with whoops of joy, smart hooters honking hard; We're off to sunny Brighton, and boy do we look proud.

Alsmart was seen with camera, a-snapping merrily; As we left the Start position, as quickly as could be.

We cruised along the roads at speed, enjoying this event; Then we stopped for some unleaded, just as we got to Kent.

Pease Pottage is the place you know, where lots of Smarties stopped; For food and drink and chatter, and some, to loos did hop!

By now we'd lost some of our tube, but off we went again; Waving, passing other Smarties, very glad it didn't rain.

And then we reached the slip road, the jam it had begun; So we threw each other sweeties, and boy did we have fun!

It took a while to reach there, the Finish line, the End; Sweet crunching kids munched in our ears; near drove us round the bend.

We watched all of the car comps, were judged by Tiff Needell; Laura's FLUFF won Zaniest, Oh! Didn't she do well!

We picnicked in the car park, we wondered round the stands; We saw Steve G from Smartimes, that magazine is grand!

By now it was our home-time; the day had been a hoot; For now the drivers of these smarts, were well and truly 'pooped'!

We've all had such a great day; we don't want it to end; But there'll be another next year that, I'm sure we'll all attend.

© Miss Polkadot 2004

Competition entries

Fluff wins 'Zaniest smart' category

Monsters get the term 'rear wheel drive' completely wrong!

The Ace Café 2004

What is the Ace Café? Well, it is an old biker's café in West London, on the North Circular Road, that was re-opened a few years ago, after undergoing a major refurbishment in the retro style of its heyday in the 50's and 60's. The Ace Café was actually built in 1938 as a roadside cafe to cater for hauliers, using the new North Circular Road. With its proximity to the county's new and fast arterial road network and opening 24 hours a day, the Ace Café soon began to attract plenty of motorcyclists, had jukeboxes playing Rock´n´Roll, and soon became the place to meet. Sadly, the expansion of the motorway network literally saw the Ace Café being by-passed, and it served its last portion of egg and chips in 1969. In 1993, driven by a passion for motorbikes and Rock 'n' Roll, Mark Wilsmore started planning to re-open the legendary Café. Twenty-five years after the Café closed, the first Ace Café Reunion was held in 1994, attracting 12,000 people. Eventually, after a complete rebuild, the famous bikers haunt had its Grand Opening in September 2001. The Ace Café now holds both car and bike events and meets throughout the year.

One of *s2trash's* friends had re-built the bar there when it was undergoing refurbishment, but he had never got round to going to check it or the café out. One morning, for no apparent reason, he suddenly thought to himself; why not plan a **smart** meet there? After a quick phone call, the Ace were more than happy for a **smart** meet to be held there, and in fact they had been trying to get a Smart Club for ages, so they said, after a few of the S2Crew members visited there a few years previously. Encouraged by their friendliness *s2trash* decided to go ahead and book a meet. The only down side with the booking, was the fact that the only time they could be fitted in coincided with a Billy Fury commemorative evening! Now that would bring in masses of **smarts**...not! True enough, as he had anticipated when he posted the arrangements on the website forums, the numbers interested in going were low, but what the heck, even if he ended up going as Billy-no-mates at least he would get to finally see his friends efforts at building the Café bar!

S2trash met up with *Miss Polkadot* enroute and they drove across town to the Ace Café, negotiating all of those rotten speed humps that **smarts** always seem to struggle with!

They arrived to find six cars already lined up along the front of the Café: *S2Herman*, *Zigzag*, *Jim808*, *Neil797*, *Captain Morgan* and *Roadrage*. What a sight! The Café itself was a lot bigger than *s2trash* had expected, and looked terrific lit up in the dark. The tattooed doorman looked at Trash wearing his Mod outfit, then he looked at *Miss P*, and neither of them was sure if he smiled or grimaced, but he let them in nether-the-less. Aaaghhhhh, screamed *s2trash* silently, as he walked into the lions den. He secretly thought that this could be Brighton 1964 all over again, and wondered for a moment if his controversial outfit might backfire! People of all ages were milling around in the Café, from 19 years to 90, wearing studded leather jackets, quiffed-up hair and turned-up jeans. With a bit of dodging and weaving he made it to the bar and ordered some drinks (a stiff one for himself), then found a table and tried to blend in! *Miss Polkadot* kept moaning that she wasn't attired in the appropriate dress code, (pink and sparkly wasn't the best choice of garb for this macho environment) and made a bee-line for the Ace Café shop, where she bought an Ace Café t-shirt. The Rock-a-Billy DJ started talking to *s2trash* giving *Miss P* the chance to scurry off and change into her newly acquired biker-chick look.

The DJ chatting to *s2trash* was quick to point out that the café food was good, so he ordered, before the place got too crowded. The food was also surprisingly cheap, which makes a change. Whilst waiting for his order to arrive, and *Miss P* to complete her make-over, *s2trash* went outside to try out his new digital camera in manual mode. Outside in the dark he suddenly realised that in a trifling moment of forgetfulness, he had forgotten his tripod, something of a necessity when shooting at very low light levels. Ever the master of invention, he went on a foray into the car park and came back brandishing a traffic cone, on top of which he balanced his camera and it worked a treat. Whilst scrabbling about on the floor with his cone, a yellow and black Roadster turned up, whose new owners called themselves

Outside the Ace Café

Inside the café

Billy and brown sauce

Fulham1971. It was getting very cold by now, as a frost had been forecast and again *s2trash* realised that in another trifling moment of forgetfulness he had left his coat behind. While wistfully thinking about the benefits of having a working memory bank, the owners of the Café came over for a chat about the cars and they began to talk about possibly organising a bigger event in the future. Now bordering on being hypothermic, *s2trash* went back inside for the huge hot-dog roll he had forgotten that he had ordered, and found it looking all forlorn...and cold! Learning to drive his new digital camera in manual mode was sure keeping *s2trash* busy, but it was probably not the best time to be trying it out. The Billy Fury evening was a charity event, and during the evening an auction of memorabilia was held. Someone paid £350 for a large framed painting of Billy Fury in all his glory! Billy Fury's Mum was gracing the event with her presence, God bless her, (she must be an age!) and they rolled her out to hand the pricey picture over to the eager purchaser. *S2trash* went back out into the cold night air, overcome with the emotional atmosphere created by the Billy Fury fans to find some bugger had moved his strategically placed traffic cone tripod! Claiming it as his very own for the night, he soon got it back and took some more photos until the frostbite started to gnaw at his digits, and he had to crawl back into the warmth of the Café and down one of their fantastic cappuccinos to thaw out.

The live band that had been booked for the evening turned up very late, around 11pm. Holy Moses! Where on earth had the Café found them! *S2trash* was expecting Vincent Price to emerge with them any moment! They must have had a combined age of 900! Everyone watched them play, and to be fair, they may have been ancient, but they were fantastic, once the Zimmer frames were removed from the stage! The band was playing to one end of the café, surrounded by a large crowd, and there in the thick of it stood *s2trash*. The trouble was, there was he, wearing Mod clothing, standing in the middle of a load of Rock-a Billy's. He wasn't a bit out of place......much!!! He then tried taking some 'action shots' of the band, until *Miss P* pointed out that the infrared focusing beam and the flash from his camera was probably irritating the hell out of them, and that he ought to put the camera away before someone did it for him! Naturally, he complied, but blinding the bass player was not intentional, and he did manage to play on regardless. Once the band finished their set, and they made their way back to their retirement homes, it was time for the **smarts** to head outside too. It was time for everyone to say their goodbyes and drive off into the smog of London. A great time had been had by all, and everyone, including all the Rock-a-Billy's in their studded leathers and drainpipes, and the Café owners, made them feel very welcome. Only a few folks had made it to this event, but they were glad they went, it was certainly an experience! Next time he goes *s2trash* might grow himself a Teddy-Boy quiff, or a get a toupee if he becomes follicley challenged by then!

Beaulieu 2004

This was the second Beaulieu Meet and what was to turn out to be a life changing experience for *s2trash*! Several traders had shown an interest in coming to this event and *s2trash* was lucky to have Smartarse Design, Smart Part Chick, and Smartimes. In hindsight, the first Beaulieu Meet was too much to try and do all in one day, all day out outside in the cold and including several hours travelling each way, so it was decided to travel down on the Saturday and stay overnight. Several other **smart** owners thought that that was a good idea and said they would make a weekend of it as it would be nice to meet up on the Saturday evening. And so the Beaulieu Meet weekend began.

Polkadot and Trash put the flags out

Early arrivals

T1NY W's impressive marquee

Saturday

S2trash left home with the intention of meeting up with *Miss Polkadot* at Brighton and driving with her down to Beaulieu. There had been a dreadful crash on the M25 which had to be closed, and *Miss P* had got caught up in the chaos. *S2trash* spent two hours waiting in Brighton for the severely delayed spotty one, who was desperately trying every route she could to get round the closed motorway. With a renowned low boredom threshold, *s2trash* decided to drive up to Pease Pottage Service Station to meet up with *Miss P* who phoned to say she had had a breakthrough with the jams and was on her way. She wasn't able to tell him exactly where she was at that precise moment, only that the scenery was pretty! Trying to keep his cool, *s2trash* just let out a very big sigh! Several hours later than planned they finally meet up and had a quick but much deserved cappuccino, before making a hasty exit as they had planned to stop in at Smartarse Design in Romsey on the way down to Beaulieu. If only they had been delayed longer and not made it to Romsey, things may have turned out differently. The trip down to the New Forest was uneventful but beautiful, that was until they tried to find Smartarse Design. They got lost, well and truly, and *s2trash's* patience, thin on the ground at the best of times, was close to being threadbare, and as he couldn't read a map for toffees the pressure was on *Miss P* again to get them there. You can see a pattern emerging here. Eventually she had the common sense to phone Smartarse and ask for 'some better directions…PLEASE!'

Having now worked out where they should have been heading, they finally made it to Smartarse Design. As always there was a very warm welcome, with Spotty getting kisses and hugs and *s2trash* just getting "when did you last shower?" Paul and David Murphy kindly showed the tired pair around their superb Smartarse workshop. After providing them with several cups of coffee Paul Murphy began raving about their new project car and asked if *s2trash* would like to go for a quick spin. Despite being tired from the tediously long journey down, he jumped at the chance.

This section is *s2trash's* personal account of what happened next

'Having left the workshop with Paul driving all had started well enough and I was certainly impressed with what they had done to the car. I guess we had only been out for about ten minutes when we came to a nice straight section of road. Paul brought the car up to speed and it was then that I became aware that there where flames shooting past my head outside the car! This took a couple of seconds to sink in. If we were going forward how come the flames were as well? I looked over to Paul and muttered 'I think we might be on fire!' Simultaneously we looked round to see that the flames had engulfed the entire back of the car! Paul brought the car to a screaming halt and told me to jump out fast. As I opened the door flames licked into passenger side resulting in me shutting it rather fast and having to tell Paul I couldn't get out. Meanwhile Paul was fighting to turn the engine off and remove the key with shaking hands. In the moments of panic, what must have been just a few seconds seemed like minutes! As soon as Paul had turned off the engine and got his door open I was across the car and out onto the roadside verge, not before ripping the arse out of my jeans on the gear stick as I scrambled out of the car. I am not sure how I ended up with the fire extinguisher but it had little to no effect and it soon became clear to Paul that the fire was being caused by a detached fuel line. As there was no chance of us putting the fire out and with flames growing ever higher we decided to attempt to close the road off, worried that with all that fuel there could be an explosion and endanger passing vehicles. By the time we had stopped the first cars the poor **smart** was well and truly alight. The Fire Brigade had been called but from what I could see there was little hope in saving the car. Both Paul and I were trying to stop the traffic but there is always one idiot who will insist that getting home is the most important thing on the planet. The road was narrow but he would not listen to me trying to explain that the car could explode any second, and proceeded to pass regardless. At one point and I am not entirely sure when, Paul phoned David Murphy back at the unit with *Miss P*, to tell him that the car was on fire. Paul turned to me and said 'I think David is under the impression that it is a small fire – he has just laughed at me!' Indeed that is what David did think – because he turned to *Miss Polkadot* and told her that

Cabbyheap wins Sound Off competition…I said CABBYHEAP WINS SOUND OFF COMPETITION!

T1NY W's Sound-Off equipment

Paul Murphy gets technical

Leomobile winner of the Exhaust Off competition

Paul said that car was alight, thinking that he was pulling a prank to wind them up. How wrong could he be! After what seemed to take for ever, the fire service finally arrived. I could hear Paul talking to them when the first bang went off which was either a tyre or the fuel tank! No matter how much water they poured onto the **smart** it was by now very clear that the fire was not going to go out on its own and the car was doomed! A small river of steaming water was forming along the roadside as the poor **smart** imitated a Viking funeral ship. All we could do was just watch it burn as dusk fell. A surreal moment in my life, for sure. As the risk of further explosions died down I wandered back over to Paul. He looked pale but concerned for my welfare, asked if I was ok. I did notice that I was shaking a lot but I guessed that having nearly frazzled my backside off it was only to be expected; plus it was getting cold and I wasn't wearing a coat. The next thing I remember is *Miss Polkadot* appearing, looking very shocked at the sight before her, running over and hugging me. As David couldn't leave the premises she had driven straight over after they had decided that maybe there was a problem after all as Paul and *s2trash* hadn't returned to the unit. As she got to the area of the fire all she could see were flames and smoke and no occupants and for one moment thought the worst. With the firemen in charge there was nothing more that could be done. Paul stayed on to liaise with the fire crew whilst *Miss Polkadot* drove me back to Smartarse where I had the unenviable task of telling David the sad news about the car. He seemed really shocked as he had thought it had just been a small engine fire.

Now, this next part of the story I hope may one day help someone. I have never discussed what happened next with anyone but close friends and family, but as we stood in the Smartarse workshop drinking tea I felt odd. I could feel my body shaking but just put it down to the cold and the shock of the fire. My speech was difficult; words were not coming out as they should, being lost for words was not something I normally suffer from, and I was really having to think hard to form a sentence. *Miss Polkadot* and I needed to get to our bed and breakfast lodgings so we drove off. *Polkadot* very kindly helped me find mine; made sure I was ok and drove off to find her abode a couple of miles away. I still didn't feel right but I had a shower and watched some TV before getting ready to meet up with some others **smart** owners for a drink that had come down that afternoon. *Miss P* volunteered to drive that evening and we headed off to a recommended pub in the middle of The New Forest. I can recall the pub being a little odd to say the least as everyone turned and stared at us as we entered and wondering if we had stepped into an episode of the BBC's 'The League of Gentleman' and that very odd village – Royston Vasey**.** This is where we meet Chris and Jane (*Roadrage*) for the first time, Chris being the man who owns at least 50 pairs of trainers and a super fast black Brabus cab. I still wasn't feeling right, and it was in the pub I was later to find out I had had a seizure, only small but the start of worse things to come.

Two weeks later, whilst at work I had what turned out to be two more seizures that were quite big. I had no idea what was happening to me at the time so I just said I had a splitting headache and went home early. I called my doctor to see if I could be seen. My own doctor was fully booked but they got me in ASAP to see another, which was just as well. I had hidden what was happening to me from my wife and all my friends as it was all felt a bit surreal. Within minutes of being with the doctor he had signed me off work indefinitely and was making arrangements to for me see a neurologist as he couldn't find a brain. I jest, he was very concerned and tentatively suggested that I was suffering from some form of neurological trauma, but was cagey as to what it could be exactly. I had to wait a month for the appointment but it transpired that I had a form of Epilepsy. I was going to need some tests done, but he was sure I was having what are known as absent seizures and it was something I may have had all my life but the shock of the car fire and recent stress at work had brought it to the front. Terrific! As I sit here and write this it has been two years since that initial diagnosis. The seizures got much worse before they got better and I am now on medication for the foreseeable future. Being a Dyslexic has not helped the situation much at all either. The medication I currently take makes my Dyslexia problems much worse. If you read the forums on the **smart** websites on a regular basis you will have noticed my poor spelling has got worse and I have been rather grumpy and short tempered at times. For many around me it has been hell too; I have these absent seizures, I am prone to temper outbursts which I cannot control and I had to give up my job (which was a

Mad Dan

Friends re-united

Biggles arrives at Beaulieu!

Proud smart owner

blessing in disguise as it wasn't doing me any good), and worst of all give up my driving licence, not that my wife is happy about that as I am now constantly under her feet. On a plus note I have had amazing help from a wonderful company called DACE who run free courses for Dyslexics, my doctor, my wife and *Miss Polkadot*, who thankfully stopped me giving up photography altogether. I am sitting here co-writing a book, (which without the massive amount re-writing and editing done by *Miss Polkadot* would be a complete pile of gobbledygook) and have learnt so many new skills that I have not been able to do before. So, the outcome of the fire has had a silver lining in a round about sort of way.

I hope that one day someone will pick up this book that maybe in a similar position as me and see that nothing should stand in your way. I am slowly learning there is no word as 'cant', and that there is always a way of overcoming a problem. This is where, in my introduction to the book I mention the fact that the **smart** has had a very dramatic affect on my life, maybe now you can see why'.

Sunday

The morning after the night before began life in a definite festive fashion. Mother Nature had provided a surprise hard frost in the early hours and it looked like Christmas had come early.

It was 7am. s2trash wandered out to the car to clean off the first frost of the season, and being totally unprepared for such a thing, was without an ice-scraper. The B & B was situated down a ruddy long dirt track drive, with huge puddles, trailing through a riding stables and horse poo. Aaaghhhhh... his lovely clean car now looked like a 16th C. wattle and daub mud hut!

Miss P and *s2trash* were the first ones to arrive at the Motor Museum. Just as they finished setting up their stand *T1NY W* and the Sussex Branch rolled into town, followed by Smartarse Design and Smartimes. While they all set up their various stands and marquees, *Dale*, two Beaulieu staff and *s2trash* manned the gate and managed to keep the cars flowing as they took money and gave out tickets at lightening speed. By 10.30 am, all of the trade stands were up and running: Spotty Badger Productions, Smartimes, Smartarse Design, Smartpartchick, Barnhill Minis, LPG Conversions, Bantam Trailers, not forgetting *T1NY W* who played hospitality to those not carrying camping stoves, and providing welcoming hot cups of tea in the bitter cold. Around 130 cars, double last year's amount attended the event, including Dave Kaye *(Mr Funkysmart)* which was a pretty good show! Despite the cold and the initial frost the sun shone very brightly in an azure sky. Lovely for the attendees, but tricky for those taking photos, with the all glare and the reflections. At 1pm it was time for the planned 'Sound Off' competition. *T1NY W* had lent *s2trash* a digital sound-measuring gizmo for the event; it sure looked the part even if *s2trash* didn't have a clue how to use it! *T1NY W* decided to retrieve the equipment from *s2trash* and do it himself, it was safer he thought. CD's were handed to the entrants so that they could set their 'ICE' up, and then they were ready for the 'off'. The entire results were very close, but *Cabbyheap* won with 127.2 Db. Now, *s2Stealth*, after losing the 'Sound-off' competition, decided it would be fun to stick the sound measuring thingy up his exhaust whilst it was running....and so a new competition was born, the 'Exhaust-off' competition. The winner of that was *Leomobile*, with an impressive 107 Db (is that legal?). It has to be said that *Leomobile* was also the one and only winner of the 'Dirtiest-car' comp, and would have won the 'Golden Potato Peeler' award, if there had been such a thing! *S2trash* quietly checked on *Miss P* ....good, she was still at the stand, so he was able to leg it away without her seeing. During the course of the day, he had been helping young *jamiebeveridge* spend his hard-earned dosh on some mods for his car. *S2trash* began to feel guilty at making this poor student spend so much, so he ended up helping *jamiebeveridge* fit his new Pipercross air filter that he had just bought from Smartpartchick. He was well pleased with all his goodies. Suddenly, as happens at these types of events, time runs away and before you know it is time to pack up. It was 4pm, and for *s2trash* that is when it all started to go horribly wrong, for the second time that weekend. His car was making a funny noise, so he asked Sasho from Smartarse Design to have a look at it. The problem turned out to be the water pump. It was at the point of giving up, and *s2trash* was in a fix. Smartarse Design said that they had a new one back at their workshop if he wanted it. Did he heck! So he decided to follow them back to their HQ. Once Sasho had had a good look at the pump and checked the new one, he said he would need *s2trash's* car for a couple of days to get the job done, due to the workload they had on at the time. At this point *s2trash* began to wonder how on earth he was going to get home. Paul Murphy came to his rescue by offering to lend him his own, rather nicely modded scratch black cabrio for the duration. Now that's what you call good service! Meanwhile, whilst *s2trash* was off in the care of Smartarse, *Miss Polkadot* had to pack up their stand and fit it into her car along with two spares tyres that *s2trash* had foolishly taken along to try and sell ~ which he did feel bad about, after he was reminded about it! By the time *s2trash* finally got back to Beaulieu it was pitch black and all of the hangers-on (the Sussex Branch and *Miss P*) accidentally drove past him through the gates, leaving him the last person there. They hadn't recognised him as he was in a different car...well that was their excuse anyway! He finally managed to catch up with his belongings, spare tyres, *Miss P* and the Sussex Branch crowd and then went for a well deserved Indian meal. This event had been much bigger and better than *s2trash* could have hoped for, including the sunny weather, so much so that in conjunction with Beaulieu Motor Museum he was again able to donate a significant amount of money to charity.

2005

Smartball Blackpool Charity Run

The Smartball Charity Run was the brainchild of Jeremy Smith. He thought that it would be a jolly wheeze to drive to Scotland and back one weekend and get sponsored for doing it.

All he needed was a few accomplices to help organise it and a few mad **smart** owners to drive it! These, as one can imagine, were not hard to locate and after several meetings in very nice pubs all the arrangements were agreed. How he wangled it remains a mystery still, but Jeremy was able to arrange for all the **smart** cars to actually be parked in Edinburgh Castle overnight on the Saturday, and become a short term tourist attraction on the Sunday morning. It did indeed sound like a jolly wheeze, and everyone got excited about the forthcoming trip. Then, about six weeks before the trip, planned for Easter weekend, the rug was pulled from under **smarts** wheels, so to speak. The city of Edinburgh was planned to be the romantic final destination of the Smartball Charity Run. Double checking the arrangements Jeremy contacted the hotel to find out that they had annoyingly double-booked the entire party, despite Jeremy having booked the rooms well in advance. It then turned out that there was not one reasonably priced hotel in the whole of Edinburgh left that could accommodate so may folks in one booking, due to it being Easter weekend. This nearly put paid to the entire trip. They called a meeting at short notice, to be held in a lovely pub in Arundel, to discuss with the folks exactly what steps to take next. The main organisers of the event: Jeremy '*The Boss*' Smith, Gary & Kat Troutman and Kimmie '*Sister*' Keil decided it was a far better idea to relocate the destination rather than cancel the event, as so many people had booked holiday time from work and collected sponsorship for the event. After much deliberation they decided to change the destination to the rather less exotic Blackpool. Not so romantic as Edinburgh but another major tourist attraction with a reasonable distance to reach it, as the whole point of the exercise was to go on a long sponsored trip after all. The final deciding factor was that it had a hotel that could cope with a large group of people at short notice. So, Blackpool it was.

Jeremy asked *s2trash* to be the official photographer for the run, who in turn press-ganged *Miss Polkadot* into being his driver for the weekend, allowing him two free arms with which to take snaps whilst on the move. The entire event was filmed by Animatus, directed by Marios Panteli, an independent film crew hired by Jeremy, who intended making a documentary about the trip for Channel 4. The start venue was the picturesque Halfway Bridge pub, near Petworth, West Sussex, and all the cars began arriving through the beautiful early morning mist at around 7.30 am. Smartball t-shirts, car graphics and souvenir programmes (designed by Stephen '*YT*' White) were handed out to cars upon arrival, along with bottles of pink champagne kindly donated by Geoff Masters. The Halfway Bridge served up a splendid breakfast for everyone, prior to the group photo and start of the adventure at 9 am.

The route on to the A3 via the back roads caused the 20 strong 'tube', including the Sussex Cars back-up team, to get split up almost immediately. Trying to keep that many cars together through villages and traffic lights is always going to be tricky especially if some cars are not re-mapped, the drivers are not used to driving in convoy-mode and and/or drive like it is a Sunday. The cars re-grouped at the first service station on the M40, where they stopped for loos, fags, food, photos and

Christine's car on the road – Stickers R us!

Magnet and Bubski console Miss P after her lengthy journey with s2trash

The death defying film crew

Jason refuses to succumb to s2trash's taunts

strange looks and comments from passers by. The plan was to follow the M40 and M6, taking in the new M6 toll road. Some drivers, including *Magnet*, managed to miss the toll by having to stop on the hard shoulder to put up the roofs on their roadsters when it rained, the wimps, and consequently missed the correct turning. They were not the only ones, all the **smart** sheep following them did the same, *s2trash* and *Miss P* being two of them! *Miss Polkadot* also managed to miss the junction for the next meeting point three times, making *s2trash* get rather wound up and mutter unrepeatable comments about women drivers. Unfortunately, these detours ate up precious time taking her to the back of the pack, and earning her the distinction of 'Most Lost Smart' on the entire Smartball Run!

The camera crew amazed everyone with their ability to be in two places at once, filming the cars flying past on the motorway, then dashing forward to position themselves on bridges and banks ahead of everyone and filming the cars again. They caught rides in several roadsters too, to get different perspectives of mad **smart** drivers, including one infamous, male photographer who shall remain nameless, sporting a rather fetching cream ladies hat belonging to *Miss Polkadot*! As the cars headed north the weather grew overcast, the drive was a little tedious and tiring but spirits were high as the next stop was a guided tour of the famous TVR car factory just outside Blackpool. A very low-key, low-tech workshop environment greeted the group, no factory robots here, but a place producing cars more akin to **smarts** – plastic panelled but with the ability to be driven MUCH faster! We realise now just how fortunate we were to see inside this unique factory as it has recently closed down completely and production transferred abroad. The Smartball convoy, now accompanied by several TVR's, owned by friends of Jeremy *'The Boss'* Smith, then headed off to The Red Lion restaurant at Bispham, a few miles up the road, for some well earned food and liquid refreshment, and another group photo in the car park. Several other **smart** owners including *Sioux* and her husband, knowing that the Smartball cars would be in Blackpool, made the effort to pop along and visit the very tired drivers – a nice gesture indeed.

Now fed and watered, the convoy made its way in the dark to the most famous place in Blackpool – The Pleasure Beach, the Illuminations and the famous Tower itself. The beach road was heaving with tourists wearing brightly coloured wigs reminiscent of candyfloss! The convoy parked along the road giving *s2trash* his hoped for photo-opportunity in front of 'The Big One', the enormous rollercoaster. Dicing with death by lying in the road to 'get' the shot, Stephen the video camera man, was overheard to say that "*s2trash must* be dedicated to his art to risk becoming road kill", and that no-one would ever catch him doing that! After causing a stir along the seafront, the convoy now headed out of the bright lights of Blackpool to Chorley; the final destination for the night – the hotel. Although some people were by now flagging, a quick wash and brush up worked wonders, and everyone piled into the fantastic pub next to the accommodation. The drinks flowed freely all evening, causing some to suffer considerable the next morning! Not such a **smart** move! Poor *Miss Polkadot*, mistakenly accused of downing too much Chardonnay and being sick, actually suffered a very nasty migraine and was rather ill, which was why she didn't appear for breakfast.

A leisurely petit déjeuner and late start preceded the trip back to Sussex the next morning. *Miss Polkadot* and s2trash didn't actually leave until gone 1.30pm, which meant that *s2trash* had the opportunity of lounging around in the bar reading the Sunday papers. Everyone stayed in a stately convoy this time, especially as *MccSmart2002's* car was suffering turbo problems and was being towed back on the Sussex Cars trailer.

Arriving back at the Halfway Bridge pub, some seven hours later, the Smartball entourage was met with a fabulous spread of food, a welcome sight indeed and well deserved by all. Despite their extremely late start, *Miss P* and *s2trash* arrived only twenty minutes later than the main group, having driven the same journey in only four hours! How's that for female driving! After a short rest, a charity auction commenced with fabulous donated gifts available such as tickets to Goodwood, St. Andrew's Golf Tournament, and several drives in an Aston Martin. A raffle also took place, with all manner of **smart** paraphernalia kindly donated by Smart of Gatwick, as prizes. A fabulous time was had by all over the weekend, and almost £4000 was raised for the four charities chosen to benefit from the adventure: British Heart Foundation, Cancer Research, Cystic Fibrosis Trust and Help a Local Child.

Crossblade cruises up country

Roadsters in hot pursuit of blond bombshell

Underneath 'The Big One'

We did it!

The M25 Run 2005

You would have thought that after the first mad rally round the M25, nobody in their right frame of mind would have wanted to do a second one, but they did, and so *s2trash* was obliged to organise it! Early in 2005 the second run was discussed and organised for the 7th May, starting at Bluewater Shopping Mall in Kent. On this occasion however, the cars would drive clock-wise just so that it would feel a little different. Amazingly, the amount of folks willing to waste their hard earned fuel coupons had doubled to 18, which just proved there are some seriously disturbed folk out there, readers. *Miss Polkadot* helped with arrangements and booked a restaurant for the end of the run, with the start time brought forward to 5pm. In theory it had been a good idea, in practice however, it was bad; Bluewater, the Holy Grail of shopping, was still full of hundreds of shoppers! With a car park crammed full of Essex housewives spending their husband's money on the latest bad taste fashion garments, everyone had little option than to double and treble park. Thank the lord **smarts** are so compact! It was great to see some new faces arrive and to admire those that had travelled considerable distances to join in the fun and games of the year's 'Most Pointless Meet'.

Both the acquisition of short wave radios and the decision of who would be positioned where in the convoy line-up had been sorted well in advance. *NeilOs* was to ride shot gun in his shat red **smart** (Shat red should read Phat red – a private joke between *s2trash* and *NeilOs*). *NeilOs* was accompanied by *Red Cookie* so *s2trash* felt safe that the rear would be taken care of. *S2rash* would, as he organised it, be chauffer driven by *Miss P* in her spottymobile and be taking the position of lead car – well you couldn't fail to miss a car looking like that now could you!

Naturally *s2trash* took compulsory photos of all the attendees so proof could be shown as to who had turned up and to use as blackmail at a later date if needed. A great deal of interest was shown in *Kym1959's* **smart** roadster from both the M25-ers and the general public. With recent major surgery the car looked resplendent in its new Rage paint colours, new rims and hot replacement Lamborghini-style doors. With all the messing about the start time was suddenly upon them – time to roll. A total of 18 **smarts** lined up in the car park – along with all the other shoppers who had decided to leave at the same time! The negotiation of the first roundabout was ok; at the second roundabout it looked as if the convoy might get split up but they stayed together, more by luck than judgement. Then disaster struck! At the third roundabout, 9 cars went left and 9 cars went right! Aghhh nooo! The 'smartarse nine' that had gone the correct way pulled up in a bus stop and some frantic calls where made, 'Mayday Mayday, calling all lost **smarts**'. When contact had finally been made it was decided that the 'smartarses' would get onto the motorway but keep the speed down to 40mph so that the 'not-so-clever-clogs' could catch up. The 'smartarse nine' made it through the toll gates at Dartford and into the tunnel without any incidence, but after 20 minutes they still hadn't re-grouped with the 'not-so-clever-clogs'. In fact it took nearly 45 minutes after leaving the start for everyone to catch up and become one happy convoy again.

The drive was being filmed by Dave Bore (Cause & Effect Video Production), who had cameras set up fore and aft inside his car. Dave, who had never been to a **smart** gathering before, was using the event as an experiment as his company car was a **smart**.

Just as he had done on the previous M25 Run *mccsmart2002* was filming the vehicular antics for the **smart** community's posterity, but this year was a passenger in *Jim808's* roadster, and could be clearly seen hanging out of the window! According to some sources, the driver of the fortwo he had hitched a lift with last year had suffered a temporary digestive disorder causing the unthoughtful expulsion of obnoxious gasses. Consequently, he told *Bubski* he would rather risk losing his locks in *Jim808's* roadster than go through another shared near-death experience with him again. Funnily enough, *Bubski* was not available for comment! With *Jim808* bombing up and down the line of cars it gave most of the **smart** drivers the opportunity to pull some amazing faces at *mccsmart2002*,

Pausing for a break

More incriminating evidence

Last outing for s2trash's car

which was humorous at the time but will be around for time immemorial, etched into one of *mccsmart2002's* comical DVDs. As the convoy settled down to negotiating the multitude of stretch limos hired by commoners across the land, the radios sparked into life and over came a message from *Helresa* that their work computers had crashed and they needed to drive back into London to sort them out, but they would try to meet back up with everyone at Bluewater for the meal. Sadly, at the first available exit they made a dash.

The first stop of the night was at South Mimms Service Station where much coffee was quaffed. It was a nice chance for a chat and the discovery that Dave Bore in the film car had been lost...*s2trash* had forgotten to give him the printed handout of the run details! A quick call found him two junctions up the motorway, where he would wait on the hard shoulder for the convoy to catch up. The smokers slowly ambled their way back to the cars, trying to bend enough time for another cigarette, but with one eye on the clock so as not to be late returning to Bluewater and upsetting the restaurant staff.

Back on the highway from hell and the **smart** convoy hit road works and speed cameras around Heathrow, just after collecting David Bore in his bright yellow **smart** covered in chevrons from the hard shoulder. Once out of the road works, which seemed to take forever, it was foot to the floor, keeping within national speed limits of course. Time was passing a little too fast and so when it was time to hit the second service area at Clacket Lane, it was decided to make it a fuel-only stop. Arrival in the petrol station caused many bemused looks from other car drivers. Some rather inquisitive ones were given an explanation of exactly what everyone was doing, much to their amusement. It was a jolly good job none of them were doctors or the entire convoy would have been sectioned under the Mental Health Act for sure! *Miss P* then phoned the restaurant to warn them that everyone would be turning up 30 minutes late and that was fine, so the pressure was off. The sun had started to set in a glorious array of colours, making the last leg of the journey that little bit more pleasant, along with all the other motorists smiling and waving at the little **smart** convoy. By the time everybody had rolled back into Bluewater at 9.20pm it was almost dark, but another group photo was taken just to prove everyone had made it in one piece, before invading the restaurant. As the group walked into the restaurant *Zigzag* was there waiting for everyone, leaning on the bar looking like he was on the pull. He hadn't done the run but had decided to meet up for the meal, and *Helresa*, after their untimely 'on-call' departure, finally made it back on time too. Slightly worried that the group's reputation had preceded them, they found ourselves sectioned off from the rest of the diners on a specially prepared table. The food, drinks and company was very agreeable, and before you could say 'Mad **smart** owners' it was 11pm and time to make a move homeward bound. Some owners had to brave travelling round the M25 again to get home – talk about déjà vu!

Sadly, as they approached the car park, they were accosted by a jobs-worth security guard, incorrectly accusing several **smart** owners of inappropriate behaviour round the car park! As if! The situation was getting very hot, until a 5 ft 1", spotty; super-woman stepped in and calmed the situation down! The absurd accusations included racing the cars and performing 'doughnuts', even though nobody had had their engines turned on! With the problem amicably resolved, the good name of **smart** ownership untarnished and restored, everyone said their goodbyes, and threatened to do it all again next year! After the usual standing around chatting in the car park, it was past midnight when the last car rolled out. It had been another really good run and everyone enjoyed themselves. This just goes to prove that you don't have to be mad to drive a **smart**, but it helps!

Billing Aquadrome 2005

As it later turned out, this weekend of the 1st-3rd July was sadly to be the last **smart** event held at Billing Aquadrome. It was Spotty Badger's first time as traders, having decided to offer people the chance to have a personalised portrait taken of their much loved car. With *s2trash* now not driving for medical reasons, a great deal of planning and clever packing was now required in order to get all of his belongings to Billing; and he had cleverly roped in *jamiebeveridge* and his friend *Jeff* to transport him and all his equipment there on the Thursday. Luckily *Jeff* had a Ford Ka to take most of the gear, as there was no way he would have fitted it all in *jamie's* car. The first part of their journey was uneventful as they headed off to meet up with *Miss Polkadot* and her son *Microdot*. You couldn't say the same thing about the second part of the journey. Not long after joining the M25 there was a very loud sounding bang as *jamie's* roof unexpectedly exploded, covering both himself and *s2trash* in glass whilst cruising along at 75mph. The glass projectiles then blasted themselves all over *Jeff's* Ka, who was following immediately behind. In total disbelief both cars pulled over onto the hard shoulder in order to remove the little glass cubes from themselves and the **smart**. The glass seemed to have gone an awfully long way, with *s2trash* even finding bits in his boxer shorts! *Jeff's* windscreen had visible damage to it but for the time being seemed safe. Poor *jamie*, who must have been in a mild state of shock at the incident and the impending costs looming for his hopefully understanding Mother, was made to pose for photos for *s2trash's* "Would you believe it!" photo album. One suspects that *jamie* would have preferred it to go in the "One I'd like to forget" folder.

With the glass removed they shakily set off again, only to see enormous black clouds forming in the very direction in which they were heading. They didn't actually have to travel that far in order to meet up with the spotty duo at Brentwood, but the impending rain wasn't a very nice thought in a car with no roof. By the time *jamie* and *s2trash* arrived the heavens opened, so they quickly took cover in a petrol station. *Miss Polkadot* arrived shortly afterwards, but she didn't immediately assimilate the fact that both *jamie* and *s2trash* were waving to her through the open roof. It took a few cog churning moments for her realise that the car was, in the roof department, deficient to the tune of one, and not a cabrio after all. Once the penny dropped, she felt concern for their health but at the same time tried to suppress a enormous guffaw of laughter, for only to *s2trash* could an incident of this magnitude have manifested itself – and it wasn't even his own car! It was finally beginning to dawn on her that *s2trash* was right all along and that he *did* carry around a hex with him wherever he went!

With their nerves finally calm, the lads repacked all the belongings that could possibly get wet into *Jeff's* car and praying that the break in the downpour remained, finally drove off on the journey up to Northampton. Providing they remained driving above 50mph the inevitable rain showers didn't blow inside the car. After many strange looks from other drivers, the two idiots in a roofless **smart** decided to stop at a service station so they could have a hot drink to warm up. Covering up the car with a ground sheet, they encountered even more strange looks, and prayed nothing from the car went missing whilst they were inside in the warm. Feeling rejuvenated, they uncloaked the car and drove the last leg to Billing without any further mishaps and in the dry. Luckily, unlike the previous year, they didn't have to wait long to get into the show ground itself and set up home for the next few days, as *Dave Kaye* was promptly on hand to organise access. With all the tents erected and everyone in a jovial mood, those folks that had turned up early lent a hand to mark out the ground plan for the trader's pitches with spray cans, poles, tape and the odd can of beer!

Traders booked for the weekend, of which there was a good selection included: Smartimes, Smarts R us, Smartarse Design, S-mann, SW Exclusive, Bantam Trailers, Murano Silver, Smart of Hertford, Smart Panels, Smart-Suits, Janspeed, The AA, Mr Dot Com, Red Dot Racing, Smarts 4 U, Smartechnique, Auto Proud, Ultraseal, Neons, MSM Insurance, Auto-Box Carrier, Funkysmart Car Club and last but not least, Spotty Badger Productions.

The driving course last year had been so popular, that *s2trash* was asked to help devise one again for this event, but with a few more safety features built in! Unfortunately, *Dave Kaye* had forgotten to bring the traffic cones and other very essential equipment needed for the course to take place, and so, much to the dismay of several keen drivers, the course was off the agenda, as the equipment could not be re-sourced at such short notice. Once all of the trader's plots where marked out it was time to take a quick trip Tesco's for food and drink. The evening was spent catching up with old friends and the latest gossip and in some instances imbibing in too much falling down water, as *s2trash* was testament to! *Wayneaucock* and *s2trash* had comfortably installed themselves inside the foyer of *Miss Polkadot's* palatial tent exchanging anecdotes and wine until she finally kicked them both out at about 1.30am. Both men began to look a little worse for wear, seemingly oblivious to the time and the amount of drink consumed, and within a short while *s2trash* was apparently spotted on all fours outside his tent re-appraising his fish and chip supper!

Friday

The following morning was the start of a lovely day, but *s2trash* awoke feeling somewhat fragile. After breakfast, courtesy of *Miss Polkadot*, the Spotty Badger emporium was opened. Positioned in a prime location, they were able to sit and watch all the comings and goings. Unfortunately *Tangerine Teal* was on holiday in the USA so she wasn't there to help *Dave Kaye* to keep a check on everything and soon the first cars started to arrive. Between taking portraits of cars, *s2trash* and *Miss Polkadot* were also on the hunt for subjects for their 2006 calendar, so **smart** spotting was the order of the day. They had help from *Miss P's* son *Microdot*, who was very good and saved them a great deal of shoe leather. At one stage *s2trash* blagged a spin in *Putzie's* new crossblade, which *Putzie* had purchased the night before driving up to Billing. Soon after that, *s2trash* was able to borrow a very unusual crossblade re-sprayed in a dark metallic gold by Smart-Suits, not bad for day one. The Friday was a chilled out day despite doing a lot of photography and it was a great chance to meet up with old friends. *Miss Polkadot* had parked up her car in front

Oops! Where's my roof gone? *Sorry Coolfart, I don't sell Union Jack pants!* *Anyone seen my smart clogs?* *Campsite cooking the student way!*

of the trading tent as it was now such a part of their company and a bit of free advertising. To hear people say "…that must be *Miss Polkadot's* car!" and pose next to it for photos was a bit of a hoot! For *s2trash*, the rest of Friday evening became a total haze and his memory cell has no recall of anything else that happened at all. You'd think he'd learn!

Saturday

Many owners who were unable to get the day off work on Friday arrived bright and early and set up their tents, swelling the numbers and intensifying that ever distinctive BBQ smell.

After removing the odd bug and showering, *s2trash* met up with *Miss Polkadot* and promptly sat down outside their trader's tent. Sometimes sitting down and watching others can be pure entertainment. It was evident by their body language and their colouring, just who had drunk too much the night before, and those milling around not knowing where to plug the toaster or kettle in were obviously those who normally didn't camp. This people watching episode just proved that this strange little car certainly draws a diverse mixture of people together, and the events are all the more fun because of it. Sadly, the s2Crew or Sussex Branch as they are sometimes known as, were unable to get to Billing as it clashed with a modified car meet held at The Hop Farm in Kent, and their wacky brand of humour was sorely missed.

Around mid-afternoon Mick and Dave, who were friends of *s2trash* and the promoters of 'The Flying Marrows', one of bands performing that night, turned up and were promptly introduced to relevant people and given a tour of the site. As the afternoon drew to a close someone suggested that it would be nice to have a meal in the Indian restaurant on the campsite instead of doing a BBQ and so a group of around 18 owners including *Miss P*, *Microdot* and *s2trash* headed for the venue. Prior to the meal *s2trash* had devised plans for a very special photo shoot with *Evilution* for later on in the evening. Dinner took longer than expected and the sky began to turn grey with rain clouds so *s2trash* bolted down his food and rushed of to find the Evil one, as *Miss Polkadot* was going to transform him into a ghoul with some expert face painting, just for the shot. With the metamorphosis complete *s2trash* borrowed a smoke machine and a generator, and with the help of Mick and Dave and a large estate car took the equipment to the location found earlier in the day. *Miss Polkadot* drove down in her car followed by *Evilution* and his girlfriend *Kat* in his car, a short while after. Whilst driving through the campsite a group of young girls pointed at *Miss Polkadot's* car with 'ooohs' and' aaahhs', only to scream their heads off when *Evil* wound down his window and grimaced at them! *Miss Polkadot* had done an amazing face paint job on him and he looked terrifying!

Now, if anything could go wrong it did that evening. First of all it started to drizzle, and then the smoke machine wouldn't work no matter how hard it was poked and probed. Even *Dave Kaye*, who had generously lent it in the first place, could not get it going. Desperately wanting smoke for his shot *s2trash* tried setting fire to a heap of damp grass, but the increasing intensity of the rain soon put paid to that idea, which was just as well because with his luck he could have caused a bush fire! By now it was dark and raining heavily and even with added illumination from car headlights *s2trash* had to admit defeat and hope what ever pictures he had taken would work. At least he had the option of adding the magic of a little photoshopping, but that was something he would only contemplate as a last resort, preferring to have taken a perfect picture at the time of exposure – still in this case it was 'needs must'. Feeling slightly moist and fed up, *s2trash* headed back to the campsite to be greeted by some new **smart** owners *Leewee* and *Kittycat,* who persuaded him to try a few alchopops to cheer himself up. This didn't seem such a **smart** move after Thursday night's jettison of comestibles but he managed to remain on the sober side of merry!

Back at the main marquee 'The Flying Marrows', a band suggested for the gig by *s2trash*, were booked as the main set. Unfortunately, they turned into 'The Diving

Puddlejumper and Candypants play Peep Bo

Champagne roadsters

Fudge performing brake surgery

Marrows' as their brand of music wasn't to most peoples taste. Booking an Indie/Ska band wasn't the best choice *s2trash* ever made! Also on the bill was 'Mad Dave' and his wacky solo take on Ska music, a 'one man Madness' but at least he received a slightly better reaction. Paul Holmes from Smarts R Us rounded up the evening playing his electric keyboard and getting everyone's toes tapping with his own unique style of performing cover versions. With his keyboard disguised as a baby grand complete with candelabra, one could have been fooled into thinking it was the Palladium all over again! The evening progressed well into the late hours and The Flying Marrows volunteered to play their greatest hits to the Essex Smarties at their camp site, some of whom, for some strange reason, decided to have an early night!

Sunday

Now at some stage during the night *s2trash* awoke to hear voices and someone trying to get into his tent, which was situated away from the main camping area. By the time he had scrambled to get some clothes on the 'voices' had made a run for it, and *s2trash* went back to bed feeling a little wary and slept with his senses on full alert. Waking bright and early Sunday morning *s2trash* stuck his head out of the tent and spotted somebody's clothes hanging on the Funkysmart marquee next door. It transpired that some unsavoury characters had been trying to break into the traders tents during the night. *Leewee* and *Otisb* managed to catch one of the perpetrators red-handed and unfortunately for him, in the pursuing struggle he had managed to lose some clothing and his mobile phone before escaping. Smarts R Us had come off the worst as they found that their new marquee had been slashed, but thankfully there was nothing stolen. Later that day *Leewee* and *Otisb* spotted the man they had temporarily apprehended that night, at the campsite shop and they managed to get him arrested.

With a bright and sunny day on the cards *s2trash* and *Miss Polkadot* busied themselves taking car portraits and borrowing more cars for shots in their forthcoming calendar. They took cars into the fair ground, round by the lakes, in fact they must have used the whole of the Billing site. As the day wound up, some of the group of **smart** owners who had completed a sponsored charity run from Land's End to John O'Groats earlier in the year, (The LEJOG Tour), handed over a cheque for a substantial amount of money to a representative of Cancer Research. *Leewee* and *Otisb*, who had been given a reward of £100 for the apprehension of the criminal who had vandalised some trader's marquees, handed over their cheque to Cancer Research too; a truly selfless act.

Apart from the problem with the criminal, all in all it had been a great weekend – as indeed all these **smart** gatherings always turn out to be. Now that it was time to depart, it suddenly dawned on *s2trash* that he was going to have trouble in getting himself and all of his equipment from the campsite all the way to *Miss Polkadot's* house where he was due to be working for a few days. He had not thought about the problem at all prior to going and therefore had not organised anything, and now he was in a fix! *Jamie*, who had brought *s2trash* and his stuff to Billing, had to take his car to Smartarse Design in Romsey to have a new roof fitted. *Jeff* had to follow along to get *Jamie* home to Hastings after dropping his car off but they offered to take all of *s2trash's* camping equipment with them and he could collect it at a later date. With two camera cases, a tripod, a ruddy huge suitcase, oh and himself still to be found transport, *s2trash* began to worry. Yes, you did read that correctly, *s2trash* took a suitcase camping! *Miss Polkadot* didn't have much room in her car as she had all her camping stuff and her son *Microdot*, but she managed to squeeze in one of the camera cases. Coming to the rescue at the eleventh hour, *Funkymonkey*, one of *Miss P's* Essex Smarties, offered to transport *s2trash* and as much luggage as he could, which would be minimal as he drove a roadster! With the tripod in the front compartment of the roadster, one camera case in the passenger foot well, *s2trash* was squeezed onto the seat and *that* suitcase shoehorned in on top! This left *s2trash* totally unable to move and just about able to breathe.

Waving goodbye to the last stragglers and trying to explain that what was in Funkymonkey's roadster was half-human/half-suitcase, they rolled out of Billing for the last time. Twenty minutes into the homeward journey *Jim808* who had been accompanying the little convoy part of the way, made everyone pull over and stop in

Smartimes car on rolling road

All the fun of the fair

Flaming cars!

a lay-by. He had just felt so sorry for *s2rash* having his 6' 4" frame being compressed into such a restricted space that he offered to change his route and take *that* 'bleedin' suitcase at least part way, as he didn't want to see *s2trash* get his circulation restricted so much that bits would begin to drop off! This kind gesture helped out *Funkeymonkey* as he didn't have much room to manoeuvre either and had trouble seeing out of his rear view mirror! After what seemed far too short a time *that* suitcase was intimately back with *s2trash*, but at least he didn't have far to go. By the time they rolled onto *Miss Polkadot's* drive *s2trash* was seized solid, and had to be surgically removed. Once out of the car but re-shaped in a rather fetching Ape-man posture, *s2trash* thanked *Funkeymonkey* for the sardine-can ride of a lifetime! Then, once the pins and needles started certain words emanated from a very pale *s2trash* including the only repeatable ones...never again!

Smartball Crossblade Meet 2005

This was definitely a first – a meet just for crossblades, with a trophy for the best turned out car. The venue was The Bluebird Café, on The King's Road, London. Originally built in 1923, the Bluebird was once Europe's largest motor garage and is thought to be where Malcolm Campbell's famous Bluebird cars were assembled. The Bluebird, a unique grade II listed London landmark now owned by Terence Conran, opened in May 1997, and depicts much of the history relating to the Bluebird car that broke the world land speed record in the 1920s.

Miss Polkadot, (who was acting as chauffer for *s2trash* for the day), was amongst the first to turn up, nabbing a great parking spot right opposite the Café. The guys from Smartechnique were there with two stunning cars, a custom sprayed fortwo and a roadster, gleaming in the early morning sun. Having arrived before the Café had opened, everyone sat around enjoying the sites, smells and sounds of the King's Road. It has a real continental feel considering it is in 'the Smoke' and is an incredibly popular place, even so early on a Sunday morning.

The first coffee of the day appeared, just as the crossblades did, from Surrey, Sussex and Buckinghamshire. Half of the Café courtyard had been reserved just for those attending the event, so naturally everyone spread out amongst the tables and enjoyed the first coffee of the day and savoured the atmosphere of wonderment that the appearing crossblades were causing. Although Jeremy Smith, organiser of this Smartball charity event had hoped for more, a respectable five crossblades turned up, along with an assortment of other smarts. All of the crossblades parked on the pavement outside the Café, causing a continuous stream of finger pointing, smiling and waving from the passing traffic. There was even a 'bag' lady so intrigued by the cars that she chatted for ages, then took away some Smartechnique brochures, and returned several times more to annoy everyone with her attention and her aroma!

From *s2trash's* point of view, trying to take pictures of the rare crossblades now became a game of dodgems, as he had no choice but to be standing in the road to get the shots he required. Even he had to admit that taking on big red buses and black cabs without getting squashed, was a minor miracle! It was a lovely day made so, not only by the weather but by meeting up with **smart** owners not seen for several weeks and also made even more enjoyable with a spot of lunch washed down with some Buck's Fizz, kindly organised by Jeremy.

As *Miss Polkadot* had designed and made the trophy, Jeremy asked her, (along with *s2trash's* help or did he mean hindrance?), to judge the competition for the **Smartball Crossblade of the Year**. It was a tough decision, but the winner was John Sullivan (*Sullij*), with his immaculate car and his much coveted number plate – **X 81ADE**. The runner-up was Rob Moore (*Brabus*), who won a scale crossblade model donated by Sussex Cars. Both prizes were presented by a representative

Crossblade septuplets

Coffee outside The Bluebird Café

SulliJ wins the Best Crossblade trophy

Heading off to Hyde Park

from The Bluebird Café. After the presentation, all the crossblades and the other **smart** owners left the Café and did a cruise to Hyde Park, accidentally losing a few in the traffic along the way... Boy, did the entourage get some looks, especially when the newly installed air-horns in *Roadrage's* car got stuck on, permanently! Once in Hyde Park the convoy stopped on yellow lines in the shade, waiting for the others to catch up. It was now mid-afternoon and incredibly hot, so everyone made a bee-line for the nearest café selling ice-cold drinks. Blowing caution to the wind, all the cars parked up on more yellow lines, praying that they would be spared the wrath of the traffic wardens. Having spent a week's wages on their drinks, but relishing every sip they took, they relaxed in the shade with one eye on the cars, prepared to make a quick get away if the traffic warden made a sudden appearance. Luckily they were spared, and made plans to escape the city, all going in different directions like multi-coloured candy coated sweets dropped on the floor. Apparently, *s2trash* seemed to think *Miss Polkadot* would make a good mini-cab driver watching the ease with which she negotiated the complicated congested London roads; *Miss P* on the other hand seemed to think *s2trash* made an even better back-seat driver, and planned on getting a sun strip made for her car bearing the slogan 'Driver from heaven – Passenger from Hell'.

Bexhill Beach Party 2005

Could this event get any longer? Yes, siree! It had now expanded to five days in length for 2005, and with many more new faces daring to venture there from as far away as Manchester, Rotherham and deepest Wales to attend.

Thursday

The Cobb's Hill Farm campsite, that had now become the official home of the event, had kindly given over a whole field to **smart** campers. The first of these arrived on the Thursday. *Leewee* and *Kittycat* had not only brought their **smart** but had towed it behind their mobile home that they had driven all the way from Rotherham, South Yorkshire. They had made a mini convoy of their journey down with *Smartie*, *Captain Pugwash* (who was carefully transporting an inflatable palm tree and a vast chocolate cake), and *Brabus* in his crossblade, towing a trailer that seemed to hold the entire contents of a camping supply shop! *S2trash* had the pleasure of four cars arriving at his house to transport him and his chattels the few miles to the campsite. Talk about be spoilt!

Down at the campsite *Leewee* and *Kittycat* had set up the campsites NAAFI; tea, coffee and currant buns. Once *Miss Polkadot* had arrived and her 'Palace' was erected, the beach beckoned as it was a fantastic hot afternoon. A few people decided to hunt out the nearest pub to the beach, whilst the rest swam and topped up their tans. Everyone prayed the weather would hold for Saturday too, that being the date for the proper Beach Party. Once back at the campsite, a few select folks were treated to a delectable slice of homemade chocolate cake made by *Captain Pugwash*, which he had very carefully and tenderly brought all the way down with him. Now that was a cake to die for! A legend in its own cake tin!

With all in high spirits, some neighbouring campers decided to pay a visit to see what was going on, as by now *Brabus* was sitting in an inflatable dingy wearing flippers, with an inflatable palm tree next to him – IN THE MIDDLE OF THE FIELD, and *Leewee* was on the 'Pimms', oh how English was this! Needless to say the visitors went away shaking their heads with laughter, finally convinced that **smart** owners were off their trolleys! As indeed some of them certainly are! The evening was a quiet affair with some folks going to the beach with fish and chips and watching the most incredible sun set.

First pub visit of the weekend

Mr. Inflatable aka Brabus

Here comes the clown!

Friday

Friday dawned with grey skies and drizzle, not what the happy campers had been expecting, and by the time more people arrived, around mid-morning, including *Tangerine Teal*, the drizzle had turned to rain. The Smart-Suits crew must have brought the Welsh rain with them, the rotters! A dry, warm pub called 'The White Hart' in the neighbouring village of Catsfield then became the venue for lunch. Here, everything from the barmaid to the WC got the 'Man-o-Bong' treatment, (a tongue-in-cheek joke, where pictures were taken of a 'Man-o-Bong' number plate in various unlikely situations). The rain cleared by early evening so *s2trash* organised a cruise to Eastbourne Marina via Pevensey Castle, where the group waited patiently to meet up with *jamiebeveridge* and his friend *Jeff*, who had got a little lost, despite it being local territory for them. Arriving en mass at the marina, the little band of desperately hungry campers made a bee-line for the Simply Italian restaurant, where they braved the elements to eat alfresco, got singed eyebrows from the heaters and caused mayhem when they requested the tables be moved to make a circle. The fabulous food and great company, followed by a gentle cruise back to the campsite, rounded the evening off nicely.

Saturday

Saturday arrived sunny and bright, the praying had paid off! Everyone got themselves ready and rushed to Cooden Beach on Herbrand Walk, via *s2trash's* special butchers, clearing the shop out of his best bangers for the beach BBQ. Although there had been the intention of having a Hawaiian theme for this party, only three brave souls dressed the part – *Miss P* being one of them! Both her and *Sally Sweet Pea* went the whole hog and wore grass skirts and flower garlands, whilst *Captain Pugwash* sported a flowery 'Hawaii-5-O' shirt and exotic straw hat. A few other chaps half-heartedly wore bright shirts, but the real joker of the day was *Brabus*. How he managed to confuse 'Hawaiian theme' with 'Circus Ring', no one will never know, but he arrived driving his crossblade wearing an inflatable clown costume! Laugh! Did we heck! Even the seaweed! A representative from the local paper came along and photographed the oddly dressed folks, which featured in the Bexhill Observer the following week. Everyone spent a very pleasant afternoon playing silly ball games, flying kites, swimming, cooking BBQ's, and if memory recalls there was the odd incident of a jet ski being hijacked and getting the 'Man-o-Bong' treatment too!

Before long it was time to pack up and join *s2trash* on his cruise to Birling Gap, a small hamlet perched on top of The Seven Sisters, the famous series of chalk cliffs between Beachy Head and Seaford. What a superb drive in the dwindling sunlight across the undulating coast. That was a truly memorable moment, seeing that multicoloured snake, formed by 22 cars, winding through the bends. At Birling Gap, most folks headed into the pub. Some folks descended the cliff onto the beach, where they caught up some of the *S2Crew*; Gary, Kat, Jason, Daryl and Nat, who, along with *Bubski*, cooked up another BBQ, whilst watching the sunset across the sea. Back up in the car park, *Sally Sweet Pea* was presented with two melons, her prize for the 'Best Dressed Hula Girl', whilst *Brabus* was awarded with two coconuts and a banana for his achievement in 'Wearing the most outrageous costume at the beach'. Just for a moment, he was lost for words!

It had been a fantastic day. Cruising back to the campsite, the evening was rounded off by sitting together around lots of tea lights, laughing, drinking and chatting well into the night. *Miss Polkadot* managed to do a clever impersonation of a flamethrower when her sleeve caught light over one of the tea-lights and burned her hand – then *s2trash*, with amazing accuracy, sprayed all the onlookers with melted wax when he stomped on the tea lights to extinguish the flames. *Brabus* played fireman and hosed down *Miss P's* arm with great efficiency, while *Sally Sweet Pea* – a real life nurse – wrapped her hand in ice. Thanks to their help, *Miss P* sustained no lasting damage, just a healthier respect for fire and wax!

Captain Pugwash with serious reading matter

Baywatch babe

Posing for the press

Brabus displays his prize for Best Beach Costume!

Sunday

On Sunday morning some folks drifted home. Some stayed on and visited the beach again. The beach visit didn't last long as the weather suddenly changed from summer to winter in a matter of minutes! *Captain Pugwash, Smartie, s2trash, Brabus, Pedro Mustard* and *Miss Polkadot* all went back to the campsite to halt the onset of hypothermia, and ended up cooking up some great camping nosh – namely hotdogs and burgers. There is nothing quite like cooking and eating food outdoors – it must be the added insects and bits of grass that make it so special! At 5pm, it was time for *Miss P* to say goodbye to some great friends and drive back to Essex, for her, the end of a superb weekend. *Smartie, Brabus* and *Captain Pugwash* stayed and camped again that night, and then met up with *s2trash* the following morning. They all had breakfast together before leaving *s2trash* in Battle, and driving all the way home back up north in the rain.

The London to Brighton 2005

Yet another new starting venue for this, the forth *L2B*, saw hundreds of **smarts** converge at Thorp Park on 25th September 2005. As *s2trash* was still not driving he had stayed at *Miss Polkadot's* house the night before in order that he could experience the luxury of being chauffeur driven in the, now famous 'Polkadot' **smart**. Although running the risk of having a back seat driver (or to be more technical a side seat driver) *Miss Polkadot* braved the extended company of *s2trash* so that he could still get to the event and photograph it for posterity. Armed with earplugs and air-fresheners, *Miss Polkadot* shoe-horned her 6' 4" companion in to her car and met up with seven of her Essex Smarties at the ungodly hour of 5.30am. Cruising along in a 'Tube' on the unpopulated road at that time in the morning, on a Sunday, when most sane people are warmly tucked up in bed, was actually rather a pleasant experience. No Lorries, no road rage, no jams. If only it was always like that!

Smart of Lakeside had kindly arranged for everyone to meet up at their showroom, where *Miss P* could also collect more Essex Smarties en route. After providing the bleary eyed drivers with much appreciated hot cups of coffee and rather large **smart** goodie bags, they headed off from Lakeside to their next rendezvous point – Clacket Lane Services on the M25. Clacket Lane had become a convenient converging point for several independent 'tubes' heading to the L2B, including cars from the Kent Meet. After such an early start and downing free coffee at Smart of Lakeside, using the facilities had become essential. All the cars then merged together and headed off as one. Typically, just as they were nearing Thorpe Park, the sky became overcast and it started to drizzle. All those painstaking hours of car cleaning smeared away in seconds – it just makes you want to cry. With the weather front forging through, the temperatures had dropped significantly, and those folks in skimpy fancy dress, in particular two topless young ladies wearing not much more than body paint and smiles, were certainly finding things a bit nippy round the ankles! Baring all as a publicity stunt favour for their brother's business, they certainly succeeded in attracting vast amounts of attention, with many a camera focused on their projecting assets!

All the **smarts** began to amass in one of the vast car parks in front of the entrance. The official total of **smarts** parked up at Thorpe Park prior to the start was 953, but when you are actually there amongst them all it seems like a hell of a lot more! There was a queue of owners armed with cameras, vying for the use of a large rubbish bin. What for dear reader? Well, you would be surprised to know that it made an excellent viewing platform to photograph an aerial view of the parked **smart** ensemble. Even *s2trash* decided to commandeer this handy location despite his already lofty height. By now of course, the bin was in a state of exhaustion,

Early morning start at smart of Lakeside

Smart superheroes

A sea of smarts

and with the worry of it imploding beneath him, *s2trash* decided to remove himself pretty sharpish before he ended up in it rather than on it.

The atmosphere at these events is just fantastic, with admiration and sometimes envy at the modifications folks have done to their cars. Why these little cars make their owners go to such lengths to make them so individual is a phenomenon that is hard to get to grips with. Let's face it, the only other models of car that this happens to is the classic VW Beetle and the old Minis. Why, we ask ourselves, when the **smart** is so unique to start with? Perhaps because it becomes part of us, we have to 'dress it up' to mirror our own identity and prove to the world it belongs go us. Surely there must be some deep psychological reason behind it all, but who cares, we love doing it, it's a bit of fun in this dreary world and it makes folk smile. Of course, there are always the few that take things a bit too far...take *Putzie* for instance! He had recently acquired a crossblade, decided it needed a bit of a make-over and embellished it with Batman logos. In order to complete the tableaux, he arrived at Thorpe Park having driven all the way from Cambridge, dressed as Batman, complete with a moulded 6-pack! Luckily for him, he met up with some very attractive, but equally batty girls dressed as Super Woman and Wonder Woman, so sometimes it pays off being daft as a brush! There were Moulin Rouge Can-Can girls, ladies wearing daisies, men wearing clothes covered in round coloured chocolate candy patterns, girls dressed as devils, car dealers dressed in dinner suits and the female half of this team sporting yet another black and white spotty outfit with matching handbag! For *Miss Polkadot* and *s2trash*, and certainly the majority of other **smart** owners, this small section of the day is the best part. The atmosphere is just amazing, and is really the only time in the year that so many enthusiastic owners can share and show their pride and joy to the rest of the **smart** community, and it is just *so* much fun!

Finally, a clement wind blew the drizzly clouds away, and presented those assembled with a sapphire blue sky and a beaming sun. This pleasant change then caused everyone to sizzle in their cars whilst they waited, and waited for the start which had become delayed due to a blissfully unaware owner who was not in his car and was blocking the proceedings! Finally, they were off, with a yellow and black chequered lead car, with yellow hazard roof lights and a 'Follow Me' sign, taking pole position. With air horns playing anything from Dixieland tunes to mooing cows, flashing lights and folks shouting with delight, the cavalcade made its way smartly onto the M25 and the journey to Brighton. Well, you guessed it... after coming off the M25 and going south on the A23, they just *had* to stop at Pease Pottage Services. Prior to the start of the run, thesmartclub had handed out route directions to all of the entrants, which gave a choice of two different approaches to Brighton Race Course, one assumes to try and spread the amount of congestion that arose the previous year. It would have been a good idea, had one of the routes given not been incorrect, sending some folks the wrong way on Brighton seafront. There was a tale of some poor chap heading west for 10 miles before realising that something was up and all the **smarts** had disappeared from view! Luckily, for her, *Miss Polkadot* took the pervious year's route to the Race Course, and remarkably, despite *s2trash*'s map reading, didn't get lost at all!

The official figures for the number of cars that crossed the Finish line at Brighton were 1341. Now, that means that somewhere between Thorpe Park and Brighton, 388 extra **smarts** overslept and sneakily joined the run halfway! Presumably some of those may have come from the Brighton area, and thought twice about wasting petrol in venturing within the M25, only then having to go back again, but hey, it was their loss, as they missed the best part of the day. Every year, (and *s2trash* and *Miss P* can now boast about being *L2B* veterans, having completed three of them), the organising of this event has gone from strength to strength. Al Young of thesmartclub and all of his staff, helpers and friends had really pulled the stops out this year enabling more traders and catering facilities the chance to attend. It is a shame Al can't pull a few more strings where the weather is concerned though, because by early afternoon although it kept dry, a strong blustery wind soon tired everybody out and *s2trash* was seen scurrying to the conveniences to re-arrange his hairnet. The purchasing of **smart** bling seemed to be the order of the day down amongst the trade stands, with anything from fancy chrome rims of all sizes to custom made aluminium air vents flying off the

The 'Follow me' smart starts the 2005 L2B

Moulin Rouge Ooh la la!

Look what I landed!

shelves. There was a unique clip-on boot extension available for the fortwo called a Clever End, body kits, re-maps and specialised trailers for those wishing to tow their **smart**. There was even the chance to buy the amazing C7 Body kit, which can turn a fortwo into a remarkably distinctive exotic roadster, providing one had the required amount of earth clams to pay for it all!

The car competitions were laid on again this year, (same categories but with slightly different titles), with representatives from DCUK judging the entrants – and there wasn't a Merc badge in sight! *Miss Polkadot* was extremely proud to find that one of her Essex Smarties, Michael Francis, had actually won the Best Kept Car category. He had gone to extraordinary lengths to exhibit a spotlessly clean car, and even showed his **smart** with one of the wheels taken off to prove its level of clinical purification. The judges remarked that the only time that they had ever seen a car that clean was straight out of the factory and they were hard pressed to accept that it was actually used on a daily basis! Now that takes dedication and a whole lot of elbow crease.

The previous year's winner of the Zaniest competition, *Fluff*, dreamed up a completely different theme for her car this year. In an amazing turnaround, the car was transformed from cute monster to cuddly fish! The car had now taken on the persona of the little clown fish Nemo from the fabulous film 'Finding Nemo'. Now covered in fluorescent orange, black and white fur fabric, and graced with numerous Nemo soft toys, the car was just a jaw-dropping sight to behold, and understandably won her category, now called Best Dressed Car, hands down!

Fortwo
Best Dressed Car - Laura Lowe (Fluff)
Best Modified Car - Harpreet Dhand
Best Kept Car - Michael Frances

Beaulieu 2005

What a turn out! Ticket sales of 255 on the day, exceeded all expectations. They produced small flyers about the event and distributed them about with gay abandon at the London to Brighton run in the September, placing them on every static car that they could. Now that the dust had settled after the collapse of Funkysmart, there were many more active **smart** car websites appearing and so *s2trash* posted topics about this years Beaulieu meet on as many as he could.

With a similar agenda planned as the previous year, *Miss Polkadot* met up with *s2trash* at his abode, on the Saturday afternoon. As explained before, the Lord of Mayhem had been temporarily relieved of his Driving Licence on medical grounds and therefore *Miss P's* spotty wagon had been commandeered to carry all the gear and chauffeur his Lordship to Beaulieu.

After a strong coffee *Miss Polkadot* squeezed, squashed, compressed and cajoled every last bit of luggage and countless hot-off-the-press calendars into her car before finally shoe-horning *s2trash* into the last remaining cubic foot of space in the passenger seat. With only the minimum amount of space left for any necessary lung expansion, *Miss P* found that with *s2trash* and his 6' 4" frame occupying the constricting space, it had a certain advantage during the long journey – it refrained her passenger from any excess verbal fluency, and she made a mental note to herself to make sure she pulled that stunt again! Of course the best place to be on any of these occasions when the car is packed to the gunnels is the driver's space, no overcrowding allowed there! Finally, with a big grin on her face and a grimace on his, they set off.

The drive down to the New Forest was initially very pleasant. As he didn't have room to relax, all *s2trash* had to do was eat *Miss Polkadot's* sweets and try not to be rude about her driving. Needless to say he failed with that task miserably, he just couldn't help himself, and *Miss P* wished that the roll of Duck tape wasn't out of her reach under all of the luggage. The plan was to meet up with some other **smart** owners who had booked into the same accommodation, namely *Bubski*, *Mr & Mrs Roadrage* and Paul and Lorraine from *Miss P's* Essex Smarties meet. Pulling up into the hotel car park, they noticed a roadster in a parking bay which they didn't recognise. Not one to miss an opportunity, *s2trash* tumbled out of the car looking remarkably like the hunchback of Notre Dame just so that he could put a Beaulieu flyer on its windscreen.

With a couple of hours to spare before meeting the others for supper, *Miss P* quickly made her escape for a deserved nap, leaving *s2trash* to morph back to his original gangly self whilst chatting to *Bubski* in the car park, putting the world to rights between them, and comparing brands of cigarettes.

Washed and groomed and with every one together in the car park, the little band of friends set off to find The Hatchet Inn. Despite the fact that the pub was only a matter of a few miles away in the village of Sherfield English, *Miss Polkadot* managed to get everyone lost within minutes. Luckily Paul and Lorraine had purchased a satellite navigation system that very day and with barely any experience in its use, took the lead and managed to steer everyone on the correct course to refreshment. Lorraine was convinced that their new gadget had beer divining properties and didn't use technology at all! Parking at the pub was tight to say the least, taking a full ten minutes to get four cars parked with some unusual manoeuvres. At least it showed the pubs popularity. Although rather cramped for space inside too, the pub has a great atmosphere and superb food, and apparently the beer wasn't bad either and everyone had a great evening. Like a repeat of the previous year, Sunday morning dawned cold and frosty and *s2trash* had to be woken with loud bangs on his door and calls to his mobile. Although the last up, he was the first person out into the cold crisp air with a cup of coffee in one hand and a fag in the other. Give this man a no smoking room and he would stand naked in snow if it was the only way he could get a nicotine fix. Not a pretty scenario... Next to show looking pale and wan was *Bubski,* with a fag in one hand and an ice scraper in the other. Oh, that first cigarette of the day. The two of them stood there like Les Dawson and his sidekick! *Bubski* had been gently pressed-ganged into parking duties for the day and so he needed to wake up and get his wits about him, a task that didn't come easily. As soon as *Miss Polkadot* emerged bright and breezy as usual, the three of them set off like musketeers across the desolate heath land of the New Forest. The scenery that early in the morning was stunning with low lying mist hovering in shallow areas across the fields. The New Forest ponies were barely awake and just opened a single eye to check the cars out as they passed, before dozing off again. Everywhere was a potential photo opportunity and *s2trash* got the hump that there wasn't time to stop. Beaulieu was only about a twenty minute drive away from the hotel so it didn't take long to arrive and be greeted by the staff. After parking the cars on the large hard standing area next to the Car Museum, *Bubski* pronounced that he wanted to wash his car. He had brought a bucket, sponge and copious quantities of other cleaning products with him; all he needed now was some water.

Bubski's water divining skills got rudely interrupted with the arrival of Smart of Maidstone and the DCUK publicity vehicle which they were manning for the day. Once *s2trash* and *Bubski* helped arrange the vehicles into the correct place in the show arena it was straight back to the important job of finding *Bubski* some H20. Surely with the size of Beaulieu there had to be an outside tap close to hand. After much head scratching and cog turning, they found it. They could see the water tap but it was down some stairs next to a metal water bowl and some large chains. Thinking that these items may belong to the security dogs, they were naturally rather hesitant in just helping themselves in case they lost a leg each! Slowly making his way down the stairs *s2rash The Brave* (or was that stupid?), couldn't help wondering if a large ravenous dog would take a juicy chunk out of his Gluteous Maximus at any moment. He needn't have worried, it turned out that the area was for dog owners to leave their prize pooches when looking around the museum. When *Bubski* had got the all clear to say that it was safe and he would be going home with all the appendages he came with, both he and the bucket ventured down the steps.

Like the calm before the storm there was a lot of standing around before the event really kicked off. *Miss Polkadot* set up the Spotty Badger stand to sell their calendars, *Bubski* smeared the dirt over his car in a poor attempt at washing it and *s2trash* did nothing but watch the DCUK stand go up, as is his prerogative as organiser. It wasn't long before the traders began turning up. Digitec were the first but unfortunately without *Jonboy* himself. Although he wasn't able make it in person he had sent down two of his colleagues with all the appropriate re-mapping equipment. The Smartball Club had asked to have an area to promote their charity and so they were given a prime spot for all to see what they are about. *T1NY W* and his roadshow turned up next, followed by Smartimes and Wellsmart.

Wellsmart, at this stage in their development, were actually three companies in one; Wellsmart, Smart Suits and Manhick Engineering. They had brought a huge amount of gear with them to say the least, but with military precision they started to set up their shop for the day inside a huge inflatable marquee. Knowing what to expect at the gate *s2trash* and the Beaulieu staff were all set and ready to do battle. Ten o'clock came and so did the cars. Within fifteen minutes *Bubski* was panicking about where to stick them all. With the view from the gate, which is higher up than the arena, *s2trash* was able to coordinate parking with some frantic arm

The Brabazon restaurant at Beaulieu Motor Museum

Leomobile's infamous Moon discs

...like a no.9 bus – all three turn up together!

waving and loud hollering (just). *Bubski* was close to running out of space and contingency plans were hastily made to use another area if needed. *Miss Polkadot* got word sent by runner to *s2trash* to say that the calendars were selling like hot cakes.

Sunday was Remembrance Day which unintentionally always falls during the Beaulieu meet. *Hot-Toddy* had asked if he could hold a two minutes silence at eleven o'clock, which everyone thought was a good idea and had no objection to. *S2trash* had spoken with the Beaulieu management in advance to see if their PA system could be utilised, which they were more than happy to agree to. Unfortunately, when the PA was tested on the day there was no sound and a call for an electrician was made. Despite many attempts to get it working it couldn't be fixed in time for the 11am Remembrance Day memorial. Despite the hiccup *Hot-Toddy's* mellow voice echoed through the clean crisp air, loud enough for all to hear. In the centre of the arena a group of ex-Service men and all of the **smart** owners, along with many other visitors to Beaulieu gathered. For *s2trash*, moments like this bring a dilemma. Capturing the moment with photographs is a lasting record to be preserved, but not wanting to be intrusive when all are standing in honour is equally difficult. At precisely 11am *Hot-Toddy*, a war veteran himself and holder of several medals, recited the poem below and instigated the two minutes silence. All stood completely still, not a word spoken; it was a very touching moment.

They shall not grow old, as we are left grow old
Age shall not weary them, nor the years condemn
At the going down of the sun and in the morning
We shall not forget them.

History of the Poppy Appeal

The first official Legion Poppy Day was held in Britain on 11 November 1921, inspired by the poem 'In Flanders' Fields' written by John McCrae, a doctor serving there with the Canadian Armed Forces. Since then the Poppy Appeal has been a key annual event in our nation's calendar. Some of the bloodiest fighting of World War One took place in the Flanders and Picardy regions of Belgium and Northern France. As you will read further on in the book, *s2trash* and *Miss Polkadot* travelled through this part of France on their way to the **smart** factory at Hambach, stopping at one of the war cemeteries to pay their respect. They both found it a very moving experience and so difficult to imagine the horrors that had played out there ninety years previously. The poppy was the only thing which grew in the fields there in the aftermath of the complete devastation. On the eleventh hour of the eleventh day of the eleventh month in 1918, the First World War ended. Civilians wanted to remember the people who had given their lives for peace and freedom. An American War Secretary, Moina Michael, inspired by John McCrae's poem, began selling poppies to friends to raise money for the ex-Service community. And so the tradition began. In 1922, Major George Howson, a young infantry officer, formed the Disabled Society, to help disabled ex-Service men and women from the First World War. Howson suggested to the Legion that members of the Disabled Society could make poppies to sell and the Poppy Factory was subsequently founded in Richmond in 1922. The original poppy was designed so that workers with a disability could easily assemble it and this principle remains today.

Remembrance Day ceremony

Making a poppy image courtesy of the British Legion media site

Digitec were very busy doing re-maps on cars during the day, and Wellsmart had all hands to the pump selling and fitting parts. *S2trash* brought himself a new ignition surround in bright shiny alloy to match the rest of his car's controls; he could still bling-it-up even if he wasn't able to drive for now. With such a diverse selection of cars available at his disposal, *s2trash* took the opportunity of borrowing a few to photograph for Smartimes magazine and for this book, thus keeping him out of harms way for a little while at least. *Justrules*, with yet another panel change, and *Binxyboo's* Urban Fairy **smart** sporting a new paint job, were amongst those that posed with pride. The early afternoon brought the 'Sound Off' competitions, again organised by *T1NY W*. This year he had brought some new equipment down with him and he promptly set about testing the cars for ear-wax removal ability. The winner of the ICE (In Car Entertainment for those not in the know) was a young guy called Lee (*chippy*) who *Miss Polkadot* and *s2trash* had met on the Smartball Charity Run to Blackpool earlier in the year, who won with a staggering 138 db. With the success of the' Exhaust Off' in 2004 it was decided to have another. *Leomobile* lost his crown, and Rob Baker (*s2Eagleye*) of Smartarse Design won with an ear splitting 114.7 db. Wellsmart donated all the prizes for the competitions, which was a lovely gesture on their part and which all the recipients were over the moon about.

S2trash had been asked if the event could be filmed for the local BBC television news station, which would include personal interviews with people at the event. Unfortunately, the actual news item that appeared on the television made everyone interviewed look like a bunch of eccentric idiots. S2trash understandably vowed never to allow filming at one of his events ever again!

For the first time since *s2trash* started organising this event, he finally found a few moments to visit the actual car museum. As it was getting late in the afternoon and was fairly quiet he dragged *Miss Polkadot* off the stand and took her in with him, as she had never managed to see the vehicle collection either. It was a welcome break as it was beginning to get quite cold outside. The collection of cars and motor bikes is second to none, but they really need to get a **smart** in there!

All good things have to come to an end and this event had been really good. Now it was time to begin packing up and heading for home. Wellsmart, as previously mentioned, had an inflatable marquee the size of a small detached house. When they started letting the air out it hadn't crossed their minds to check to see if anyone was in it. *Kittycat*, who had worked her socks off for them all day, got buried as it sunk to the ground, and little muffled meows of 'Help get me out of here!' could be faintly heard from the mountain of deflated vinyl. She was finally rescued when everyone eventually stopped rolling around the ground in hysterics. The final task of rolling the marquee up to expel the remaining air pockets was accomplished by half a dozen adults running and jumping on it, which was most comical to watch. Once everyone was packed up and *s2trash* had offered his thanks to the Beaulieu staff for all of their help towards making a brilliant day and booking the event for the following year, he joined *Miss Polkadot* and a few folks who were going to the nearest pub. This had been the best day out at Beaulieu so far and *s2trash* felt pleased that this annual end of year meet had now become established as a major **smart** event in the UK calendar.

Fudge and Massive

Leomobile undergoing tests for the Exhaust Off competition

Chippy wins Sound Off competition

s2Eagleye becomes the new Exhaust Off winner

2006

Hambach Trip

Sharing a remarkable resemblance to Dorothy and the Tin Man, *Miss Polkadot* and *s2trash* began their journey along the fabled yellow brick road to the birthplace of the little car that changed their lives. The chance to actually witness and photograph **smarts** in the making was a dream come true. After months of organising and preparation the time had come, but only just. With several weeks of mysterious electrical problems with *Miss P's* car leading up to the journey, and last minute problems with an oil sump, the trip looked in jeopardy, and many a finger nail got chewed with anxiety. Not for the first time, *Smartarse Design* pulled out all the stops and managed to fix the car at the eleventh hour. And so it was, on a misty Monday morning, (it really was, honest!), *Miss P* collected *s2trash* from Ashford International station and they made their way on the first leg of their journey to Hambach.

The **smart** factory, the most environmentally car manufacturing plant in Europe, sits nestled next to the quaint little country village of Hambach, in the region of Lorraine. For the past four years thesmartclub has organised a trip to the factory, and so the pair had some knowledge about what to expect from friends that had already been there. It didn't dampen their excitement though to get the chance to actually see it for themselves. There were a few, very restricted photographs of the plant, supplied by **smart** directly, that had made their way into a few publications that they had seen, but none taken by an independent photographer. Not since the initial factory opening had any individuals been allowed to capture the scenes of the manufacturing process, and so the intrepid duo of *Dot* and *Trash* felt highly privileged indeed, to be allowed visitation rites on such hallowed turf!

The Ferry

Down to the docks the dotty car drove, to the ferry, and wary of knocks;
Up on the ramp and into the boat, where a crew member said 'Where's its box?'
The cheeky young chappy, thought the car was so small;
That a box was required, for the length of the haul
'Don't worry my friend, that smart is robust;
But with you for this journey, my car I'll entrust'
With a glint in his eye, to his mate he did wink;
For he knew if he didn't, I'd kick up a stink!

© Miss Polkadot 2006

Dover

Historic French town of
Cassell

Super size pâtissierie

French mist

Travelling with Norfolk Line, *s2trash* and *Miss P* were very impressed with the first class feel the ferry fronted. It was obviously a new-ish vessel, but it was modern, clean and very stylish and produced a mean cappuccino served in white china on a white china tray! They had to pinch themselves to prove that they weren't in first class by mistake. Gliding across the millpond that the channel thankfully served up, made the endless prayers to Neptune during the week worthwhile after all. As they had arrived at the docks with several hours to spare before departure, they were allowed to take the crossing 2 hours earlier than they had originally booked. *S2trash*, in his infinite wisdom, and he has a great deal of this, decided that as there would be 2 hours extra in France, a brief stopover in Lille for a spot of lunch would be a hoot. *Note to editor....don't let the pair deviate from prior plans!*

Craving caffeine and tobacco fumes, *s2trash* spotted a small town called Cassel, perched on a hill in the distance and persuaded *Miss P* to stop and find a café. Turning right into the approach to the town they were immediately confronted by an ancient cobbled road, the only entry to the town square, where lay the target of urgent cravings. The exclamations of how quaint the cobbles looked soon turned to exclamations of horror as the full extent of driving over the huge stones took effect. The urge to reach the facilities of the nearest cloakroom now took top priority from the caffeine and cigarettes. Driving across the cobbles for half a mile up a 30% incline almost proved too much for the pair and the poor car! How all the screws remained in situ and their brains didn't turn to blancmange is a complete mystery.

The ride to the town centre, although akin to being inside a washing machine on full spin, was worth it. An enormous ancient square surrounded by beautiful historical buildings that appeared to have escaped the ravages of two world wars, played host to a spotty little car and two desperate humans in dire need of a rest. After downing a wonderful cappuccino served outdoors and with their nerve endings settled, it was time to be off. Feeling famished, *Miss P* made a bee-line to a Pâtisserie, where she bought two of the world's largest cakes. *S2trash* thought it a grand wheeze to photograph *Miss P* trying to bravely eat hers in a ladylike manner, which was almost impossible considering that this cake was the size of her head. As they walked back to the car it suddenly dawned on them that they had to leave the town way they came...across the cobbles! It may have only been ten minutes, but that journey will forever be etched in the memory as the most tortuous travelling ever done!

Now, on the map, Lille looks a nice medium sized town. In reality, and due to the fact that *Miss P's* sat nav guided them through the delights of town's suburbia and light industrial areas, it just seemed to go on, and on and on. Never, in 28 years of driving had *Miss P* driven over so many pedestrian crossings or stopped at so many traffic lights, as the ordeal through Lille! Every single road junction had a pedestrian crossing either side of it, some controlled with traffic signals and some without. It had both of them scratching their heads as to who had priority, pedestrians or cars, as the French drivers seemed to take no notice of those patient souls waiting to traverse the road. The grand idea of having lunch in Lille finally disappeared when they found themselves smack bang in the very centre of this bustling, cosmopolitan town with absolutely no chance of parking. It was not dissimilar to driving through London at rush hour on the busiest day of the year. With *Miss P* concentrating on her driving skills, *s2trash* was able to sit and watch the effect the car had on the people around. As they were stuck in lots of traffic jams through the town there was ample time for incredulous looks, baffled glances and humorous smiles from the folks busily going about their business. He was gradually beginning to wish he had brought a paper bag to hide under. Having had enough of this city-like traffic, they ditched the idea of stopping for lunch, re-routed the sat nav and headed out of Lille to the more tranquil villages en route to St Quentin, the first overnight destination.

Packing up

Aubérive cemetery

Lost in France

Cross country

After a well deserved night sleep, *s2trash* awoke with the dawn chorus and sped outside to capture *Miss P's* car shrouded in mist in the hotel car park. He could have so easily done with another of those paper bags when he was caught by another guest in a nearby room posing beside the car with the self timer set up! After a crispy croissant for her, and a whole basket full of bread for him, the pair set off for the long journey to Saarbrücken, the town just north of Hambach across the border in Germany that they had chosen to stay at. Hambach is such a small village that it doesn't support hotels and so the nearest viable place is Saarbrücken. It is only about 13 miles from Hambach, but being in Germany, it is a completely different place culturally.

Once the mist had broken and the car was re-fuelled, the sun broke through and blue skies appeared; perfect weather for driving. With all large towns dismissed from the chosen route where possible, the pair set off in the knowledge that today's 214 mile drive would, hopefully, be less stressful that the day before. What a difference a day makes, as that old tune goes. Gone were the inner cities and the plethora's of pedestrian crossings, today it was open countryside and quaint villages combined with glorious weather. Heading south from St. Quentin past Laon and down to Reims, the famous home of Champagne, they passed the most beautiful château or champagne houses, built by some of the most famous champagne makers in the world, such as Veuve Clicquot, Taittinger, Dom Pérignon, Krug and Mumm. Sadly, there was no time to stop and make time to experience the sweet bubbles burst on their tongues, the only thing about to burst was the bladder belonging to *s2trash*!

Having skirted around Reims they joined the D931/N3 road heading east. This road, also called 'Voie de la Liberté' or 'The Road of Liberty' follows the route taken by General George Patton's 3rd Army, from Cherbourg in Normandy across France to Metz and north to Bastogne in Belgium during the liberation of France in WW II. The French government have placed a stone marker or 'borne' at every one of the 1.446 kilometres of the roads length. When they first saw these markers they naively thought they were post boxes, until they realised that firstly there were just too many of them and then that there was no where to insert any letters – a case of live, learn and be humble. Driving through such beautiful countryside it was exceedingly difficult to imagine the horrors that occurred here. Feeling in such a pensive mood, they thought it appropriate to stop and visit one of the many WW I cemeteries lining their route. The Aubérive memorial cemetery lies about 15 miles outside of Reims and is situated along a beautiful country road lined with poplars. Immaculately manicured and cared for, this relatively small cemetery was the final resting place for thousands of both French and German soldiers. At first *Miss P* was hesitant about parking her car so near to such a hallowed place, at the risk of it looking too irreverent, but *s2trash* persuaded her that they were only paying their respects after all and not to worry, plus with his eye ever vigilant for a photo opportunity he was very persuasive. Despite being such a thought provoking place, the cemetery exuded a mesmerising calmness in the beautiful spring sunshine, a perfect interval before the rest of the journey to Saarbrücken.

With lunchtime rapidly approaching and with *s2trash* having a stomach like a bottomless pit, *Miss P* thought a swift stop over for some light lunch was in order. Now, both *P* and *Trash* love coffee, cappuccino in particular, but the French insist on serving up small, dark, thick espresso coffee without milk. Gradually, it became a standing joke that in her poor school-girl French and lots of arm gesturing, *Miss P* had to firmly insist in vast quantities of the white stuff to accompany the coffee, which was accompanied every time with much head shaking and eyebrow raising by the server. Luckily, this time they stopped at a small village called les Islettes, where a sweet young man served them up hot steaming milky coffee and fabulous hot panninis filled with jambon and Gruyère cheese, which they ate sitting in the sun beside a small canal – ah this was the life...

With time gradually slipping away, they had to get a move on if they intended reaching Saarbrücken before the end of the next week, tempting as it was to stay. With her back seat driver feeling like Winnie the Pooh after a huge pot of honey, *Miss P* and *s2trash* continued on road eastwards past Verdun and on towards and

Overwhelmed

Coffee break, French style

Smart parking Saarbrücken

Smart spotted in the rain

through the town of Metz, crossing the River Moselle. Here the pedestrian crossings reared their ugly heads again, but not with the frequency as they had done in Lille, and it wasn't long before they were speeding towards the German border. The pair were amazed at how run down and poor the majority of the small towns and villages were that they drove through. In a lot of instances many of the houses and cottages were close to dereliction, left over from the ravages of the war for more than 60 years with apparently no-one to renovate them and give them new life. They look very quaint, but alien to us; it is a site Brits are not used to in this country and it makes one realise how lucky we are.

With just one more stop for a cold drink outside a café in yet another one-horse-town, causing most of the inhabitants to stare in awe at the spottymobile, *Miss P* and *s2trash* were able to reflect that they had probably only spotted about 5 other **smarts** so far. Considering they were in **smart** territory they found it a bit odd not to have spotted more. It turns out that there are very few **smart** dealers in the north west sector of France, with only the larger showrooms appearing in larger towns and cities like Paris where the cars are too numerous to count; a scenario only too similar in this country.

Having finished their ice cold drinks and watching closely the approaching black storm clouds, they sharply legged it back to the car before the heavens opened. *Miss P* was rather pleased with the impending precipitation; she was vainly hoping that the rain may dislodge some of the millions of dead flies now gracing the front of her car in such a dense formation as to make the viewing of her number plate impossible without the aid of an infrared camera! No such luck, they were well and truly baked on. They would take more than just a quick wipe with a soapy sponge to remove, what was needed was some of that special *s2trash* elbow grease – ha! Chance would be a fine thing, *Trash* is allergic to that! Still, no point on scraping the bugs off now, there was still 40 miles to go of fly-saturated air before they reached Saarbrücken.

It was a pretty uneventful and at times a tedious journey through St. Avold, and on up to Forbach, a small built up town full of light industrial commerce and not particularly attractive.

At last, the border approached. One blink and the pair would have missed it completely. Gone are the days when one had to stop and produce passports and documentation, the checkpoint was closed and it seemed no-one gave two hoots about who went where. In a way it was rather disappointing not to be made to feel that you had done a momentous thing crossing from one country to another, still the locals must have thought it a great idea not to go through that each time they visited their neighbours. Although there was now no physical barrier, there was a distinct difference in the physical appearance of the place. No more derelict houses, unkempt appearances and very few old cars. This was uber-tidy Germany and boy did it show, even within a few yards of the border line it was very noticeable, and not at all unpleasant. With only 13 miles to go to the centre of Saarbrücken and the site of the hotel *Miss P* and *s2trash* had booked, relief set in, as by now tiredness was creeping in because *Miss P* is no spring chicken and driving foreign was beginning to take its toll. The hotel wasn't as easy to find as the directions had led them to believe, and déjà vu ruled as the spottymobile circled the town encountering virtually all the one-way systems it had to offer. To add insult to injury, when finally tracked down, the hotel didn't offer the myriad of parking spaces it had led the tired two to believe when it was booked. The six hotel allocated spaces were... surprisingly enough...allocated, and the spottymobile ended up parking on the high street pavement outside the hotel building. With **smarts** to be seen everywhere in this town, this was an acceptable thing to do, luckily, and Polkadot was neither clamped, towed, nor ticketed.

Fashion faux pas

French farmhouse circa 1784

Smartville

The smart factory

A very early start after a very long journey driving on the wrong side of the road the previous day, made it very difficult for *Miss P* to want to get up and get ready, but the thought of where she would be actually going today was like a cold refreshing shower and all thoughts of aching bones disappeared and genuine excitement reigned. Not so *s2trash*; three phone calls and a knock on his door was required to rouse that tired bod. After an amusing but delicious German breakfast of what seemed like a full wedding buffet (is it normal to have coleslaw for breakfast?), the pair set off for the 13 mile journey to Hambach. Back across the almost non-existent border and on French soil again, it didn't take long to reach the sleepy little village. With all its street furniture painted red and its exquisitely kept gardens, one could have been fooled into thinking that one was in toy town. Now just where was Monsieur Plod le Policeman? After driving right through the village, there on the left was the very site of **Smartville** – birthplace of Polkadot and thousands of other little **smarts** like her – the end of the rainbow!

After months of planning, they had at last arrived and were in awe at the size of the place. They were met at the main gate by Ulrike Bianchi, Head of Communications for the plant. A delightful lady with a great sense of humour and perfect command of English, which was a great help as both *Miss P* and *s2trash* could just about struggle to order milky coffee – pathetic really! The gate operator went from jaw drop to beaming smile when they arrived, as did the myriad of employees coming and going. What *Miss Polkadot* and *s2trash* were naively unaware of was the fact that over in France and indeed in Germany too, most **smart** cars remained the same as the day that they were made; customised cars were a rarity, and so Polkadot became a bit of a showstopper! With just the briefest introductions they followed Ulrike and drove around the outside of the plant to the entrance to the main assembly, the central cross of the building.

After they had parked, got out, and *s2trash* assembled his tripod, Ulrike could contain herself no longer, and came over to properly introduce herself to these two mad people from Grande Bretagne. Her face said it all. Beaming from ear to ear, it was impossible for her not to scrutinise the spottymobile from every angle. Although they had previously warned her about how spotty the car was, she just wasn't prepared to see it for real. She loved it and kept pointing out all of the mods that had been done to it; she certainly knew her stuff about **smarts**.

For four years Ulrike originally worked for Magna Système Chassis, the fabrication body shop for the tridion safety cell and one of the system partners within the factory, before joining **smart** France itself in July 2000. She had been Head of Communications for **Smartville** since that time and appeared to wear many hats; as she very competently arranged factory visits, organized internal and external events, and was the Press Officer for the plant too. Having worked for the **smart** project for ten years one can understand why she was so knowledgeable about **smart** production as she enthusiastically guided *Miss Polkadot* and *s2rash* around the factory with almost encyclopedic knowledge. Although **Smartville** accommodates approximately 12,000 visitors, on between 400-600 guided tours each year, Ulrike prefers to just take specialist tours, such as this photographic one by Spotty Badger Productions, leaving the twice daily public tours to her staff.

As mentioned before, it is so rare for cars to be seen with modifications that even the smallest alteration that *Miss P* had done to her car caused Ulrike to exclaim in astonishment; but in a nice appreciative way, not a sneery what-a-pair-of-loonies way – well that was until she took a glance at interior of the car! She instantly recognised the fact that, not only *Miss P* and *s2trash*, but all the other folks that modified their cars, did it out of sheer love and affection for this highly original, cute, amazing car. As they were chatting, they started to notice a few faces peering out of the office windows, and then, surprise surprise, it was obvious some folks just couldn't contain their curiosity any longer and came out to view the car that appeared to be living in a '60s timewarp!

Hallowed turf!

Smartville

Seeing double

Smart express

1 The start of the production line in 'The cross' area

2 Tridion pre-fitted with cockpit unit

3 Smart in suspense

4 Red guard protects Tridion during production

5 Petrol tanks waiting for installation

6 Engine module

7 Drive train

8 Suspension

9 Tridion married to the drive train...aghhh

10 Smart roller coaster ride

11 Gear stick/box added

12 Window seals fitted

13 Glass roof offered up to the car

14 Windscreen fitted

15 Pure roof

16 Rear glass tailgate awaiting fitting

17 Floor pans fitted

18 Heading towards the wheel fitting area

19 Wheel bolts fitted by machine

20 Seats at last!

21 Doors fitted

22 First test line

23 System partners payment signage

24 Waiting for rear panel

The Inner Sanctum

Sometime later… their hearts in their mouths with excitement, entry to the very birthing room commenced. There, before them, was all the paraphernalia laid bare in preparation for the creation of this prized little car. Comparatively speaking, it was rather like being in a hospital, subdued lighting and music, background conversations interspersed with guffaws of laughter and the tinkle of tools poised to bring the components closer to creating the little car with personality and charm. The factory floor just oozed peace and calmness; the workers genuinely looked like they enjoyed their work, not a sentence one would normally use to describe a car factory. It was indeed becoming understandable why this plant was the most environmentally friendly car factory in Europe, no smell, no noise; it was clean and so well thought out. The very clever interior design gave a human dimension to the scale of it all, so one didn't feel either claustrophobic or like a pea in St Paul's Cathedral, it felt just right, light and airy and a very comfortable environment in which to work.

Originally designed and constructed by Johann Tomforde, and opened in October 1997, the factory was conceived in such a way as to halve the construction time normally set by the industry standard for car production. By segregating the manufacturers and suppliers but keeping them on site situated in system modules set around the centre of the factory where the actually final production took place, Johan Tomforde was able to slash the 'normal' vehicle production time from 15 to 8 hours! Out of that eight hours only four hours would be completed by **smart** employees, the rest would be supplied by the system partners. Not only that, each system partner was just that, a partner, having a voice in development and production along the way. This was also financially beneficial for **smart** as each system partner didn't invoice for its time and components until each car rolled of the production line, meaning less financial outlay for **smart**, and more say so for the partners. It appears to be a very clever, productive and viable symbiotic relationship for all concerned – in other words – it works!

The first system partner in the chain is MAGNA COSMA EUROPE. Here the **smarts** distinct structure, the tridion safety cell, is produced by the initial pressing of the steel sections. These steel components are then welded together to form the actual chassis platform and tridion. This completed 'shell' is then passed next door to the module containing the next system partner EISENMANN SURTEMA. Here the tridion safety cell undergoes a unique powder coating process, in either silver or black, an innovative and highly environmentally friendly process causing no emissions from this state-of-the-art plant. It is from here that the **smart-to-be** begins its clever journey to the outside world.

The factory is designed in the shape of a cross, with each system partner feeding its contribution to the production of the car directly into the centre or main hub of the factory, by the clever use of overhead hanging conveyor belts. When they saw the tridions appear, suspended by the firm grip of two metal arms,

25 First test drive

26 Brake testing

27 Heading for the water test

28 Drying out after the water test

29 The Finish line

30 The finished article!

they could have been mistaken for thinking they were at a fairground and broad smiles began to develop across the face of *Miss Polkadot* and *s2trash* – oh how cute, they really looked like toy cars being assembled!

The powder coated tridion makes its way to the next partner SIEMANS-VDO where the dashboard, instruments, heating and air-con assembly, known as the cockpit module, is fitted by SIEMANS-VDO own personnel, the only point in the **smart** voyage where this occurs.

Continuing its fairground ride around the plant, the tridion now complete with its cockpit arrives inside the main hub of the cross-like layout of the plant. Here all the rest of its innards are installed by employees of **smart**; the electrical wiring, brake and cable systems, front suspension, brakes, fuel tank and rear end module. Supplied by a warehouse next door belonging to THYSSEN KRUPP AUTOMOTIVE, the rear end module consists of the all important hand-bag sized engine, transmission, rear suspension, brakes and finally wheels, which are added further on down the line. Once the rear end module has been completed the actual body is lowered onto the chassis ready to be bolted together. It is here that a unique feature comes into play in the plant. **Smartville** has only one robotic machine in the whole fabrication line and it is here that it makes its appearance. Its sole job is to fix the 15 bolts that hold the tridion to the chassis, a process that **smart** thought would be executed far better by machine to the exacting parameters it set, than risk any human error.

Now that the tridion and chassis are married together, it continues along its fairground ride to meet up with its front end module; the headlights, radiator, air-con condenser and then the windscreen and roof panel. Depending on the choice of the customer this can be either a solid, glass or electric sliding version. The back screen is also added here as is the Cabrio roof where applicable. The next items to be added are the four wheels, no spare don't forget, unless one counts the one round some owners middle! Again, the wheel style is a variable chosen by the customer, and supplied to the line fully fitted with inflated Continental tyres. Next in line are the seats which are supplied by FAURECIA, followed by the external plastic panels. These plastic panels; front, rear, doors and tailgate, are another of the **smarts** innovative designs, and without which would have demoted the **smart** to being just another boring vehicle amid the millions of others already carrying the same genes. Breaking free from the stereotypes is what makes **smart smart**.

All of the panels are precision moulded on site in four different substrate colours by another system partner DYNAMITE NOBEL. To date there are 7 choices of colour, plus any special editions. Back in 1998 there was a choice of vibrant patterned panels created by another system partner CUBIC; Numeric Blue, Aqua Orange, Aqua Green and Aqua Vanilla and the unusual Scratch Black, and were hence called the CUBIC colours. It was a highly complex and costly system of production involving the panels actually absorbing the patterns and not being printed on, which is what most folks seem to think. The patterns were floated on a body of liquid in an almost sterile, vacuum-like environment and then the panel was guided through the floating pattern. One sneeze and it would be curtains for the operative! It was and still is a highly secretive process that has not been reproduced by anyone else so far. Unfortunately, the amount of customer orders for these fantastic panels was as few as 5% of the total orders and therefore could not sustain the high cost of manufacture. Typically, now that these Cubic panels are no longer in production, they seem to be in great demand in the second hand market, and will of course in time become collector's items. What is ironic is that it was the whacky coloured panels that first drew everyone's attention to the car in the first place and now that those panels are no longer in production, only flat restricted colours, there is more of a market of home customisation and re-sprays instead.

Back on the line, once all the body panels are fitted, the doors, which were sent separately to the next system partner MAGNA UNIPORT to be united with the actual door modules, rejoin the line suspended beneath another overhead conveyor belt and are attached to the car to complete the body. Once the grills are attached and the car is checked over, the engine is started for the first time and driven round to the testing station. Here the rear quarter light windows are fitted

Miss Polkadot on the test track

Miss Polkadot tests her brakes and her courage on the gradient track

Head of Communications Ulrike Bianchi and Miss P

The famous smart Tower

prior to being put on a rolling road to check gears and brakes, and then is subjected to a car wash to test for leaks. Once cleaned and buffed each **smart** makes its way round for its final end of line sign off. After only 8 hours and with all the boxes ticked, a brand new **smart** will finally be born. From the end of the line it will drive a few meters to the awaiting transporter where it will be whisked away to its new and very excited owner.

Some interesting facts....

- Every car that passes through the factory has its own unique code number and can be traced within the production line at any time.
- Every car has been specifically ordered, they are not made just because they can be.
- It takes 8 hours to produce one **smart** from start to finish.
- On average 500 **smarts** are produced each day.
- The maximum number of **smarts** ever produced in one day was 582.
- Within the factory, any damaged parts are collected and recycled to make new parts.
- At any one time the production line can contain fortwos of any variety; pure, pulse, passion or cabrio, left hand drive, right hand drive, hard top and Brabus, in varying combinations and amounts.

The Great Outdoors

With the fantastic tour over, Ulrike took the pair for coffee up in the atrium. She then took them up to her office which has a fabulous view over the factory complex and the countryside beyond. Here *Miss Polkadot* presented her with a copy of the current Spotty Badger Smart Car Calendar, which she immediately opened and excitedly showed to her colleague. After a few moments chatting and smiling, Ulrike asked if it would be possible for her colleague to take a photo of *Miss P* and *s2trash* beside the car for the next edition of their monthly newsletter. It would been rude to say no, but the boot was definitely on the other foot as far as *s2trash* was concerned, as he is normally behind the lens, not in front of it. Funny really, ending up in a **smart** publication when what *Miss Polkadot* and *s2trash* were doing there would end up in a publication about **smart**! After fooling around outside having their picture taken, Ulrike guided the pair back into the factory complex and up into the stunning atrium where they were treated to lunch in the amazing factory restaurant. A restaurant the like of which one would not expect inside a car factory – French chic are two words that would describe the place very well indeed. They sat at a table looking down into the atrium space, at the bottom of which are parked a few cars pulled off the production line for minor hiccups or to randomly test cars for quality control. Sitting so high up the cars looked so small, like the little Kinder Surprise **smarts** found inside the chocolate eggs. Sadly, photography was out of bounds in this area as it would have made a great picture.

After being wined and dined, it was off outside for a look around the complex. Whilst looking out of Ulrike's office window earlier on, *s2trash* had spotted the test track and had asked if he could take a look. Ulrike smiled and said of course, so jumping into the car *Miss Polkadot* and *s2trash* followed Ulrike through the 'streets' of **Smartville** and drove across the complex to the site of the track. General handling, performance, wheels and brakes are all tested here, and *Miss Polkadot* was privileged to be given the chance to try out her head for heights on the gradient slopes that ranged from 10% to 40% gradient. It certainly gave her more faith in the car and her own driving ability after its sterling performance.

Glancing around the factory site, it is understandable as to why **Smartville** had received so many accolades for being so environmentally friendly. Even outside, the landscaping has been done to compliment the surrounding environment, native wild flowers have been sewn and grown, and indigenous species of small wild animals that had become extinct prior to the factory being built have re-colonised the land within the factory grounds itself. Now that is something to boast about and quite rightly **Smartville** was given an award in recognition of its endeavours. After being suitably impressed by the entire place, and *s2trash* pleased indeed with all the photos he was allowed to take, Ulrike took them both to the bar area in Communications building where they were treated to refreshments. What a fantastic tour! Ulrike went out of her way to be friendly and incredibly informative and both *Miss Polkadot* and *s2trash* thanked her profusely for her hospitality before saying their goodbyes. There was one thing they had to do before they left, and that was photograph the iconic **smart** tower that stood meters away from where they were. Of all the things that symbolise the **smart** brand, the **smart** tower is at the top of the list, and yet rules, regulations and silly red tape prohibit the construction of such a thing in the UK. Shame really. With numerous tower shots in the bag, the two very happy **smart** enthusiasts made their way back across the border, heads full of fantastic sights and experiences, and so pleased they had had the opportunity to visit this very special place.

The Return Journey

After a slap up meal and a good night's sleep, *Miss Polkadot* and *s2trash* packed up the following morning and made way for the journey back to blighty. With another rather large breakfast buffet under their belts they paid a visit to the **smart** centre in Saarbrücken, who are lucky enough to have a **smart** tower in their forecourt. The manager kindly let *s2trash* take photos inside and out, and although they had made arrangements before the trip, *Miss Polkadot's* car couldn't be put in the tower for a picture to be taken as they had had a large delivery of cars and there was no room for manoeuvre. Feeling slightly disappointed, *s2trash* cheered her up by taking a photo of her car in front of the tower instead. After being given cups of coffee and a free keyring, the spotty pair finally hit the road, and this time it was a motorway; well when they eventually managed to get on it that was.

After driving on the busy route from Saarbrücken to Metz, *Miss Polkadot* decided to take a detour on to some quieter roads after she had nearly collided with a large sheet of corrugated iron that had fallen off a lorry. This wasn't the sort of start to the day she really had in mind considering it was her birthday. It seemed a less stressful option to get onto a smaller road and give her the opportunity to stop for a break and for *s2trash* to unfold his cooped up limbs. Having booked rooms at a motor inn just outside Sedan, they headed off cross country guided by the sat nav and stopped in a small village not long after turning onto the N43. With still a fair way to go, they didn't linger over their coffee. It wasn't long before the road started meandering through proper countryside again and they could relax.

As *Miss P* had programmed the sat nav to get to Sedan via the shortest distance, she began to notice that they were driving on more rural roads that she had anticipated; in fact they felt like they were almost driving through the middle of private farms. As they passed through a village with no more than ten houses that were perched on a hill in the middle of nowhere, the road suddenly took on the character of a scrambling track. Never mind, the sat nav knew exactly where it was going. With memories of the 40% gradient test slope at **Smartville** still fresh in her mind, *Miss Polkadot* reached the end of the village road and had to turn sharp left and along yet another track masquerading as a road, that disappeared off into some woods. Never mind, the sat nav knew exactly where it was going. Not this time it didn't, it had blatantly lied its head off! This would be no gentle country drive but a full on off-road experience – the sort of thing Jeremy Clarkson would engineer with Richard Hammond for a few laughs. The road gently transformed into a flat gravel track, then a muddy lane and then into a muddy track with two ruts two feet deep. They knew things didn't look good when they were stared at by two lumberjacks who stood and shook their heads and who must have surely been muttering 'they can't be going up there, can they?' As the men made no attempt to stop the car from carrying on, *Miss P* carried on, as she certainly could not turn round or reverse; she had gone too far. The tiny track became a bit of a concern. The ruts were now so deep the floor pan of the car was rubbing along the ground. At this point in the procedure, *Miss P* adopted the off-road driving style of 'thumbs out' as the wheel was getting whipped out of her hands as she tried to negotiate the heavily rutted track without getting grounded. She dared not stop for fear of setting the car on the mound between the ruts, like a kid swinging its legs on an oversized chair, and wondered if she had enough stamina to endure the test for the full two and a half miles that was the length of this hellish, so called road. That sat nav certainly had a lot to answer for!

To be honest, neither of them thought they were going to make it to civilization and were concerned that the car would get damaged or stuck and they would be stranded in the scary woods all alone at night in the dark and the bears would come and get them! Well, that only happens in the movies doesn't it? The thought of being stranded alone in the woods with an *s2trash* was an even more frightening thought and one that kept *Miss Polkadot's* foot flat to the accelerator! Finally, the

Smart dealer at Saarbrücken

Saarbrücken smart tower

Relief at the end of Polkadot's off-road experience

Castle Fort Sedan

heavy woods diminished to reveal a beautiful green valley and *Miss P* stopped the car to catch her breath and pray that her pride and joy was still in one piece. This was certainly turning into a very memorable birthday.

A mere few miles away was the Citadel town of Montmedy, where they made a beeline straight for a café serving strong coffee; and ended up with a dog trying to chew the legs off *Miss P's* trousers! The little Shihtsu then took a liking to *s2trash* and tried to get over familiar with his suede shoes. There is obviously no peace for the wicked!

Moving swiftly on from the devil dog café, they drove straight on to Sedan. This is a town like no other. Although staying just outside Sedan, they just had to make time whilst it was still light to visit this small town, home to Europe's largest fortified castle. It has an area of 35,000 square meters, on seven levels, three of them are above ground and four of them underground, and boasts that it can shelter up to 4000 men. It is the only remaining part of the once enormous fortifications in and around the town. Construction started in 1424 and the castle's defences were constantly improved over the ages. Nowadays, part of the castle is a museum, and another a very upmarket hotel. Using *Miss Polkadot's* birthday as an excuse, they drove up into the fort and parked in the rather large courtyard, and stopped in the swanky hotel for a much needed coffee. As they had patronised the hotel *s2trash* felt quite within his rights to take some teriffic photographs of the car within this overwhelming enclosed space. *Miss Polkadot's* car certainly received a great deal of attention from the hotel patrons, in fact an American gentleman was so taken back by its endearing looks and green credentials that he definitely wanted to buy one for his wife, who was already a fan of **smart** cars. If only **smart** GmbH knew just how much *Miss Polkadot* and *s2trash* promoted their products, they would be giving them jobs as top sales staff! They were so impressed with the hotel, a five star establishment it appeared, that they went back there that evening for a birthday bar meal, as they certainly couldn't afford the top dollar à la carte menu. The hotel has been sympathetically restored and everywhere in the hotel revealed the original stone walls of the fort and in the bar area, which had originally been the prison within the fort, the shackle rings in the walls still remained. (*Miss P* was sorely tempted to enquire whether they would be strong enough to restrain a mad British photographer, but had a change of heart when she realised the UK **smart** scene wouldn't be the same without one).

With ultra modern décor that complimented the ancient construction, this certainly was an amazing place, normally reserved for the rich and famous, neither of which categories could be applied to either *Miss P* or *s2trash* for sure!

After a good night's sleep, it was an early start the following morning for the drive back to Dunkerque. After a brief spell of motorway driving from Sedan to Charleville Mezieres, the A32 turned into the N43/E44 road, a pleasant route through more of the gorgeous countryside. Knowing they had a ferry to catch at 8pm local time, they decided not to stop too often, bladders permitting, and cover as many miles as possible. The journey took them through beautiful towns and villages via incredibly straight Roman roads, the end of which could be seen ahead for miles. After passing through Cambrai they headed north towards the dreaded Lille.

This time, however, they skirted round the outside, finding a delectable little car park to stop for a glug of water and to stretch their legs. Not wanting to waste much time, they set off promptly joining the D933, the equivalent of a British 'B' road, which conveniently took them back to Cassel – that unforgetable town with the cobbled streets! As they had made good time over the main part of the journey they decided to brave the hideous drive through the town to have a look round at the architecture and get something to eat and drink. Talk about gluttons for punishment!. They had to agree it was worth the ordeal; the town is beautiful, and *s2trash*, who has a thing about taking photographs of old doors, found several amazing examples for his collection. *Miss Polkadot* found a little café named after her called Jules Café, thus giving her that five minutes of fame everyone apparently deserves. The weather had turned much colder and the wind was biting, causing *s2trash* to suffer a bad hair day. Stopping at a café for chocolate crêpes and coffee, *s2trash* set the camera up on the timer and took a photo of the two of them. For some bizarre reason *s2trash* appears to be sporting the startled look – he blames the wind for re-arranging his hair!

With Cassel only about 17 miles from Dunkerque, it didn't take them long to reach the ferry terminal without any incidents or detours through country tracks. It had been a good but tiring days journey, and after waiting for over an hour for the ferry to arrive, the comfortable seats and wonderful coffee served on board the cosily warm vessel, was a welcome luxury to the tired pair. With another two hour drive ahead once on home soil, both of them decided to try and get forty winks. They both agreed that it had been a fantastic trip, and were so lucky to have been to **Smartville**. The scenery, the towns, the mad detours and off-roading, the people, the food, – it all added to life's rich tapestry and was an experience neither of them will ever forget.

Lindisfarne 2006

With this book and the planning of next years calendar creeping up, the need for more photographs of cars in great locations became top priority, and so a mini trip to the more northern reaches of the UK was planned. Lindisfarne Priory on Holy Island, just south of Berwick-upon-Tweed, was decided on as the main location for a shoot as it gave folks in the Borders and the southern part of Scotland the chance of coming along. Just as soon as *s2trash* made some tentative posts on the website forums there were people replying that they were very interested in coming, including *Littlerou* and *ste862* from Scotland and *Drageron* from Southampton.

Miss P and *s2trash* had arranged to meet up with a few **smart** owners in the car park of Ikea in the Metro Centre in Newcastle, so that they could all drive together up to Lindisfarne. The only problem with this was the time they had to meet up...6.30am! This hideously early start was all due to the tide times across the causeway that joined Lindisfarne to the mainland. There was a tide window of 6 hours from 7am to 2pm in which cars could cross, so plenty of time had to be built in to the plans to allow for meeting and chatting and the second meeting point an hours drive north from Newcastle. There were several owners already poised in the car park when *Miss P* and *s2trash* arrived, including *Puddlejumper,* and a very nice chap with the unusual user name of *Mike'n'Helen*, who had a rather tasty, custom sprayed fortwo in an amazing shade of claret. *Maccymoo* and his lovely girlfriend were there along with *smartmp,* and *alienbob* who turned up just as everyone was close to leaving.

Heading out of Newcastle it was off to The Blue Bell Hotel at Belford for the next meet up point, about an hours drive away. The driving was good as the roads were quiet with lots of sensible people still tucked up in bed. The section of A1 from Newcastle to Berwick is notorious for the amount of accidents that occur along it. On many occasions sharp intakes of breath were heard when signs reporting the amount of road fatalities were spotted on route. The first sign read 35 fatalities, but increased to 3 figures further along! What on earth were drivers doing up here – needless to say the convoy drove very, very carefully!

At 8.30 am the convoy finally rolled into the car park of The Blue Bell Hotel to find *Drageron's* car parked outside, where he had spent the previous night in the lap of luxury in the hotel.

Even at what was an ungodly hour the group of bleary eyed drivers were greeted by a member of the hotel staff who, when asked if it was possible for them to rustle up some coffee, said 'Aye it was' and beckoned us in. Smartly dressed in tweed and brogues, did anyone who saw him think he looked like a game warden? As everyone made a beeline for the lovely warm hotel bar, *Drageron* suddenly filled the doorway with his manly frame and huge grin. Good lord! He certainly knows how to deliver a bear hug! He could crush your ribs with one of those vice-like grips! Several more folks arrived but *s2trash* in his own inimitable way, couldn't work out to whom he had and hadn't said hello to! *Miss Polkadot* in her normal professional way greeted every one with 'Hi, I am *Jules/Miss Polkadot*, and that festering thing in the corner with a cigarette hanging out his mouth is *s2trash*!'

While enjoying his fifth cup of coffee, *s2trash* got a text from *Littlerou* saying that her group of **smarts** were waiting in another pub car park at the road junction for Lindisfarne, having run a little late on their way down from Scotland. Not wanting to be rude *s2trash* phoned her to say that everyone would soon be joining her. !*??*##* ??*!"*??! !*?* came the reply! Och aye tha noo! That girl has one strong accent! To this day *s2trash* has no idea what she said, and maybe that was for the best.

With the battle-ready troops in their cars the convoy headed south. South? Without anyone noticing the driver of the spottymobile had misheard the satnav instructions and had gone the wrong way! Oops! Finally back on track, and the mistake unnoticed, they found the Scottish mob waiting for them. Greeting the

Lined up on the causeway

Time for contemplation

The Wild Ones

Scottish contingent was short and sweet as the time was pressing on and there were the tidal restrictions to consider. The first part of road that led to the island was like any normal country road, a winding lane dressed with high hedges. This lane however had a sting in its tail! It was bisected by the mother of all railway crossings that left the occupants of every car recounting their early breakfast!

The first sighting of Lindisfarne and The Causeway was breathtaking as the convoy broke free of the claustrophobic lane. Acres and acres of sand flats stretched before the little cars, and underneath a horizon that seemed to stretch to eternity sat Holy Island and the Lindisfarne Priory. As the cars snaked their way along The Causeway, *Miss Polkadot* stopped the tube so a picture or two could be taken, as the light was in s2*trash's* favour, with nice soft tones. Once the cars got going again, a hello yellow **smart** parked up on the sand was spotted patiently waiting for everyone and joined the group on the last hop to the island.

As previously mentioned this meet was planned with the intention of getting some great pictures for book and the calendar. With hindsight, a little more investigation of the venue would have revealed the limitations of the place. The Priory was a car free zone, as was the village itself – strictly residents only. The rocky outcrop that supported the Priory was so far away from the car park that it made it impossible to use it as a backdrop. As car movement was so restricted the car park itself became an outside studio. With some nice photos in the bag, everyone took a stroll through the village and up to the Priory, accompanied by *s2trash* lamenting the inaccessibility of the place. The next hour was spent playing mountain goats high up on the massive rock formation upon which the monks built their famous home. *Littlerou* decided to play what one presumes is a Scottish traditional game of 'Chucking the Snails' – related to 'Tossing the Caber' but modified for vertically challenged folks! A few owners decided to shell out for the hefty entrance fee and visit the Priory itself, but in common with those amongst the group from north of the border, most kept their wallets firmly shut and chatting amongst themselves proved a better and more entertaining option.

All too soon it was time to start thinking of getting back to The Blue Bell for lunch and getting off the island before the tide came back, but not before a fantastic cup of tea for 60p was had first. With everyone accounted for, the convoy headed back along The Causeway. The scenery here was just fantastic so *s2trash* pulled everyone over for one last photo session. Taking several cars onto the sand caused mayhem with other motorists trying to pass, but it was for the sake of art 'luvvy', and the photos taken here turned out to be some of the best ones of the day.

Having been pre-warned by the hotel that they had a wedding on that day, and that there might be a lack of parking space, the nice hotel manager in the tweed ensemble, explained that a side alley could be used for extra parking as the cars were so small. It was a fantastic idea at the time and six cars managed to squeeze nose to tail in the space. Once parked up there was a mad scramble to the bar, ordering food, drinks and taking over all of the tables, even if it did mean evicting the odd granny in the process! After a few giggles and a nice chance to chat, it was time for everyone to start making their way home. A start is as far as a lot of cars made. Remember those six **smarts** parked in the alleyway beside the hotel? The last car in the queue, a roadster, who shall remain nameless to cover his embarrassment, had accidentally locked his keys in boot! Sorry dear reader, you are thinking that's unfair not to name and shame aren't you...Ok then, it was *Maccymoo*, you will see a photo of him looking embarrassed anyway, so you can now just put a name to the face!

On several occasions *s2trash* has had course to help a few people in distress when they have locked their keys in a fortwo, but a roadster was new territory and try as he did, had to eventually admit defeat. Some very frantic phone calls where made to Smarts R us, Smartarse Design and *T1NY W,* but they were all answered with 'Its impossible without taking the rear apart', 'Its bloody hard without any tools' or 'We have never done it!'. Aghhh, but it is blocking in five other cars! Oh heck!

Eventually a desperate call was made to the AA, the national breakdown and recovery organisation. *S2trash* didn't hold out a great deal of hope that the AA would succeed without smashing a window. The highly embarrassed owner phoned a friend to see if he would do a two hour drive with a spare key if needed. The ensuing answer didn't appear to be polite! Anyway, with time to kill while waiting for the arrival of the AA man, commiserations abounded for those trapped and waiting to go

Mike and Puddlejumper

How many more can we squeeze in?

The Automobile Association comes to the rescue

Is the tide coming in?

home, whilst some made good use of the bar, and in his defence *maccymoo* took it in good spirit despite dreading the incident appearing in any forthcoming publications! (Hehehe…)

After about an hour or so the AA turned up to find some very stuck and restless **smart** owners. The engineer was a little bit fazed to find that he had an audience who were all very keen to see just how he was going to break in to this vehicle. Now, for security reasons it would be irresponsible to publish just how the AA engineer managed to get into the car, but if you have a roadster and lock your keys in it, the details of gaining entry are now on the AA's computer system, should you ever require it. The engineer was a very amenable chap and with a lot of persistence and deftness of hand finally opened the car after forty five long, frustrating minutes and with absolutely no damage done either! He did feel a little awkward when he received three cheers from the very pleased onlookers in praise of a job well done, and at one that was thought to be almost impossible at that!

Finally, able to make a move homeward, the Scots headed north and the rest of the southerners took a nice drive in what was left of the spring sunshine, along the beautiful scenic coastal road past Bamburgh Castle and down to Newcastle, where the group eventually went their separate ways home.

Bexhill Custom and Classic Car Show 2006

Firstly, a brief history of the involvement Bexhill had with motoring. In May 1902, the 8th Earl De La Warr colluded with the Automobile Club of Great Britain and Ireland, to organise the very first automobile racing on British soil. Such an auspicious event caused thousands of interested people to flock to Bexhill to witness a unique spectacle. Straight sprint races were run from east to west against the clock but cars also raced side by side in the opposite direction, similar to the start of Grand Prix races today. Distinguished names appeared on the entry list including Lord Northcliffe in his Mercedes, the founder of the Daily Mail Newspaper and Monsieur Leon Serpollet piloting his steam driven "Easter Egg" with a top speed of 54mph! With more than 200 entries competing in that inaugural meeting, Bexhill saw a massive influx of curious voyeurs who had come to witness the spectacle of motor cars racing at speeds in excess of 50mph for the first time on British soil, when the speed limit of the day was an astonishing 12mph. The huge success of the meeting encouraged Earl De La Warr to make Bexhill the motoring centre for British racing drivers of the day. By 1906 plans were drawn up for a brand new racing circuit almost reaching Beachy Head, along with garages, restaurants and hotel accommodation. The circuit unfortunately never saw the light of day and the motoring set moved to the new Brooklands circuit in 1907. A few attempts were made to resurrect the races and the last competition was held in 1925 after which the Royal Automobile Club withdrew permits on public highways.

In 1990, four local motoring enthusiasts decided to celebrate this little known piece of motoring history and started "The Bexhill 100" on the sea front, along the original road where motor racing was introduced all those years ago. In May 1995, Bexhill-on-Sea was at last officially recognised as the 'Birthplace of British Motor Racing', and road signs to this effect were erected at the entrances to Bexhill, along with obelisks that are appropriately placed along the sea front to indicate the start and finish lines of the infamous races run in 1902. Bexhill's other claim to fame is that it was also one of the first places **smarts** where imported privately in this country. The Bexhill 100 Car Show itself used to be much larger event, attracting thousands of spectators, but lack of funds and rising costs have meant that it is now held at the Polgrove Sports Ground and not the entire sea front.

Although not strictly classed as Classic cars, the **smarts** were invited when *s2trash* contacted the organisers to enquire if they would be interested in a group of them attending; particularly having a connection with Bexhill regarding it being one of the first places the cars were to be seen on our shores. A tentative post was made on the **smart** website forums to see if there were any folks who might be interested and within a few days, there were enough cars to go ahead and make plans. This event proved a joyous occasion for *s2trash*, as he would be allowed to transport his beloved moth-balled **smart** to the show, with the help of Paul and Kate from Wellsmart. *Miss Polkadot* arrived at Badger Towers mid-afternoon the day before, and despite there being a hose pipe ban in East Sussex, set about preparing her car for the next days show. Whilst busying herself with the cleaning routine, *Miss P* had a discreet chuckle to herself when she spied the 'trash can' being wheeled out of the garage into the sunlight and polished for apparently the 4th time that week! With both cars now in mint condition all they now had to do was proceed with a spot of self valeting and rendezvous at *s2trash's* local hostelry in Battle with some other **smart** owners who had come down early for the show. Whilst ordering drinks at the bar, a rare occurrence, *s2trash* managed, without the help of adult supervision to get the order partly incorrect, i.e. red wine instead of white and brown beer instead of lager! He did however manage to spot *Brabusmatt* lurking in the shadows and dragged him outside to meet the others. *Lil.smartie* and Paul were there with their black Labrador puppy.

Knowing that *Bubski*, *Vicky*, *Binxyboo* and her boyfriend Martin were all staying overnight in a B&B in Bexhill, *s2trash* tried giving them a call to find out where they were, because as yet they hadn't appeared at the pub. After a few attempts, *Bubski* finally answered his mobile.

"Oh Wow! I've got a lava lamp and a wizard in my room…this place is far out man!"

It became immediately apparent that all four friends would not be joining those already at the pub, preferring to admire the décor in their accommodation!

Nosmallo, the fastest Numeric in the south was next to arrive at the pub. A newbie to the world of **smarts**, she fits right in with her wacky sense of humour. Everyone ordered food, which was eaten whilst being serenaded by the sounds of the Battle Proms concert. The entertainment continued with a low flying WWII Spitfire being put through its paces to the sound of The Battle of Britain score What a spectacular sight and sound! Long before the evening got too late, everyone said their goodnights knowing they all had an early start the next day.

Bank Holiday Monday – 7am

Being kicked out off bed to the strains of the alarm was bad enough, but then stumbling over to his window to be confronted by rain was most disheartening. All that hard graft car cleaning the previous day had been in vain. Car cleaning that even *NeilOs*, a **smart** owner who could clean for England, would have been proud of. Without the ability to alter the weather *s2trash* focused his thoughts on making tea, only to mix up the entire family's cups so that everyone had the wrong combination of requirements. It must be a man thing, selective thought processes working in the binary system i.e. only one thing at a time.

Feeling positive that the rain would desist before long, both *s2trash* and *Miss Polkadot* were ready and raring to go by 8am when Paul and Kate arrived. They had offered to apply their trade plates to *s2trash's* car in order for it to be legally taken to the show. Kate drove the 'trash can', filling the criteria of only being the third person ever allowed to drive it! Trying to avoid muddy lanes, *s2trash* lead the mini convoy on the cleanest route to Bexhill. As the now, unavoidably soiled **smarts** arrived on the sea front, there were already some others that had arrived earlier and parked up with owners in the sea front café having breakfast. Still fretting that his car appeared less than pristine, *s2trash's* demeanour brightened somewhat once he spotted *T1NY W* roll up looking like he had taken his car 'off road' to get there. It was no exaggeration to say that he could have grown spuds on his rear wheel arches! Well ok then, it was a bit….but it sure was filthy!

With teas, coffees and food finally consumed, all the cars lined up in preparation for entering the show ground on mass. The multi-coloured convoy was directed to a far corner of the field. *S2trash* began to wonder if the organisers thought that they may have had a bunch of hoodlums on their hands…as if! At least all the cars were together in one area. *Ykciv123* had cleverly thought to bring with her a bucket and a magic gravity-feed hose with a brush on the end, which she kindly lent *T1NY W* to clean his car. *S2trash* had also amazingly thought ahead, and went off in search of water with which to fill both his and *T1NY W's* bucket. Twenty minutes later carrying a bucket dry as a bone, he returned with a show marshal who was sure that there was a tap hidden in the hedge near to where the **smarts** were parked. On closer inspection the pipe work was there but the tap was non existent – the council having forgotten to install it for the event! After a few moments of head scratching, *T1NY W* and *s2trash* came up the cunning plan of filling their buckets in the men's showers in the sports pavilion! Just as they finished washing the cars, the rain stopped and the sun came out. Talk about good timing! *Miss Polkadot*, who owns a genuine five foot **smart** flag, commandeered a new **smart** owner to hammer a stake into the ground, so that she could erect the flag on a fifteen foot carbon carp pole in the middle of the parked **smarts**. It certainly added a little bit of prestige to the colourful group of cars.

Finally, after much buffing the cars were squeaky clean and glinted in the now brightening sun. Just as a few folks got out their fold up chairs and picnic sets, another show marshal wandered over to question why the group was so far from the rest of the show. Explaining that they had only been following orders, they agreed to decamp, and at the risk of getting the cars dirty again, moved closer to the rest of the show. Poor old *Polkadot* was spotted struggling to relocate her **smart** flag and pole in the increasing wind, until brave *Sir s2trash* gallantly intervened and erected it on her behalf, just in case she got carried away in the breeze.

Later on in the afternoon, in between dodging the erratic showers and having to re-chamois off the cars, all the **smart** owners had the privilege of being introduced to the Mayor and Mayoress of Bexhill. As it had been *s2trash* that had organised their appearance at this event, the Mayor was interested to know if it

Looks of admiration

Mayor of Bexhill and his wife

T1NY W entertaining the crowds

would be possible for him to arrange a much larger **smart** car event in Bexhill in the near future. It was apparent that the Mayor was rather taken with not just the cars but the group of owners too, surprised maybe, that they were not Burberry-wearing, tattooed teenagers, muttering monosyllabic expletives whist signalling with gesticulating digits! Being an obvious car enthusiast, the Mayor was aware that Bexhill had seen some of the first **smarts** way back when they were first produced and seemed very keen to see as many as possible gracing his seafront. Not one to miss an opportunity of promoting **smarts** whilst having a good time into the bargain, *s2trash's* brain began to splutter into action and he spent several hours trying to formulate a plan.

Organising as he does, the Bexhill Beach party event, *s2trash* had an idea to maybe combine the meet on the seafront with that one and holding it over the August Bank Holiday weekend. This could be a great combination as it would be the 5th Beach Party meeting at Bexhill in 2007, but with the beach party in a slightly more prestigious location, an appearance at the Bexhill car show and the camping still at Cobb's Farm.

Back at the car show, the weather turned in their favour with blue skies, fluffy clouds and sunshine, causing some to get mild sunburn. Visitors to the car show made a bee-line to see the **smarts**, encouraged by the numerous announcements made over the PA system by the show marshals, "go look at the **smarts**, every one is different and non standard!"

During the afternoon, Paul Woolley brought out a bag of tools and set about sorting out a sickly roadster that was cutting out due to a problem with a re-map. He also replaced the dashboard LED's in *Polkadot's* car before plugging in his diagnostics machine and doing some tests on the 'trash can'. Despite standing there watching in trepidation, *s2trash's* worries were unfounded as all was fine with the wee beast after its year in storage.

Despite the fickle weather some amazing classic and customed cars of all shapes sizes and ages had turned up, but the main topic of conversation at the show was the **smart** invasion of 12 cars, the biggest single group of the same make appearing that year. They certainly had made an impact.

In the middle of the afternoon, an organiser strolled over and asked if there was a **smart** volunteer who would help judge 'The Best in Show' as they had a three-way tie. *Bubski* was unanimously volunteered and armed with a '99' ice cream he had just bought with his pocket money, shuffled off muttering "Why me, man?" Upon his return he wouldn't say who had won, despite being threatened with short back and sides if he didn't tell! When the announcement was finally made, the winner was a very nice vintage Aston Martin. When questioned as to why he voted for it *Bubski* replied "I really liked the wheels, dude"... a good enough reason one supposes.

An announcement of apology was then made by the car show officials concerning the fact that the belly dancers that had been booked for the afternoon entertainment couldn't make it. What a shame some said, others just looked agog! Two members of the Bexhill 100 Club offered to demonstrate a Salsa routine, to fill in for the belly dancers, and an official pleaded for more people to join them, homing in the **smart** owners lounging around chilling out and looking cool. Suddenly, everyone switched on their invisibility cloaks and sank down as far as they could into their seats – everyone except *T1NY W* ...

Across the PA system, for all to hear, one of the marshals had jokingly asked if there was a dancing **smart** among the group willing to join in. He had obviously not seen *T1NY W*'s car in action with his newly installed hydraulics. Suddenly, the invisibility cloaks were thrown off and everyone's fingers pointed at *T1NY W* shouting "Yes, we really do have a dancing **smart**!" Blushing ever so slightly behind his cool dude shades, *T1NY W* drove his car over to the main arena. Positioning the car beside the two dancers, *T1NY W* performed his magic by remote control, making the car bump and grind to the sounds of Ricky Martin, and to rapturous applause of the growing audience. It was definitely one of those 'you had to have been there' moments, and one that will never be forgotten!

Like all good things the day came to an end, and the little **smarts** were one of the last groups of cars to leave the showground, waving and tooting to those left behind. Each car was stopped at the exit gates upon leaving and presented with a complimentary commemorative plaque, which was a lovely gesture and touching momento of a great day out.

Newark 2006

With new folks now running the old Funkysmart website, now called Smartmaniacs, a decision was made to re-locate the annual **smart** camping pilgrimage from Billing Aquadrome in Northampton to Newark Showground in Lincolnshire, and everyone was really looking forward to it. In the months leading up to the event, *Vladaria* from Smartmaniacs had worked up to fourteen hours a day on preparing and organising what was hoped to be, the best show in the UK.

Thursday

For the spotty duo the road was long...as the song lyrics tell us. *Miss P* had to collect *s2trash* from Orpington Station, as he had made his way laden with baggage up from Battle by train. As they were trading they had to get to the venue on the Thursday a day earlier that those just camping. A three and a half hour drive, under normal driving conditions, lay ahead from Orpington to Newark after shoehorning both *s2trash* and his assorted rubbish into the car. As they were travelling up alone this year, it meant they were unable to offload any of the gear into anyone else's car. This was one of those times when the **smart** upheld its reputation of imitating a Tardis. In the front with the 6' 4" *s2trash* was one camera flight case, two sleeping bags, one smartware bag, one rear boot cover and the poles to keep the Spotty Badger sign erect and vertical. Within an hour the sardine like conditions had caused lack of circulation in all but the passenger's vocal department, and with *s2trash* moaning about cramp, a service station stop was required. This simple task in itself needed *Polkadot* to open the passenger door and remove most of the packed items before *s2trash* could even get out and stretch. After a quick trip to the loo and a session of yoga, *s2trash* got back in the car and *Miss P* re-packed all the chattels around him.

The journey turned out to be very, very slow. The traffic was horrendous due to three separate accidents on route and it was one of the hottest days of the year. True to form *s2trash* moaned non stop and *Miss P* was relieved when her passenger demanded another stopover. The next stop was more of a 'oh! There's a pub, that will do' moment. What a pub! A hypochondriac landlord, and décor that your granny would be proud of. While he served the well deserved cold drinks, his full medical history came pouring out and a tale about how his head chef was in hospital. That last bit of information finally convinced the peckish pair not to sample the menu there that day! As it was a no smoking pub they headed outside, not only to avoid looking at the interior design but to de-stress *Miss P* and let *s2trash* have a smoke. Whilst *s2trash* daydreamed, *Miss P* popped into the pub to use the facilities provided for ladies convenience, not before being pre-warned that they too were in a 'granny time-warp' as the men's sported duck egg blue paintwork and charming net curtains! Now all alone, *s2trash* made the mistake of catching the landlord's eye and enquiring about an unusual tree in the grounds. 'I say my good man, what is that fine tree over there?' The landlord looked *s2trash* square in the eye and said 'Ah! It is a walnut tree that is over two hundred years old' and from that moment on there was no stopping the man. Mesmerised by the salmon pink room, with frills on just about everything bar the loo paper, *Miss Polkadot* was gone for at least ten minutes while *s2trash* suffered the landlord's non stop chatter about the tree, his grounds and the **smart**. Finally *Miss Polkadot* came back, and *s2trash* was able to side step and let her take the full barrage of the history of the tree, the village, land he wanted to buy etc, all over again! *S2trash* had skilfully re-packed himself into the car by the time she broke free, in an attempt to escape. In a cloud of dust they left the pub and got back onto the A1, with *s2trash* managing to go a fair way this time before cramp started to set in and he wanted to get out yet again.

Now, the next stop was a real surprise, they came across an original American diner, a proper metal bullet caravan one. The car caused its normal amount of

There was only just enough room left for me!

Smartimes stand

S-mann's new publicity stunt

interest as *Miss Polkadot* parked it right outside the entrance. *S2trash* was fascinated with the diner and the diners where fascinated with the car! With tummies full to the brim with burgers, fries, hotdogs and shakes and all feelings returned to *s2trash's* limbs it was back on road for last part of the journey. It turned out the their destination was only about half an hours drive away, much to *s2trash's* relief and it wasn't long before they were looking for the entrance gate into Newark Show Ground. Although completely worn out by their long, hot, tiring journey, which had ended up taking over eight hours from start to finish, they decided to erect the tent immediately, because they knew if they stopped to relax before that, they just wouldn't have had enough energy and would have ended up sleeping in the car. Although it was very late afternoon, the temperature was still in the eighties and so everything was a real effort. Once completed, they went and chatted with some other folks who had turned up, rustled up some campsite food and agreed on an early night.

Friday

Friday morning dawned rather hot, late and tetchy for *s2trash*. Feeling like he had the body of an eighty year old from his cramped journey up the day before, and discovering that the air had seeped out of his inflatable bed during the night made *s2trash* a bit of a cross patch and gave him reason to moan about everything he could. And folk think women are temperamental! The first plan of the day was to look around the site for locations for photos, so in the car they jumped, only to get 20 feet before *Vladaria* came running and waving her arms at them. 'Stop! I've got something for *s2trash* to try on; a red latex nurse's uniform for him to wear during the charity car wash!' *Miss Polkadot* did her Roger Moore impression and just raised an eyebrow whilst *s2trash* was out of the car and on with the outfit in seconds! Superman couldn't have got changed any faster. *Miss P* was hot off the mark to spot a winning photo-opportunity here and with a quick photo sneakily taken (bribery – for the use of), the uniform was carefully peeled off *s2trash* in the ever increasing heat and he was forcefully put back into the safety of the car. After driving all of fifty feet they spotted the guys from S-mann who had come over from Holland and the chaps from Smarts R us from Nottingham. Hugs and kisses were exchanged in greetings and a long afternoon of chatting began.

The first thing to catch *s2trash's* eye was a customised Limited 1 edition belonging to *Tinks43* sporting many S-mann parts. He has combined forces with S-mann and is importing their parts to the USA. His car is featured in the custom section of this book so we will save all the details for now. Imro Penders, the clog-wearing top banana and all round nice guy from S-mann was explaining about their concept and design process and just how much work goes into their product development, which explains why the quality of their finished parts is so good. *Miss Polkadot* is one of their very satisfied customers with a nice set of side-skirts – the car variety!

Some **smart** car owners had a long journey to get to Newark, and so midday saw the arrival of some who had been given permission to come early and set up their weekend home.

By late afternoon a supermarket run was on the cards to stock up on provisions. *Miss Polkadot* is the kind of gal who knows what she wants and doesn't dither about in supermarkets, so luckily the shopping didn't take to long and not long after getting back to the site and cooking and consuming their supper, they went off on a hunt for things to photograph. What an evening! Smarts R us gave *Miss Polkadot* the keys to their beautiful gold Lambo door roadster coupé, which looked stunning in the late evening light. Next, *Miss Polkadot* drove their new C7 Kit car round into a hard standing area for *s2trash* to photograph, a car he is in love with and definitely features on his wish list. Then the real fun began; they were loaned a massive three wheeled motorcycle trike, built based on **smart** components. The keys of a TRIKEtec C2 three wheeled roadster were handed to *Miss Polkadot* along with a quick lesson about the controls. Despite her never having driven a vehicle like this before, the owners were quite happy for *Miss Polkadot* to drive off into the sunset with their prized possession. Standing at a meagre 5' 2", *Miss P*

DCUK publicity vehicle

Kym1959 buys more bling from Smarts R us

Smartie and Puddlejumper test out the kids equipment

felt rather overwhelmed by the sheer size if this beast. Despite her diminutive stature she was easily able to reach the controls and in a true have-a-go style, set off, with poor *s2trash* sitting in the rear seat clinging on to his camera for dear life! Biker babe maybe not, but she did control the trike rather well once *s2trash* had screamed 'let me off!' a few times. With the safe return of the C2 and some great photos in the bag, they then had the pleasure of being taken out on the C3. They were both passengers this time, being chauffeured by a much more seasoned driver. Holy Moly did it shift! What an amazing machine! It was a cross between a super-fast bike and a fairground ride! Having set up the SBP stand earlier in the day, and with very little light left, there was nothing left to do but commence with a spot of socialising around the campsite. The evening ended up with a jolly Pow-Wow with all the guys from Smartarse Design, who plied everyone with cigarettes, coffee and beer. *Massive*, with the able assistance of some falling down water managed to put the world to rights before tottering off to his abode, skipping between the invisible guy ropes.

Saturday

Even before the birds were up, it was hot! Not having TV or radio whilst away, an up to date weather forecast wasn't available, but everyone just knew it was going to be a scorcher!

After breakfast and showers everyone made their way to their stands ready for the big day ahead. No sooner had *s2trash* appeared than he got collared by *Vladaria* to go and look for a broom to sweep the area where Ross Swift was to perform his stunts later that day. With a broom found and cleverly passed on *s2trash* returned to his stand and the important task of getting his equipment ready for the day ahead resumed. One of the first people to come over and say hello was *Sioux* and her hubby John who had driven down from Blackpool via the Peak District in their cabrio. *Sioux* has been a good friend and very supportive helper whenever *s2trash* makes a big mess of his computer.

The traders inside the main show area were all set up and ready to roll. *T1NY W* was there with his car and new modifications, *Smartypartfast* and his stand full of **smart** merchandise from Smart of Hertford, Blown Away – a T-shirt printing company, Murano Silver, Smartarse Design, a toy stall and a car insurance company. There was also a Scalextric track set up for people to try. For a £1 you could drive 20 laps with the fastest times being recorded. The winner at the end of the weekend won a Scalextric set worth £100. Both being avid Scalextric fans, *s2trash* and *Hoagiekat* got into a duel, with *s2trash* sending one car off the track on to the floor causing major damage to the toy! It did start to dawn on everyone by mid-morning that there wasn't a lot of people around, not the numbers that were expected anyway. Then messages started to filter through that there were major problems on the roads getting to Newark from the south, thanks to a large lorry fire causing a seven mile tail back. Later on in the day more news arrived to say that the roads had been closed twice more during the course of the day, which had made it almost impossible to get to the venue. Many folks had either not bothered and stayed home and watched the football match or had turned back and gone home. Whatever the reason, the turnout was very disappointing and everyone's sales figures were affected. With time to kill and a need to move around *s2rash* went off with his cameras to see what there was on offer. Smartmania had set up a club stand with a 1959 Messerschmitt car sitting amongst the **smarts**. Although a **smart** owner, this vehicle belongs to the publisher of this very book, *Messerschmitt owner*, who decided to take that with him instead of his **smart**, so he could do some work on it over the weekend!

Another group who set up a club stand was the East Anglian mob, with the likes of *Sprintmick*, *Fudge*, *NeilOs* and *Red Cookie*, to name a but a few. Next it was a visit to the Smartimes stand who should have been positioned next to the Spotty Badger stand. Thanks to some traders not wanting to be next to each other,

Poised and ready

Crowd participate in judging car competitions

RichG's winning photo

Massive had been moved miles from the main arena. *Massive* had several cars on his stand that had been featured in previous editions of smartimes magazine, including *smint roadster's* mint coloured roadster with its one piece rear looking gorgeous in the summer sun, Coolfart's Union Jack car 'Brit-tiny' along with his own ever changing smartimes car. Further down the line Wellsmart had a fortwo coupé in white, made up with graphics to look like 'Herbie' with a tiny matching caravan called a 'Bed-Bug', which was very cool. They also had a forfour that was undergoing some modifications but wasn't fully finished at the show. By early afternoon the heat was seriously getting a problem, and drinking water to stop dehydration was the top priority. Outside it was becoming unbearable, and neither *s2trash* nor *Miss Polkadot* had any shade to hide under. Temperatures reached a staggering 37°C. As there was room to spare, *Miss P* and *s2trash* decided to move their stand into the main indoor arena so that they could get out of the sun, they didn't want to run the risk of getting sunstroke. They may have been out of the direct sunlight, but it was just as hot, completely stifling in fact.

During 2006 the websites clubs had seen a lot of new owners come on board and it was nice to meet up with and put faces to a few of the new names that had wandered into the pavilion with the same idea of getting out of the sun. This weekend event unfortunately clashed with the football World Cup and England were playing Portugal this particular afternoon. *T1NY W* had set up a huge TV screen in the main pavilion for all who wanted to watch the match. *Miss Polkadot*, *Drageron* and *s2trash* all sat at the back watching from afar with *Drageron* telling many of his humorous tales, most of which could never be put into print. *Drageron* eventually went wandering and then out of the blue appeared Andy Peace, the man originally behind the famous Blindschleiche exhausts. He had sold the company a while back but had come to the event just for the day to say hi to old friends. This is what makes events such a great thing to go to; you don't see people for ages, yet once a year you get to meet up and chat like old friends and catch up on what's been happening to them and their cars.

Back to the football... the second half was well underway and *s2trash* was with *Messerschmitt owner* and one off his wee Scottish friends, just at the moment Wayne Rooney was sent off. The friend lets rip with a loud 'YES!' in his deep Scottish accent while the rest of the hall fell silent. A timely exit was due for fear of being hung. England lost on penalties in the end for anyone who might have the slightest interest in football. The later part of the afternoon saw the competitions and games start with sack and space hopper races organised by *Vladaria*. The trouble was, it was so hot, jumping around in sacks wasn't the first thing folks wanted to do and getting enough to participate in the games was a tough call. *Mad Max* won one of the races and had to present himself to two DJ's to be interviewed. *Mad Max* was wearing an England shirt. *Messerschmitt owner* decided to shout out 'That's the only person in an England shirt who will win anything today!' Oh dear, again time to split. Why did we land ourselves a publisher with a death wish? With the temperature finally beginning to cool, it was time for the Car Competitions, Best Clean Car and Best Filthy Car. It will be of no surprise to those know her, that *Smartie* won the Filthiest Car category with her Viper **smart** , a car that doesn't 'do' clean! Voting was done by groups standing next to cars and the group who made the most noise won for the cars owner, well we think that was what went on. Once the competitions finished everyone packed up for the day and relished in the cool of the ensuing night. With ablutions over *s2trash* went in search of food, finally finding *NeilOs* and *Red Cookie* and helping himself to their sausages! Paul Holmes (from Smarts R us) and his band provided the evenings entertainment, and with the bar open until late, everyone had a merry time indeed. The Scottish contingent dressed in their kilts, which during the evening could be spotted being worn by various other folk apart from their original owners. A case of musical kilts no doubt!

Sunday

The Sunday got off to a similar start with *s2trash* moaning about the milk having gone off, the air bed leaking again and getting out of it the wrong side. This sourpuss obviously didn't appreciate the finer points of camping! *Miss Polkadot* however, ignored the petulance and in her normal mild mannered way suggested *s2trash* go and find a cow and get some really fresh milk, knowing full well that he would be gone for hours, leaving behind a tranquil scene around the camp site. It then dawned on her that letting *s2trash* loose in a field with farm yard animals maybe wasn't such a wise move and that escorting him to the camp site shop was a far safer option. With *s2grumpy-chops* coercively propelled round to where the car was parked and forcibly thrust into the spotty wagon, *Miss P* headed for the shop and the showers with her passenger looking decidedly *s2sheepish*. Under normal circumstances, taking a shower is a routine affair, even at a campsite. This was one of those occasions outside the envelope. *Miss Polkadot* walked into the ladies area to be met by a lady filling up buckets of water with a jug from the taps on one of the sinks; and like a doddery character from' Acorn Antiques' most of the water ended up on the floor. Out of polite curiosity she asked what she was doing. The reply she received what not what had expected to hear. 'The water is for washing my goats', there being a goat version of a Show 'n' Shine competition at the showground that same weekend. Still feeling a trifle puzzled, *Miss Polkadot* said 'Oh! Don't they have taps over by your goats then?' Being such a large showground, famous for showing animals you would have thought they would have. The lady replied 'Yes they do, but we want hot water, we couldn't possibly wash our goats in cold water!' One has to bear in mind that this was the hottest weekend of the year. *Miss P* stood there too incredulous to speak and continued to watch the goat lady slosh more water all over the floor. Talk about pampered pets. In the meantime *s2trash* was having his own strange encounters in the male shower block. As he walked in, the floor was soaking and doing a double-take he spotted what appeared to be hoof marks on the floor! Wondering if he had walked into the aftermath of a voodoo ritual he waded through the water and the odd tussock of grass to a shower cubical. As the door almost fell of in his hand, hanging as it was on only one hinge, he noticed more hoof marks! What on earth had been going on in there he dared not think too hard about. Living as he does in a strange world at the best of times, this scenario was weird even for him. Feeling strangely unnerved about the whole situation *s2trash* was jolted back into reality when he realised that he had forgotten his shower gel and had to use soap from a hand dispenser, which he had to pour into a paper towel in order to use it in a shower with a secure door. By the time he came out he was wondering if the day could get any more surreal.

By the time *Miss Polkadot* had finished doing what ever ladies do which takes so long, it was time to exchange the tales of the showers, buy those much need provisions from the shop and head back to camp for breakfast before the days events began. Luckily the animal antics in the shower had revived *s2sourpuss* no end and *s2happychap* re-emerged.

On the Saturday evening both *s2trash* and *Miss Polkadot* had been asked to judge a photographic competition. The winner, chosen from a large selection of pictures taken by **smart** owners at the event during the day and viewed on a computer in the evening, was won by *RichG* with a great photo of *Mad Max's* car. His winning prize was a personal portrait of his prized car, a star blue roadster, and for *s2trash*, that was the next thing on Sunday's agenda. *S2trash* took *RichG* (Smartmaniacs moderator and all round good egg) and his car to a nice secluded spot surrounded by green shrubs and trees and got the shot he wanted. With that job out of the way out it was time to head to the indoor arena for the day. The Smartimes stand had also moved into the pavilion to escape the heat but *Massive* was noticeable by his absence. The previous days sun and evening beverages had taken their toll on him and he had gone home feeling the worse for wear. It was another extremely hot and humid day and *s2trash* and *Miss Polkadot* remained indoors for most of the time, enjoying just sitting in the shade of the pavilion and talking to people.

People who had just come for the day were kept entertained with the hydraulic antics of *T1NY W's* car. The slot car racing challenge was hotting up but *s2trash* stayed off it having smashed up one of the cars by accident the day before! Later on in the afternoon, *Miss Polkadot* spent some of her birthday money she had been saving, on some flash side skirts from *S-mann*. She had also bought some front spats from *Smartypartfast* and cheekily got Imro Penders from *S-mann* to personally fit them at the same time as the skirts. While she was having her latest mods fitted, she had a few chips on her windscreen repaired for free by a company called Optic-Kleer, who specialise in windscreen repairs, and an amazing job they did as well. On the Saturday, *Smartie*, who had won the 'Dirtiest Car' competition, had been given a car washing kit as her prize. By some minor miracle, *Smartie* then entered the 'Cleanest Car' competition held on the Sunday afternoon, and won that too! It was definitely a weekend for her to remember.

With the first Newark rally drawing to a close, stands were taken down and packed up. With the heat of the day still affecting everyone it looked like everything was being conducted in slow motion. Feeling rather peckish, and with some left over provisions that would not be taken home, *s2trash* decided to rustle up a plate of something vaguely resembling an omelette, which he kindly shared with his diminutive side-kick, who regretted packing up her chisel so early. In no rush to set off home, only to sit a hot car for hours, they sat in the shade for a while to relax and unwind, and were joined by *Smartie*, *Puddlejumper* and *Captain Pugwash*, who also couldn't be bothered to go just yet and had had the same idea. There is nothing like a nice cup of tea, and what *s2trash* made for everyone was nothing like a nice cup of tea! Ah, the old jokes are the best. He actually made a great cuppa and everyone was most appreciative of it as they sat and mulled over the weekends memorable events.

After finally packing up the camping equipment and squeezing into her car, *Miss Polkadot* had one of those déjà vu moments when she shoe-horned *s2trash* into the passenger seat for the second time within days. As *s2trash* was travelling back with *Miss Polkadot* all the way to her house in Essex to work on this book with her, she hoped he didn't get too grumpy with the long journey ahead. Ready and loaded up, they drove round the campsite to say goodbye and safe journey to those still left behind and headed off...in the wrong direction! For some reason, maybe the heat, *Miss Polkadot's* newly acquired sat nav decided to play up and wouldn't connect to the satellites. Consequently, with the only map in the car buried under two tonnes of gear, they got lost almost instantly, and ended up travelling around twenty miles further than they needed to, which the sat nav kindly informed them of when it eventually decided to work. Several stops had to be made to let *s2trash* get out of his **smart** sardine can and stretch his cramped muscles. *Miss P* had a very quiet drive back as *s2trash* had become too tired to talk, a most unusual scenario and one that she made the most of. Finally after a great, hot and unusual weekend they rolled onto *Polkadot's* drive and thought about the work they had lined up ahead of them before crashing out – no need for counting sheep or **smart** cars this time – heat exhaustion ruled ok!

Summary of Events 2006

You should by now have got the jest of some of the regular events, so here is a brief round-up of more scandalous activities that occurred in 2006.

The M25 Run

Year four for this event and still people want to do it! *S2trash* had posted on the website forums that he wouldn't be organising this completely bonkers trip on a circular by-pass in 2006, as he couldn't drive the route himself and had to rely on getting a lift. However, due to popular demand for doing daft things, he was persuaded to go ahead and arrange it again. It just goes to show that people obviously enjoyed themselves previously despite it being such a mad-cap thing to do.
Here are some of the highlights:

- *s2trash* got a lift to Bluewater with *jamiebeveridge* – you remember him; he was the lad who lost his roof whilst travelling to Billing in 2005 whilst giving *s2trash* a lift. *S2trash* must surely carry a jinx, as poor *jamiebeveridge's* car overheated and they had to travel from East Sussex to the Bluewater Shopping Mall in a car that was running with the heating on fall blast to keep the temperature down – in JUNE!
- The convoy of **smarts** all managed to go the same way out of Bluewater and stay together for once.
- Whilst driving his crossblade *Putzie* was nearly overcome by the overpowering fumes of newly distributed manure wafting across the motorway – experiences the like of which cars with roofs tend to miss out on – luckily! Apparently his next modification involves a thin plastic tube, face mask and small oxygen cylinder discreetly bolted to his seat.
- Twenty nine **smart** owners and their passengers invaded Pizza Express back at Bluewater at the end of run without having booked, scaring the living daylights out of the staff who were not quite prepared for such a large influx all at once! They were actually brilliant about it all and as the country was in the grip of a heatwave, set up tables outside for alfresco dining as it was just so hot even at 9.30 at night.

The Bexhill Beach Party

The earlier heatwave typically disappeared just in time for the Beach Party! Cold, wet, cold, wet, wet, cold, sun and wet; a typical English summer really but the event proved to be just as popular as *Smartie* and *Captain Pugwash* made a mini holiday of it and stayed for 8 days. The weather on the Saturday afternoon turned so cold that even the die-hard Beach Party veterans had to concede defeat and return to the campsite early afternoon to avoid hypothermia, and ended firing up their BBQ's just to keep warm. Everyone was most impressed when *s2Escargo*, an engineer by trade, brought along the teardrop caravan that he had designed and made completely from scratch, towed behind his roadster coupé with one of his own self made tow bars, which he will make to order if asked nicely.
Here are some of the highlights:

- *S2trash* got 'told on' by some naughty kids after they were asked to move out of the way of a shot he was setting up outside the De la Warr Pavilion in Bexhill on the Friday evening. He then found himself being grabbed by the lapels by one of the parents of the naughty kids who had been fed some porky pies about what *s2trash* had said to the kids, then discovered that a cavalry of 28 **smart** car owners turned up to rescue him from a potential black eye!
- The photographic shots for the front cover of this book using *Bat* and her car in front of the De La Warr were taken in fifteen minutes in a force ten gale, and she still looked beautiful!
- The Saturday evening cruise to Bodiam Castle proved interesting with everyone going different ways across East Sussex, as was the reaction of some residents of Battle as the cars pulled up outside the Abbey waiting to re-group.
- *Bubski* got tipsy on a bottle of fine Claret and was watched with great amusement as he wandered around the campsite like Charlie Chaplin.
- The night time chats at the campsite sitting huddled around tea lights, which would have been censored if aired on television.
- *Drageron's* jokes and hysterical mobile phone ring tones!
- Side splitting comments heard late Sunday evening emanating from *s2trash* as he alligator wrestled with his air bed and mechanical pump. *Miss P* was overheard saying that she put down the inability of the nozzle to remain in the hole purely down to operator error!
- Packing up on the Monday in a torrential rain storm and creating a **smart** sauna with the damp camping equipment.

The London to Brighton

For the second year running *Miss Polkadot* chauffeured *s2trash* to the start accompanied by a sweet selection of Essex Smarties. *Magnet* kindly supplied everyone with coffee from his workplace conveniently opposite the first meeting point at smart of Lakeside, which at 6am was shut. The start venue this year was at the new

Mercedes Benz World on the site of the old Brooklands race track. Sadly, it was not quite finished and was closed to the public, so we were not allowed into the futuristic building, but were parked up two by two along the snake-like outdoor test track. Here are some of the highlights:

- Trouble trying to find the entrance to the start at Brooklands, even with a sat nav, as there were two entrances and **smarts** driving around in all directions.
- The great drive down to Pease Pottage Services and being amazed that the mini convoy had managed to keep together.
- Parking next to a group of Harley Davidson bikers and a very large Hummer!
- Getting to the finish line without incident; and not having to queue for as long as normal on the approach road to Brighton Race Course.
- Meeting up with old faces, who, having sold their **smarts**, still made the effort to come along for the day.
- Taking the opportunity to look round at the hundreds of shiny cars, gleaming in the late summer sun.
- Admiring the couple that had recently married then entered and won the Best Dressed **smart** wearing their wedding outfits.
- Seeing the electric **smart** for the first time.
- Trying to hide from *Miss P* wearing her Polkadot cowboy hat.
- Watching *fq101* setting up their club marquee just as it was time to go home.
- Chilling out watching the world go by for most of the afternoon and getting to drive the World's First right hand drive diesel **smart** constructed by Wellsmart.
- The drive back with *Magnet* following, and unfortunately losing him after stopping for a bite to eat on the Sussex Downs.

Beaulieu

Cadging a lift from *Bubski* and following *Miss Polkadot* and *Miss Radley* on the journey down to Beaulieu in the New Forest, *s2trash* had too much caffeine and combined with his driver's forthright driving skills, desperately tried not to be car sick – one of those rare moments when *s2trash* was lost for words. This was the best ever Beaulieu despite the numbers being slightly down and the PA system refusing to work yet again. Here are some of the highlights:

- Taking over the hotel with **smart** owners from all over the country.
- The fantastic Saturday evening meal at The New Forest Inn.
- Finding out how well the Spotty Badger calendars burnt when *Kittycat* was given a new one to look at and held it over a burning candle on the table at the pub.
- Finding out how much fire really hurts when *Mr Smart-Suits* put the flames out with his fingers.
- *Bubski* secretly having his car washed at 1am in the morning by the Wellsmart gang, therefore boycotting *Bubski's* plans to win The Dirtiest Car competition – the rotters!
- *Bubski* going outside for a cigarette at 1am and catching them at it!
- Being blessed with beautiful sunny weather yet again.
- Wellsmart trading out of a mosque! Well, it looked like one and did cause the odd person fall on their knees and pray to Mecca.
- *T1NY W* and his amazing performing car, his trendy black marquee that was full of sweets and biscuits and free refreshments.
- A great show of attendance from individual local **smart** clubs, setting up their own displays.
- Smartarse performing free clutch adjustments, which had them run off their feet.
- The gorgeous birthday cake for *ykciv123* that was cut up and shared out in the afternoon, and turned into the feeding of the five thousand.

Polkadot gets escorted by stretched limos

Re-grouping outside Battle Abbey

Miss Radley hops to it at Brooklands

Winner of the 'Dirtiest Car' competition receives washing kit with instructions

6 Modifying the smart

By the very action of ordering a **smart** from new, **smart** themselves have said that there are approximately 5,000 different part options to be decided upon when putting together any one car. This alone would be enough for most folks, but having relaxed laws regarding modifying cars in the UK, owners here in Britain have gone to town on making their cars far more individual than anywhere else in the world, although Italy does have some very nice modified cars too.

Trying to analyse the reason for this modding madness is difficult. The **smart** to start with is unique, so why make it more so?

The only possible reasons are that: because owners can, because the car comes out of the factory with all of its performance settings fixed very low allowing the engine to be electronically upgraded or re-mapped, because parts are easily interchangeable and accessible making life easy to upgrade exhaust and air intakes, because the car itself is diminutive and re-spray costs are low due to the small quantity of paint required, a reason in itself that allows the use of very expensive flip paints. One could assume that a great deal of owners are erring on the middle aged side of life with dependants no more and with a little more disposable income with which to personalise something just for themselves. Let's face it, who wouldn't want the chance to throw out the boring old family saloon in favour of a cute, quirky, economical, two seater, designer vehicle with bags of character that made the occupants grin every time they got in it, and not feel guilty that it didn't fit in with the family's requirements. Having said that, there are also many younger owners with a great deal of disposable income willing to spend, spend, spend on modding to the max just like with other vehicle makes, such as the Corsa.

Basically, what we are saying is that the **smart** just lends itself to have things customised ~ just how many cars could get away with sporting an exterior covered in spots, green peas, sharks or skeletons? None we would suspect! In fact, when you think about it, how many cars have you had in a lifetime that you have actually done any modifications to? The answer is probably none – until you bought a **smart**. There does tend to be a bit of the herding instinct going on regarding modifying though. When owners turn up at events and meetings with standard cars and with the intention of keeping their car that way, and they see just what can be changed on a car similar to their own, (some very cheap mods and others extravagantly expensive, but mostly easy to do but of course there will some that are more difficult), they get caught up in the excitement of it all and go home thinking 'oh! I could do that!' At that precise moment the owner will be on the start of a journey of jolly modification with the hopes that they have some very deep pockets and very understanding partners! Go to any meet in this country and you will be hard pressed to find any two cars the same, such is the spread of this phenomenon.

So, what exactly is modifying? In its simplest form it is anything fitted on a car that diversifies from the makers original specifications.

In this chapter we will showcase some of the UK's leading modified cars and their specifications, which we hope will show you some of the diverse ways to customise a **smart**, from DIY modifications to hand made custom parts. These cars range from those with basic modifications up to those with complicated and extreme ones, just to give you an overview of what can be done.

Colour coded roadster light surround

Air scoop

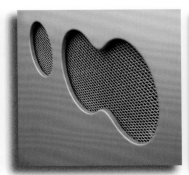

Massives unique side air vent

Air scoop

** *One quick word of warning – when making any changes to your car, you should immediately inform your insurance company, as non-disclosure of modifications can void the insurance in the event of a claim. Some companies will not even insure modified cars, so if in doubt, check with them first before undertaking any work.*

One grey area to watch out for in the world of customising is the **smart** warranty. Some modifications can void the warranty, others do not. For example: EU laws allow some changes to be carried out without affecting the warranty i.e. performance air filters and re-maps, as **smart** now sell them as aft-market additions themselves. However, do check on your countries laws before you make any modifications, because in Germany for example, modifications are strictly forbidden to any make of car unless factory fitted or are government approved parts!

Just out of interest, *s2trash* decided to conduct a short Poll on the Smartmaniacs website to see just how many people had actually made any modifications to their car. It was a plain yes or no situation, but the modifications allowed included any non-standard factory fitted options. The poll only ran for seven days but during that time 104 owners took part. The results were quite astounding. A staggering 98 people had made modifications and only 6 remained completely standard. It just goes to show modifying is very, very catching.

On the cheap...

Before we move on to the really hot Customised cars, here are a few of the more simplistic and non-expensive ways that you can modify your car.

Vinyl

You don't have to spend mega bucks to make your **smart** individual; *Miss Polkadot* for instance designed the exterior graphics on her own car, had them cut out of high-quality vinyl for the meagre sum of £30, fitted them herself symmetrically on the car (as only *Miss P* would do), made and covered her seats in Dalmatian fur fabric, again at minimum costs, and created one of the most recognisable cars in the UK. Using vinyl is one of the cheapest ways to customise your exterior and can be a simple or as complex as you like. Another early car that used vinyl was *Sally Sweet Pea*; her stream green panels had vinyl peas on them which had also been air brushed to give a 3D effect. Costing more but very effective none the less was *s2stealth's* Gumball **smart**. Being a graphic designer like *Miss Polkadot*, *s2stealth* created another stunning car using copies of company logos to recreate the feel of a Gumball Rally car.

Wolfrace Alloy wheel

Rear speakers

Evil Twin rear valance

Roadster air scoop

Performance enhancements

De-lipping the air intake on the side of the car (not to be confused with the fuel intake that **smart** got worried about one year and sent out a special 'Fuel Only' sticker for owners to place beside the fuel cap to stop confusion!), fitting an air scoop and an after market performance air filter can add 2 to 5 bhp on the fortwo. On the roadster the air intake is different but can be modified with larger pipes and some fairly simple adjustments. Better airflow means better performance. On the forfour there isn't a side air intake so just replacing the air filter will suffice. Still on the cheap, a 'tik' pipe from a roadster (a replacement air induction pipe and again an original **smart** part) fits rather nicely into a fortwo; *s2trash* actually has a Brabus one. A totally free modification is to de-lip the gasket in the throttle body. All you need to do is remove a couple of jubilee clips that hold the top intercooler pipe in place, remove the pipe and with a craft knife de-lip the rubber gasket. This simple little job increases the air flow which means better performance for free.

There are far too many alterations to mention them all here, (check out the website clubs for more), so we will let the following pictures and car specifications show you what can be done. Maybe they will give you a few ideas of your own on how to enhance your car's performance or looks, although there is still nothing wrong with a standard **smart,** that is why most of us brought them to start with, but just got a bit carried away. However, be warned, the modding bug can bite you hard on the bottom and may lead to many late nights in cold dark garages. Unless you have a very understanding significant other, hiding the credit card statements may not be such a bad idea when furthering your modding schedule!

Sally Sweet Pea and her custom vinyl peas

Air filter

Light cluster

Schmidt Alloy wheel

7 Customised smarts

It would be actually be impossible to list all of the modifications that could be made to any of the cars in the **smart** range. There are potentially so many of them and more appear on a daily basis, that there would be enough to write a whole book about them. So, what we have done here is gathered together a cross section of cars and let the specifications actually supplied by the owners themselves do the talking.

S2trash

Having owned it from new the 'trash can', one of the first right hand drive cars in the UK, has slowly taken shape with modifications added over a period of four years. *S2trash* put the modifications on this car together on a budget costing around £870 in total for parts. Much searching, a bit of begging, occasionally getting trade prices on items and kindly being given bits and pieces has helped keep the cost down. Having added **smart** bass bins, Sony 13cm speakers and a fairly standard JVC head unit, the sound system is superb due to the car having a solid roof and creating great acoustics. People often think it is fitted with more ICE than it has. The moral of this car is 'seek and you will find', or in plain English, you do not need to 'flash the cash' to get a car to your own personal specification.

Model: smart fortwo pure – Built June 2002 – Registered July 2002

Colour: All Black

Engine
• *Digitec* Re-map • *Piper Cross* Air Filter • De-lipped Air Intake • Carbon Air Scoop from **thesmartclub** • *Brabus* roadster Tik Pipe• Bigger Cycle Valve

Exterior
• Lower Front Grille Meshed • Carbon Eyebrows • Carbon Wing Mirror Covers • Hand made Exhaust Trim • Stubby Aerial • Roadster Chrome Badge on Front and Back Panels • **smart** rear Mud Flaps • Custom made Axel Caps • *Ripspeed* Kick Plates • Smoked Side Repeaters with Chrome Surrounds • **smart** starline Alloy Wheels • Custom made Front Wheel Bolt Covers sprayed Green • *Brabus* Wheel Arch Extensions • *Wellsmart* Sonic Fake Rear Brake discs • Custom Gold Scorpion Graphics by *Ordnryjoe* • *Smartimes* Custom Rear Valance • Fancy Black and Chrome Door Protectors

Interior
• *JVC* Head Unit • **smart** Bass Bins • *Sony* 3-way Speakers • **smart** Drinks Holder • **smart** Full Length Mats • *Ripspeed* Gear Knob • Alloy Hand Brake Button • Alloy Wing Mirror Controls • Alloy Ignition Surround • Alloy Heater Controls • Hand made Seat Covers from Germany • Custom Door Inserts •

smart Boot Cover • **smart** Boot Protector • Red LED Interior bulbs • **smart** Pod and Dash Surrounds in Limited Edition Green • **smart** Parking Ticket Holder • *Ripspeed* Tax Disc Holder

Mad Max

Originally starting life as a red and black pulse this car has remained pretty much standard, until you look at the paint job! An unquestionable Mad Max fan, Mart just could not prevent himself from turning his **smart** into a miniature version of the Interceptor car named 'The Dark One' driven by Mel Gibson who starred in the series of Mad Max films. With the help of Smarts R Us, who produced the paintwork on the car, they helped him bring his dream to life. As soon as his finished car appeared on the Smarts R us website, *Mad Max* became inundated with interested fans, both **smart** and film, from America, France, Germany, Australia and of course here in the UK. All he needs now is an equity card!

Model: smart fortwo pulse coupé – 2004

Colour: Yellow, blue & red

Engine

• 698cc petrol • *Evil Twin* ECU Re-Map • *Powertec* Filter • *K+N* Air Intake

Exterior

• 'Mad Max' paint job – 4 Colours individually masked and painted • Custom made 'Interceptor' Graphics • See-through Vision Vinyl on Glass Roof • 16" *Titan* Wheels • *Dunlop* sp9000 Tyres • *K+N* Air Intake

S2Herman

One of the 'old school gang' of early **smart** owners, *s2Herman's* car has one claim to fame – it was the first car *s2trash* ever photographed for the first 2005 Spotty Badger Smart Car Calendar. *S2Herman* himself has several claims to fame including starting the hysterically funny website 'Funkyknitting' that was a comical parody of the famous Funkysmart site; and constantly being spotted alongside *Bubski* in eating mode! *S2Herman* sadly sold his car before we finished this book and moved on from the **smart** scene, but that slight oversight doesn't stop him from still coming along to **smart** events and meeting up with his many friends. *S2Herman's* car has only had subtle visible changes done to it but they give it a certain sleekness and originality that is instantly recognisable.

Model: smart fortwo passion coupé – 2001

Colour: All silver

Engine

• 599cc • *Smarts R Us* Re-map to approx 78bhp (estimated) • *K&N* Air Filter orignally, then changed to *Pipercross* Air Filter • Vertical Wiper Modification • 90% Tinted Glass to rear • 50% Tinted Glass to front windows • 6" Sunstrip to front windscreen • Custom made Chequer Plated Floor Mats

Exterior

• River Silver panels • *MS Design* front spoiler and sideskirts • Rear Valance colour coded to Tridion • 16" *Adikt* Type E Alloy Wheels
• 165/40 16 *Pirelli P-Zero* tyres to the front and 215/35 *Dunlop SP* to the rear • *Knightrider* light custom-made inside grille made by owner

Interior

• Alloy Gear Knob of unknown origin

Tinks43

This limited edition car is modified to a very high specification. It is a nice mix of the early original car and the S-mann body kit parts that have been added to it, showing them off to their best and giving the car its unusual look. We bumped into *Tinks43* by chance when we were at the Newark 'Smartbeat' **smart** Rally in 2006, but instantly new this subtley modified car had to be in the book for you to see.

Model: smart fortwo coupé Limited One – No. 3842

Colour: All black

Engine

- 599cc • **K&N** Air Filter • Up rated Spark Plugs • **Evil Twin** Re-Map

Exterior

- Black Tridion & Black Panels • 16" **TSW** Fury Alloys, custom sprayed Titanium Colour with 3 to 5 stud adapters & spacers • **EBC** drilled & grooved brake discs with **Green Stuff** Brake Pads • Up rated **Bilstein** Gas Shocks all round • **RS** Rear lowering springs • De-Lipped Air Intake • **Blindschleiche** Twin centre exhaust & valance • Fog Lights_• **S-mann** Front Grille (New Range)_• **S-mann** Front Spoiler (New Range)_• **S-mann** Side Skirts (New Range) • **S-mann** Air Scoop • Black short Aerial • Black tinted windows • Black tinted rear light clusters • Personalised Number plate – **S1 4TWO**

Interior

- Standard Limited One Blue interior with half yellow leather trim on the Seats, Door Pockets, Steering Wheel & Gear Knob • Blue LED interiorbulbs in Dash, Pods, Lights & Switch • Clock & Rev Counter Pods • 7" Screen & DVD Player with MP3 • Slim-line Playstation 2 • 6x9 Speakers on rear tailgate • 8" Kicker Solo Baric Subwoofer • Sound Pack Upgrade • Air Conditioning • **MDC** Cruise Control

Mike'n'Helen

Originally an ex-demonstrator car from Smart Birmingham and produced in silver, this car had had it panels swapped for hello yellow ones when *Mike'n'Helen* bought it on October 2004. Feeling a little uncomfortable with the bright panels, they decided to have them re-sprayed in a colour a little less harsh on the eye and made a few modifications along the way. The paint job is to die for! It looks like the colour of vintage Claret, velvet and silk all rolled into one! It looks delicious, which is a strange term to use when describing a car, and voluptuously luxurious! It is an all-round nicely modified car, which is done to such a high standard that it gives it an air of a 'Top-of-the-range' executive car about it. We think it certainly has **smart** style - hope you agree.

Model: smart fortwo Passion coupé 2002 – 51 plate

Colour: Custom Red

Engine

- 599 cc • **K&N** Air Filter

Exterior

- Panels re-sprayed in Maple Red with a Blue Pearl lacquer top coat • 16" **ATS** Titan alloys • 195/40 x 16's Tyres • **Black Stuff** Brake Pads • **MS Design** Side Skirts • Chrome Surrounds on Side Indicators • Twin exit Exhaust Extension • De-lipped Air Intake

Interior

- Custom made Black heated Leather Seats, including Door and Dash Trim • Purple Piping on Seats, Doors and Car Mats to match exterior colour • Chrome Surrounds on Speedo, Rev Counter and Clock • Alloy Air Vents • Alloy Heater Knobs • **Kenwood** Stereo with 6 disc Multi-changer and upgraded Speakers

smartsRcool

smartsRcool purchased his **smart** not long before the London to Brighton Run in 2002. When he arrived there with his very standard looking car, he immediately made the decision that he just had to personalize his car and the sooner the better. He has added a full Brabus body kit in silver which nicely matches the tridion, for a little added muscle. He now has such an extensive inventory of chrome accessories that he must surely have to wear sunglasses at all times to avoid the chrome flare burning out his retinas inside the car! At some stage smartsRcool must have thought that he needed just a tad more chrome, so he went and purchased some stunning custom designed 3D chrome flame graphics from America to grace his door panels; a modification that was not a common site at that time. It is certainly safe to say that now; this car certainly stands out from the crowd. He had to admit to scaring himself when writing down his spec list, not realizing quite the amount of bling his car carried! Something I'm sure the majority of car owners featured in this section will identify with!

Model: smart fortwo coupé pulse 2001

Colour: True blue

Engine

• 599cc • **Evil Twin** Re-Map • Dump Valve • Adjusted Waist-gate • **Powertec** Filter • **S-mann** Air Scoop

Exterior

• Custom made American 3D Vinyl Airbrushed Graphics • **Brabus** Side Skirts • **Brabus** Front Spoiler • Quad **Blindschleiche** Exhaust • **Schmidt** Space 16 "Alloy Wheels • Up-rated Front Brakes (**EBC** drilled disc & **Green** brake pads) • **Brabus** Suspension • **Evil Twin** Chrome Fuel Cap Cover • Chrome Aerial

Interior

• Boost Gauge • **Pioneer** CD player • **Pioneer** 6/9 Speakers • **Pioneer** 10" Sub • **Pioneer** High Power Front Speakers • **Pioneer** Tweeters • 760 watt Amp • **Brabus** Handbrake • **Brabus** Gear Knob • **Brabus** Pedals • **Brabus** Blue leather interior with silver stitching, including door cards • **Evil Twin** White Dial Kit • Traction Control Switch • Chrome Accessories include: Door Handles, Heater Knobs, Heat Gauge Inserts, Air Vents Balls, Air Vent Rings, Heated Rear Window Button, Rings round the Air Con Button, Wing Mirror Adjusters, **Brabus** Wing Mirror Covers, End Caps on Wiper Arms, Indicator Surrounds, Rev Counter and Clock Rings, Speedo Cover, Seat Inserts, Inserts near Wing Mirrors and Sill Covers near the doors

Richard Bright

Miss Polkadot fell in love *Richard Bright's* car when she spotted it at a Donnington Park meet in May 2006. *Richard* had obviously polished it to within an inch of its life and had enjoyed every muscle aching moment of doing so. With its 'just out of the showroom' gleam and beautifully carried out modifications this car was just begging to be photographed and *Richard* was extremely obliging in letting *s2trash* have him park his uber-clean roadster on some horribly dusty ground, just to get the effect! *Richard* was no newbie to car modding, having previously completed various projects on other cars. He was at the time working on a very unusual custom made fibreglass module to house a set of speakers in the rear of the car, and although not completed, his attention to detail was astounding. Any future modifications that he has in mind will no doubt be of an equally high standard and hopefully he will get to show them off to an equally appreciative audience very soon.

Model: smart roadster 2005
Colour: Silver and black

Engine

• 698cc • *K & N* Induction Kit • *Forge* Dump Valve

Exterior

• Leister Body Kit Colour-coded Black • *Fuel 7* colour changing L.E.D under body lighting kit with 100 functions • Rear Boot Spoiler

Interior

• Handbrake and Handbrake Surround Colour-coded Black • Interior Door Handles Colour-coded Black • Centre of the dash, from the windscreen to the bottom tray Colour-coded Black • Boost, Temp, Speedo and Rev Counter Dial Surrounds all Colour-coded Black • Glove Box Colour-coded Black • Plastics under the steering wheel Colour-coded Black • *Sparco* 4 Point Harnesses • *Panasonic* Head Unit • *Crunch* 600 Watt Mono Block Amp. • 10" *Audiobahn* Chrome Sub, Mounted Magnet Out • *JBL* 13cm Components up front and a set in the rear • Fibre Glass Install, Colour-coded Black • All New Speaker Wires Installed From Head Unit to Components • 2X 3" TFT Screens Built into Sun visors • *XBOX* and *Playstation 2* Installed • *Janspeed* Stealth Exhaust System

• Mods to Come Soon: 17"/18" Wheels with *Evil Twin* 3 To 5 Stud Adaptors • Headlight and Rear Section Colour Coded Black

Otisb

Otisb has now sold this car but this is how it looked in May 2006 when we photographed it at the monthly **smart** Donni Meet held at Donnington Park Race Track. Maybe it will still be seen around the **smart** world and hopefully kept as it is or added to in such a way as to enhance it. It really is a looker! Starting life in grey with his own custom-made camouflage graphics adorning it, *Otisb* went to town with this make-over! The fantastic tinted windows certainly show the re-sprayed green panels off to a tee. Having recently sold this car after making such a good job of modifying it, we think it made him regret his decision and he is now back with another **smart**. We are waiting with bated breath to see just what he will do to that one!

Model: smart fortwo Pulse coupé 2004

Colour: Custom green

Engine

- 698cc Petrol • **PowerTec** Air Filter • **Smarts R Us** Roadster Re-Map

Exterior

- Air Scoop
- De-lipped Air Intake • Panels Re-Sprayed in Blue/green/gold/purple Flip Paint by **Smarts R Us** • Colour Coded Side Skirts and Front Splitter • Tinted Windows • Meshed **RS** grille • **AZEV A** 16" Alloy Wheels • **Tarox** G88 Grooved Disks • **Black Stuff** Brake Pads

Interior

- **UFO** Kit • **Road Angel** • **Sony** Head Unit • **Alpine** Front Speakers • Bass Bins • **Alpine** 700 watt Amp • **Alpine** 700 watt Sub • DVD Player • **Cobra** alarm (cat one) • Factory fitted Electric Sun roof • Under Seat Drawer • Private Number Plate

lil.smartie

There are probably a few lurking around in the UK, but customised forfours are a rare breed indeed. This stunning sparkly pink one has to be one of the best. It is still an ongoing project, so no doubt by the time this book is published there will be some more modifications. Along with the forfour, *lil.smartie* also owns a fortwo that was one of the first cars to come off the production line at Hambach. Having owned the fortwo for seven years has given *lil.smartie* a good grounding in everything **smart** related. Combining that knowledge with a job overseeing the maintaining, repairing and customising of **smarts** at Wellsmart, this lady certainly knows how to produce a stunning car and has proved that the forfour, sometimes unfairly labelled as an old mans or reps car, can have street cred. She has proved that although the actual Brabus version is great to look at, modifying it oneself takes the process a whole step further and has given her a whole bucket load of satisfaction.

Model: smart forfour Passion 1.5 Cdi – Lounge concept – 2004

Colour: Custom pink

Engine

- 1.5 litre diesel – 95bhp version • Semi Automatic gearbox

Exterior

- Titanium Tridion • Magenta Metallic paint with Pink Rose **House of Kolor** metal flake • 15mm **Manhick** Wheel Spacers • 17" **SWT** Racing Vegas Wheels • **Yokohama** Tyres • **Cannon** Mud Flaps front and rear • Light pack • **Brabus** body kit • **Brabus** Stickers

Interior

- Multi-media Navigator • Multi-function Steering Wheel with Paddle Shift • **Brabus** Floor Mats • Twin face Arm Rest • **Brabus** Gear Knob • Luggage Cover • Custom made MP3 Lead • **Kenwood** Speakers and Tweeters • **Clarion** Active Sub

Mccsmartarse

Claire and Simon were amongst the first owners *s2trash* ever met. Claire or *mccsmartarse* as she is known on the website forums, has the world's most infectious laughter and livens up every event she attends. Owning several sets of different coloured panels, the car is shown here wearing its aqua orange outfit. The front panel has been ingeniously modified to accommodate an extra set of lights. Most of the work has been undertaken by Simon, with Claire standing by in a supervisory capacity and poised with numerous cups of tea. This is one car *s2trash* really wanted for the book because customised aquas are few and far between, and this one is the bee's knees.

Model: smart fortwo passion coupé 2001 (Mk 4) – Belgium Import from Antwerp

Colour: Aqua Orange

Engine

• 599cc • *Digitec* remap phase I, II & III • *K&N* Green Air Filter

Exterior

• Choice of Panel Colours: Aqua Orange, Aqua Green, Jack Black • *Compomotive* ml 15x6j Wheels • *Yokohoma* 195 Tyres • *EBC* Grooved Disks and Green Stuff Pads • *Brabus* Spats • *Brabus* Front Spoiler • *Brabus* Rear Valance (Recently switched from custom rear Valance from Bruce S2Z) • *Brabus* Twin Exit Mk7 Performance Exhaust • *Michalak* Front Grille with Driving Lights • *Michalak* Quad Headlights with Eyebrows • *SW Exclusive* Stainless Steel Air Scoop • *smart* Mark 6 Wing Mirrors • *smart* Mark 6 Rear Lights • Window Tints in Titanium Colour • Private registration plate – **T33 NYY**

Interior

• *Prapia* Leather Seats and Steering Wheel • *Brabus* Prapia Side Pockets • *Brabus* Handbrake • *Brabus* Pedals • Custom Foot Rest • Custom S2Y Gearbox Insert • *Kenwood* Speakers KFC HQ698 6x9 4 in total • *Kenwood* KFCW1225Db 12" Sub • *Kenwood* KACPS650D 1200 Watt 5 Channel Amp • *Kenwood* KDC7024 Stereo Head Unit • *Kenwood* Ipod Adaptor IP500 • *Apple* Ipod Video 30 GB

Warbird

Not long after purchasing an aqua green fortwo in 2005 and naming it 'The Hulk', *Warbird* was seriously attacked with the modifying bug, a serious disease that creeps up on even those most resistant to applying extraneous bits to their cars. This disease is contagious, and drivers of all ages from seventeen to seventy are susceptible to its grip! Sadly, there is no known cure; it's a bug for life! Warbird added bling here, wide wheels there, a Brabus exhaust and some upmarket ICE. However, after attending a GAS (Gloucester Area Smarts) meet with a friend who had a cabrio, he lost his heart to the soft top, and part exchanged his 'Hulk' for a passion cabrio with lots of toys already onboard. Still with a liking for green, *Warbird* decided to have the car re-sprayed in green pearl, a stunning colour he had admired on a customized Ford Thunderbird, and Smart-Suits then added a layer of micro rainbow flake and nine layers of lacquer! When the sun hits this paint it shimmers from green to gold like crystallized fruit, and so naturally *Warbird* decided to christen this car 'The Crazy Grape'.

Model: smart fortwo passion cabrio – 2003

Colour: Green pearl

Engine

• 698cc • De-lipped Air Intake • *Pipercross* Air Filter • *Smarts R Us* Re-Map

Exterior

• *Smart-Suits* Custom painted panels • *Smart-Suits* Custom painted graphics front and rear • *Brabus* Exhaust System • *Michalak* Titan 16" Wheels • *Toyo* 225 x 40 x 16 Rear Tyres • *Toyo* 195 x 40 x 16 Front Tyres • *Roto* Brake Discs and Green Pads to front • *smart* standard brakes to rear • *Michalak* RS Chrome Grille • *S-mann* Side Skirts

Interior

• Alloy Air Vents • Alloy Mirror Control Ends • Alloy Heater controls • *Metal Monkey* Instrument faces • Boost Gauge • Colour-coded Instrument Surrounds • Paddleshift Steering with monogrammed paddles • *TomTom* 700 GPS Sat Nav

Binxyboo ~ The Urban Fairy

Binxyboo bought her second hand **smart** when it was 6 months old with 6000 miles on the clock, from Smartarse Design. It was Paul Murphy who initially designed and applied the original star graphics. When *Binxyboo* had the car resprayed, she had to remove all of the original stars but the fairies stayed in place. She bought some extra stars from Smartarse, which she then re-applied on the new sparkly panels with the help of her Dad. The car was resprayed at Absolute Vehicle Care in Romsey by Paul Johnson. A rainbow metal flake paint was used over the original black panel colouring, and then several layers of clear lacquer applied on top of the metal flake and the stars, giving the car a three dimensional look. The mixture of paint and vinyl graphics makes this car a real head turner and along with all its other modifications, re-map and a pair of fairy wings behind the drivers seat, this is one very fast Urban Fairy!

Model: smart fortwo pulse 2003 – Mk 7

Colour: Black

Exterior

• De-badged • Air Intake pipe 'De-lipped' • 15" *Kahn* Alloy Wheels • Silver Wing Mirror Covers • Stubby Chrome Aerial • Axle Caps • Fake Rear Brake Discs • *thesmartclub* black Air Scoop • Chrome Number Plate Surround • Rear Valance re-sprayed in 'Tridion Silver' • Stars and Fairy Graphics • Rainbow Metal Flake Paintwork

Interior

• *smart* Floor Mats • *smart* Seat Belt Pads • *Metal Monkey* Speedo, Clock, Rev Counter and Heater Inserts • Alloy Heater Control and Radio Buttons • *Evilution* MP3 Cable • Alloy Wing Mirror and Handbrake Buttons • Alloy Window Control Buttons • Alloy Indicator Stalk Buttons • Alloy Pod and Speedo Surround • Chrome Ignition Surround • Fairies on the dash • Fairy wings on the drivers seat

Engine

• 599cc • *Red Dot Racing* Re-map • *Pipercross* Sports Air filter

Miss Polkadot

Well, this car has been called spotty, dotty, the bubble car and the boil mobile, to name but a few, but with its use of a simple vinyl graphic design, it has become one of the UK's most recognisable cars, and pops up just about everywhere from the internet to magazines. This car isn't just about looks though, it is a bit of a wolf in spots clothing, if you excuse the pun. *Miss P* can never be accused of being a namby, pamby Sunday afternoon driver, she is in the car and off, a woman with a mission, and has shown many a BMW her tail lights, especially with the Digitec re-map that allows the car to reach speeds up to 105mph, not that she has actually taken the car to that speed! Many a driver has been taken aback as she hurtles along in the outside lane; a case of spots behind you, beside you, and before your very eyes.

Model: smart fortwo passion coupé – 2001 – Mk 5 – LHD
Colour: Jack black panels with white vinyl graphics

Engine

• *Brabus SB1* Re-map changed to *Digitec* Re-map • *Forge* Dump Valve • *Pipercross* Sports Air Filter • *Brabus* Twin Pipe Sports Exhaust

Exterior

• Customised Black Body Panels with White Vinyl 60's Retro Circles and Dots – • Design symmetrical both sides of vehicle and fitted by owner • *Brabus* Stainless Steel Exhaust Heat Shield • *S-mann* Side Skirts in Black with mesh insert • Pair of *smart* Spats attached to lower front panels • *thesmartclub* Carbon Air Scoop • Air Intake Pipe De-lipped • Pair of Shark Fins on roof, with multi-light function • Red and White Oval Side Reflectors (for Lawful perpendicular parking along kerbsides) • *Michelin* Tyres • *smart* Starline Alloys • Lower Front Grille Meshed with Circular Patterned Aluminium sheet – Homemade Modification • Silver Chromed Rear Axel Covers – Homemade Modification • Red Wheel Nut Covers – Homemade Modification • Front Brake Callipers and Rear Brake Drums painted Red • Silver Chrome Edging applied around Wheel Arches • Replacement 'Stubby' Aerial • Replacement Chrome 3D *smart* Badges on Front and Rear Panels • *Brabus* Handle for Rear Glass Panel • Fancy Black and Chrome Door Protectors • Red Chrome Number Plate Surround to Front • Silver Chrome Number Plate Surround to Rear • Personalised Number Plate – **P60 LKA**

Interior

• Customised Interior with Black and White 'Dalmatian' Fabric covering: Seats – Sun Visors – Door Pockets – Door Handles – Electric Window Buttons - Hand Brake Cover – Boot Cover – All custom made and fitted by owner • Black and White 'Dalmatian' style Steering Wheel Cover • Custom sprayed Air Vents and Pocket Surrounds in Silver • Polished Aluminium Hand Brake Button • Polished Aluminium Ignition Surround • Polished Aluminium Wing Mirror and Heater Controls • *smart* Parking Ticket Holder • Silver Chromed Edging applied on Cockpit Surround • Replacement Interior Bulbs with Bright Blue LEDs • *smart* Bass Bins • Replacement Alpine Speakers with Tweeters • Custom made *Evilution* MP3 cable • Silver Chromed Floor Mats

s2stealth

This is a car that was forever changing in its looks. A graphic designer by trade, and a man with a passion for the Gumball rallies inspired *s2stealth* to cover his car in authentic looking graphics, along with a matching number plate with the Gumball logo. *S2stealth*, friend and sparring partner of *s2trash*, was one of the original s2crew but has sadly sold this car during the writing of this book, another sad loss to the **smart** scene. *S2tealth* himself is famous for a) falling asleep at the drop of a hat, particularly under canvas and b) just like Felicity Kendal, has a famous rear end. Unlike Felicity Kendal, *s2stealth's* not so pert rear end has unintentionally appeared in too many DVDs made of **smart** events and luckily, so we were reliably informed, was pimple free! The s2steathmobile is now stripped back to its original specification and spookily been sold to someone in *s2trash's* home town.

Model: smart fortwo pulse coupe – Sept 2003
Colour: Jack Black/ River Silver

Engine

- 698cc • Air Scoop • **K&N** Air Filter • De-lipped Air Intake • Enlarged Intercooler Scoop • **Blindschleiche** Twin Exit Exhaust

Exterior

- **Lorinser** Speedy 17" Alloy Wheels (First set in the UK) • **Pirelli** Nero 195/40/17 Tyres • **EBC** Black Brake Pads • **Eibach** Springs • **Brabus** Front Spoiler • **S-mann** grille • **Michelak** Eye Brows • **Hella** Secondary Indicators (Lower Air Intake) • **PIAA** Blue Chrome Indicator Bulbs • **Hofle** Side Skirts • **Hyper Style** M6 Mirrors • **Brabus** Arch Extensions • Custom **Blindschleiche** Valance • Roadster **smart** Rear Badge • Blacked Out Rear Quarter Windows • Light Smoked Rear Screen • 2005 Gumball Livery Summer '05 and or Silver Doors/Corner Panels • Personalised Number Plate – **S2 SYT**

Interior

- **Blitz ID** Blue EL Illuminated Boost Gauge – Window Mounted • **Brabus** 3 Spoke Paddle Shift Steering Wheel • **Brabus** Gear Knob • **Michelak** Alloy Heater Knobs • S2Crew/ Brabus & Gumball Badging • **smart** Sound Upgrade with Speaker/Tweeters • **Caliber** Tweeters Mounted In Headrests • **Medion** GPS Navigation Unit

phildperv

Funky, fun, fantastic! Three little words that capture *phildperv's* fabulous **smart** with the red blobs! Only *phildperv* could have come up with such a simple but stunning idea and have it carried it out with so much accuracy. It cleverly mimics cartoons and realism all at once and the viewer often expects one of those naughty animated characters to step out of the car and create mayhem. Mayhem is a description that isn't far off from reality when *phildperv* himself steps out of the car! This larger than life character has a wicked sense of humour and is reputed to have been beamed to this planet from the same one that *s2trash* came from. Originally with bay grey panels, the stunning paint job on this car was done by Dave Webber at Smart-Suits, who arranged for an airbrush artist to put the finishing touches on the paint blobs to give them such a realistic 3D effect. Alongside the paintwork, *phildperv* has added many modifications, and like most that start down this road, he is now searching for a mature money tree to plant in his garden!

Model: smart fortwo passion 2004 – Mk 7

Colour: Red and silver

Engine

• 698cc • *Pipercross* Air Filter • *Digitec* Re-Map

Exterior

• De-Lipped Air Intake • Air Scoop from *thesmartclub* • Custom Paintwork by *Smart-Suits* • *MDC* Brushed Alloy Petrol Filler Flap • *S-mann* Side Skirts • *S-mann* Front Splitter • *Brabus* Monoblock VI Alloy Wheels • *Brabus* Gear Knob • Alloy Chassis End Caps • Upgraded Horn – now loud Two-Tone Horn • Custom fortwo Metal Lettering to Rear • Colour-coded Door Handle Inserts • *Blindschleiche* Exhaust • *Blindschleiche* Rear Valance • Personalised Number Plate – **S2 4TWO**

Interior

• *Brabus* Alloy Pedals • Bluetooth Hands Free Kit • Recalibrated Speedo (Up To 120mph) • *Metal Monkey* Alloy Speedo Face • Alloy Air Vents and Surrounds • Alloy Clock & Rev Counter Surrounds and Faces • Alloy Heater Knobs and Slide Faces • Alloy Gear Console Trim • Alloy Wiper Stalk Ends • Alloy Speedo Casing • Alloy Door Pockets • Alloy Door Handles • Alloy Handbrake Button • Alloy Window Buttons • *Wellsmart* Alloy Paddleshift Kit Fitted • *MDC* Dual Window Switch Upgrade • *smart* Embroidered Seat Belt Covers • *JVC* Head Unit • DIY Headrest Speaker Install • *S-mann* Dash Mounted Speaker Shelf & Upgraded Speakers • *Alpine* SWD1600 Active Sub fitted under the passenger seat • *Vauxhall Corsa* Sunglasses Holder

ZorroReturns

We happened to spot this car while making our way to the shower block at Newark 2006. Well, we say spot, it was impossible to miss it! Re-sprayed in eye throbbing luminous green paint both inside and out, and nick named 'The Green Thing', it almost takes ones breath away. The attention to detail is amazing and to see the tridion re-sprayed inside the car is most unusual. However, 'Free sunglasses supplied with every viewing' should be a notice that *ZorroReturns* should have attached to this vehicle! *S2trash* was able to capture the car in the diffused evening light that was perfect to show off the paintwork to its glorious best. This car is a perfect example of what SW Exclusive can do for your **smart** – once seen never forgotten!

Model: smart fortwo silverpulse coupé – 2005 (Mk7) Registered in Germany
Colour: Custom green

Engine

• 698cc • 61PS **SW Exclusive** Tuning = 88PS • 95Nm **SW Exclusive** Tuning = 128nm • Redline – 6,700rpm • V-max – 109mph (174km/h) • Standard 45kw Turbo • 74kw **Brabus** TIK Pipe • **SW Exclusive** fortwo Performance Tuning • Viper Kit (using Standard Side inlet)

Exterior

• **SW Exclusive** Custom Green Panels • **SW Exclusive** Custom Green Interior Dash Trims • **SW Exclusive** Custom Green Interior Roof Trims • **Brabus** Aerodynamic Font Bumper/Spoiler • **Brabus** Aerodynamic Wide Arch Kit • **Brabus** Aerodynamic Front Side Flaps • **Michalak** Eyebrow Spoilers • **smart** 17" Roadster Runline Alloy Wheels (tricky to make fit!) • Vertical Wiper Modification • **SW Exclusive** fortwo Greenline Springs • **SW Exclusive** fortwo Performance Air Scoop • **Janspeed** Twin Exit Exhaust (with catalyst)

Interior

• **Brabus** Chrome Gear Knob (soft-tip) • **Brabus** Chrome Pedals • **smart** Paddle-Shift Steering Wheel

27lennie

27lennie has been around the **smart** scene for some time and this gorgeous yellow fortwo with jigsaw graphics on the tailgate is a new project for him. What really caught our attention was his amazing custom made front air intakes. *27lennie* has designed and fitted blanking plates instead of the standard grilles, and boy does it alter the overall look of the car, giving it a sleek, no-nonsense finish. It is one of those small simple modifications that can make a huge impact and no doubt it could well be popping up on other cars in the very near future.

Model: smart fortwo passion 2003 – Mk 7

Colour: Custom yellow

Engine

• 698cc • *SW Exclusive* Re-map – 85 bhp at flywheel • 85mph speed limiter removed (speed 100mph plus) • *Brabus* Roadster Tik pipe (74) • Immobiliser

Exterior

• Custom Yellow Re-Spray • De-lipped Air Intake • Air Scoop • *SW* prototype Sports Air Filter • *Blindschleiche* Twin Centre Exit Exhaust • *SW* Stainless Rear Valance • *S-mann* Front Grille • *Brabus* Front Spoiler and mesh • Eyebrows on headlights • *CDI* Spoilers front and rear (mud flaps) • Door Handle Inserts • Custom made Front Air Intake Blanks fitted • *Brabus* Rear Arch Extensions fitted front and rear • Tinted windows • *SW* Stainless Cover on fuel cap • Short Aerial • *Bilstein* Adjustable Gas Suspension • 7"x16" *Tecnomagnesio* Alloy Wheels front and rear with spacer adaptors for 5 stud wheels • Locking wheel nuts with *SW* Centre Caps • 195/45x16 *Dunlop* Tyres on the front, and 215/35x16 on the rears • *EBC* Competition Disc Brakes with black pads • Drums and Callipers painted in yellow • Personalised Number Plate – **R10 UST**

Interior

• Clock, Rev Counter Rings, Air Vents, and Speedo Trim Surround colour-coded in custom yellow to match panel re-spray • Heated leather seats • 6 stack C/D system • Air Conditioning • Power Steering • Electric Mirrors • Tilt and slide Sun Roof

Justrules

Justrules, one of the younger members of the modifying set, is forever changing, modifying and having things done to his car that it is hard keeping tabs on him. There had already been a two panel changes on the doors, one of which was to support the England team in the World Cup and appropriately were white with a red cross. *Justrules* always has an interesting take on modifying and is always happy to chat; just don't get him started on television reality programs unless you have two free hours and some ear plugs! This is one fast **smart** that grips like a go-kart. The car has a verified top speed of 117mph using 16" alloys and with two people in it at the time!

Model: smart fortwo passion 2002
Colour: Ferrari Rosso red

Engine

• 698cc conversion on 599cc gearbox and electronics • **Brabus** Roadster Turbo, Injectors, Cam Shaft and Valve Springs • 74kw TIK Pipe • **Brabus** Clutch • Mk1 Fuel Rail and Map Sensor • De-Catted **Janspeed** Stealth Exhaust • Full sized **Pipercross** Viper • **Mocal** Intercooler Pipes • **Mocal** Oil Cooler Kit • 4 bar Fuel Pressure Regulator • Silicone HT leads • **Blitz** Turbo Timer

Exterior

• Full re-spray in **Ferrari** Rosso Red • 16" Front and 17" Rear custom painted **Brabus** Monoblock VI Alloy Wheels • **Brabus** Widestar Rear Arches • **Brabus** Front Spoiler, Spats and Front Grille

Interior

• **Brabus** roadster Leather Seats • **Brabus** leather Door Cards and Dash • **Brabus** Gear Knob, Handbrake and Pedals • **Brabus** Floor Mats • Colour coded interior set • **Metal Monkey** Brushed Metal Dials • X-Gauge

Jimmy Wong

When we started this book we had a list of some cars that we would like for the custom section but knew that by going to all of the big events during the year others would crop up; this is one of those. *Jimmy's* car reminded us of some of the early customised **smarts**, with its colour coded trim, which had been one of the 'in' things when we first appeared on the scene. *Jimmy Wong* is a very quite chap but then with a gorgeous, bright yellow car like this, you don't need to be loud to be noticed.

Model: smart fortwo passion coupé 2002
Colour: Custom yellow

Engine

• 599cc • **Digitec** Re-map • **Piper Cross** Air Filter • Flying Saucer Induction Kit • 60kW Induction Pipe • *Mocal* Silicone Intercooler Pipes • **Blindschleiche** Twin Oval Exit Exhaust • **Spin On** Oil Filter Conversion

Exterior

• **Tarox** G88 Brake Disks • **EBC Greenstuff** Pads • **Mocal** Braided Brake Hoses • **Bilstein** Streetline Suspension • **smart** Roadster Spineline Alloy Wheels • **Lorinser** Body Kit – Sides Skirts and Front Splitter • Colour Coded Bodywork • **Phillips** Bluevision Sidelights • **Osram** Diadem Indicators • **smart** Roadster Chicken Head Logo Fuel Flap • Heated Electric wing mirrors

Interior

• Foot well Lighting • LED Dash and Interior Bulbs • **Alpine** Component Speakers • Passenger Window Switch
• Paddle shift • Heated leather seats • Sound upgrade pack • CD player with 6 disc Multi-changer • Additional Side Airbags

Coolfart

Instantly recognisable as the 'Union Jack' **smart**, this car is fine example of a theme taken right to the limit! Everything about this car and its owner is linked to the British flag. From the amazing exterior paintwork right down to the custom drilled aluminium air vents and colour co-ordinated leather interior, not to mention *Coolfart's* famous Union Jack hat, trousers and even socks! Originally fabricated in vinyl on standard painted panels, this car has recently undergone an amazing transformation with a fabulous sparkly re-spray by those clever Welsh guys from Smart-Suits that took around 60 man hours of work! This car is a real crowd puller and regularly appears at **smart** meets and charity events.

Model: smart fortwo pulse 2002 – Mk 5

Colour: Red, white & blue

Engine

• 599cc • *Digitec* Re-Map • Hybrid Turbo Conversion • *Powertec* Air Filter • *S-mann* Air Scoop • *Evil Twin* Dump Valve • Iridium Plugs • Oil filter adaptor to metal canister filter

Exterior

• Panels re-sprayed in metallic colours, then coated in rainbow flake and around 12 coats of lacquer, courtesy of **smart-suits.com** • *RS* Grille – also rainbow flaked and stripe to match flag • *Lester* Front Spoiler and **smart** Arch Extensions fitted and sprayed to match Tridion and Side Skirts sprayed in blue pearl with metal flake over the top • Custom 'one-off' Rear Valance • *Blindschleiche* Exhaust • LED Indicator Repeaters • Polished Alloy Axle End Caps • 7 x 15" *Compomotive* Alloys with factory finish rainbow flake paint over black • *EBC* Discs with *'Green Stuff'* pads • Up-rated *Bilstein* Shocks and *Eibach* Lowering Springs • Personalised Number Plate – **GB TNY**

Interior

• Seats, Door Panels and Dash re-trimmed in red and blue leather with white piping • Blue décor Kit to Dash • Brit-Tiny logo on Custom Floor Mats and Seat Belt Pads • Brit-Tiny logo Engraved Alloy Plates to Door Sills, Inside Tailgate and Gear Change Plate • *Metal Monkey* Stainless Steel Dial Inserts with Blue Numerals • Stainless Steel Heater Inserts • Alloy Heater Control Knobs and Handbrake Button • Alloy Rings to Central Dials and Air Vents • Custom, 'one off' Alloy 'Flag' Air Vents • Button Gearshift to Steering Wheel • X-Gauge installed in Clock Pod • Blue Alloy Tax Disc Holder, Wipers and Aerial • *Panasonic* CD Player with additional Speakers under seats

Bubski

This was the first fortwo that *s2trash* had ever been in that could reach 110mph! No wonder that *Bubski's* **smart** was named after a German WWII rocket, the V2, as it certainly goes like one. *Bubski* has been on the **smart** scene for a long time and has become a close friend of both *s2trash* and *Miss P*, turning up to most of the organised events that there has ever been. He gets affectionately teased about his chilled-out manner and is often heard muttering the phrases 'Hey man', 'Hello dude' and 'What's up?' With his long involvement with **smarts** he has certainly had plenty of time to make the myriad of modifications to his car that you can see below, turning it into one hell of a ride! Photographed here with green front and back wings instead of its normal all black panels, it gives it a very striking pose. It just goes to show that by swapping standard panels around you can instantly give the car a whole new look. If you can manage to mutually swap your panels with another owner, you can achieve a completely different look for free. Panel swapping is normally a feature on most **smart** car website forums, so keep an eye out for them and reincarnate your car!

Model: smart fortwo pulse – May 2001

Colour: Jack black

Engine

• 599cc • *Red Dot* Racing Custom Re-Map • *Red Dot* Racing Brake Discs • *Red Dot* Racing Black Brake Pads • *Venom* Air Filter with Relocated ECU • 74kw TIK Pipe • Roadster 80bhp Turbo • *Janspeed* Intercooler Pipes • *Janspeed* Stealth Exhaust • *SPAX* Adjustable Suspension (Ride Height/ Dampening) • *SmartShift* Paddle Shift (Original *Smarttronik* PCB)

Exterior

• Go Faster Sun Strip • Vertically Parked *Michalak* Aero Twin Wipers • Meshed Service Grilles • Black Eyebrows • Front Indicator Diffusers removed • Front Chrome Indicator Bulbs • *S2Stealth's* Black Headlight Interior • Big Front Grille •

Meshed Lower Grille • Ring Micro Driving Lights (E Marked) • Personalised Number plate **V2 BUB** • Black Number Plate Surround • *Digitec* Front Spoiler • Wheel Bolt Hole Plugs • *S-mann* Side Skirts • Black Rear Lock Cover • Black *Digitec* Rear Valance • Cool Smart Parts Didion End Caps • Black Painted Rear Brake Drums / Drive Shafts • *Maximus* Air Intake • Black Bee Sting Aerial

Interior

• Light Smoke Window Tint on Sides, Rear Quarters and Rear • *Lockwood* 120mph Speedo Face Plate • Brushed Metal *Richbrook* Tax Disc Holder and Handbrake Handle • Big Rear View Mirror • Big Gear Knob • Black *Michalak* Air Vents • *Michalak* Boot Panel Storage/Luggage Net • *Smart* Bass Boxes • *Smart* Mobile Phone Console • Door Mounted Phone Holder • Black Carpeted Speaker Vents • Black Spray Painted Speedo Ring, XGauge Ring, Stalk Caps, Gear Shift Surrounds, Ignition Key Surround and Safety Island

Electrical mods

• XGauge • *Smarttronik* Passenger Window Switch • Hard Wired Extendable Phone Charger • Hardwired 1.5v SD Card WMA Player • *Evilution* MP3 Lead • Custom 4 Way LED Switch replacing **smart** 12V Socket • Custom Enclosure housing 3 Regulated Power Supplies • Extendable 12V Socket • Relocated Softouch Button • Relocated Interior Light Switch • Relocated Fig Light Button • Switch to Disable Trust and then Enable XGauge • Hardwired Temperature Sensor (Pre Intercooler Pipe) • Hardwired Temperature Sensor (Air Above Intercooler Array) • Hardwired Temperature Sensor (Post Intercooler Pipe) • Hardwired Temperature Sensor (*Venom* Air Filter Casing) • Hardwired Temperature Sensor (Engine Bay Air Near Side) • Hardwired Temperature Sensor (Engine Bay Air Off Side) • *Nautilus* Air Horn

Evilution

Evilution is fast becoming one of the hottest modders in the UK, contributing to the designing and fitting of most of the parts himself. This guy is a font of **smart** knowledge which he willingly shares with others by hosting his own web site www.evilution.co.uk

If you have a problem with your **smart** looking here first could save you a lot of time and trouble. Both s*2trash* and *Miss P* have cured problems on their cars by using the amazing wealth of information he has put together and have saved trips to garages and shed loads of cash. The only thing pure about his car though is the name of the model! This could be the fastest pure in the UK, so if you are near Dartford late at night and an all black **smart** spitting hell fire and brimstone flies past you, it could be *Evilution*… or the Devil himself!

Model: smart fortwo pure coupé 2003 – Mk 7

Colour: All black

Engine

• 698cc • Decorative Engine plate • **Wiltec** Sequential Dump Valve • **ITG** Filter • Custom **Red Dot** Re-Map

Exterior

• **Lorenser** Front Splitter • **S-mann** Side Skirts • **Blindschleiche** Twin Oval Exhaust and Matching Valance • **S-mann** Top Spoiler • **Carbontec** Scoop • Headlight Eyebrows • **smart** Arch Extensions • 16" **Adikt** Alloys Powder Coated in Black (incl. 3-5 stud converters) • Tinted Rear and Side Indicators • LED Focus Style Repeaters in front of the wing mirrors • Shortened Aerial • Tinted Windows • **Michelak** Smooth Wipers • Tinted Show Plates • De-badged and roadster "smart" badge applied to back • Quick Fill Fuel Filler Cap • "Evil Inside" Domed Resin Badges on Side Skirts

• Personalised Number Plate – **S2 RCO**

Interior

• X-Gauge • Leather 3 Spoke Steering Wheel • Paddle Gear Shift • Roadster Leather Heated Seats • Smaller Rear View Mirror • Stainless Steel Speedo, Revs and Clock Gauge Faces • Metal Heater Control Covers • Aluminium Handbrake Button • **Ripspeed** Handbrake Cover • Padded Neoprene Draw Insert • Aluminium **Evilution** Kick Strips • Aluminium Heater Pods • Aluminium Heater Surrounds • Aluminium Pod Surrounds • Aluminium **Evilution** Gear Shift Plate • Aluminium Handbrake Base Decoration • Metal Wing Mirror Adjuster Covers • 8-Ball Handbrake Knob • Aluminium Chair Inserts • Aluminium Stalk Ends • Knurled Brushed Metal Stereo Volume Knob • Blue LED Interior Lights • M-station 10gig MP3 Player • **Grundig** Compact Subwoofer • External **Tomtom** Aerial and Custom Centre Console Mount • **Vauxhall** Sunglasses Holder

smint roadster

As one of the Smartimes contributers cars, this must be the UK's most highly original modified roadster, from the gorgeous sminty blue re-spray to the amazing re-modelled rear end and front section that appears to be in one piece. Having used bucket loads of body filler, fibreglass and cash, *smint roadster* managed to achieve this fabulous look mostly within the confines of his spare room! It also took a great deal of determination, time and skill and it shows. Finished off with a groovy re-spray by Smarts R us, his radically different roadster certainly shouts out 'Oi! Look at me!'

Model: smart roadster 2003

Colour: Porsche Peppermint

Engine

• 698cc • Air temperature sensor bracket and shield blocking intake removed • *Pipercross* MkII Air Filter • *Smartarse Design* Re-Map

Exterior

• Colour-coded Headlamp Surrounds • Custom Front Grille with modular *Hella* indicators mounted behind • Main Beam Lamps replaced with model incorporating side lights • Bonnet Badge removed • Smoothed side repeater and aerial holes • Gloss Black *DTM* Mirrors with built in indicators mounted on customised standard mirror quarters • Gloss Black Plastic Panels above door handles • *Brabus* side skirts • Gloss Black Plastic Spoiler Trim • Shark Fin Aerial fitted to plastic spoiler trim • Smoothed and colour-coded rear Number Plate Panel • *Lester* rear valance smoothed into rear panels • Exhaust Valance Panels replaced with mesh • Rear Number Plate relocated to mesh between panels and valance and illuminated by a universal lamp • Boot Badge removed • Colour-coded Boot Hinge Covers • All panels and colour-coded parts re-sprayed in *Porsche* Peppermint • 15" x 7" *Compomotive ML* Alloy Wheels powder coated in gloss black • 195/50 Front Tyres & 205/50 Rear Tyres • Rear Wheels spaced out by 10mm each side • Lowered 40mm on Eibach springs

Interior

• Brushed Aluminium Heater Controls • Brushed Aluminium Stalk Trims • Silver Gear Stick Surround • Silver Speedometer Peak • Brushed Aluminium *MOMO King* Gear Knob • Gear Shaft shortened by 30mm • Door Cards trimmed in Black *Alcantara* • Dash Tops trimmed in Black *Alcantara* • Polished Aluminium Drilled Gear Change Paddles • Underside of boot lid features decals of products and companies used • *Pioneer* P77MP head unit • *Apple iPod* located in central air vent connected to head unit • *Kenwood* KSC-WA62RC amplified sub-woofer in passenger foot well behind stealth board • *JBL* GTO-525e 2-way door speakers • *Pioneer* tweeters mounted in 'A' pillars

smint roadster's famous rear end

Smarts-R-Us

Unlike all the other cars in this section, this gold roadster coupé was customised by the garage with the intention of selling it. 'Goldfrapp' is the name of this demonstrator car, and we can see why. 'We love the band Goldfrapp and it's the perfect name for this sensational car, said Paul Holmes as the spotty pair stood and drooled over it. 'We combined Exclusive Line paint with Lambo doors and BBS wheels to create this showstopper', and that is exactly what it is. Both Paul and Liam love the car so much that they have now decided to keep it. Not only is the outside of the car great to look at, the inside is fantastic too; with new upholstery custom made in black, yellow and grey and colour-coded accessories.

The performance is about 115bhp with a top speed of about 125mph, so it is pretty nifty too! Smarts R us were the first company in the UK to fit Lambo doors to a **smart.** In 2005 they went to Germany and collected the first set of LSD Lambo doors and fitted them to a bright yellow customed sprayed roadster and proved to the **smart** community just how well these elegant looking doors suited the car; and as the evidence shows, it finishes off the whole car to a tee.

Model: smart roadster coupé 2005

Colour: Suzuka Sun yellow

Engine

• 698cc • *Evil Twin* Hybrid Turbo • *Powertec* Induction Kit • *Evil Twin* ECU Re-Map

Exterior

• *LSD* Lambo doors • *Standox* Exclusive Line Limited Edition Suzuka Sun paint on panels, tridion • Special paint treatment of rear quarter lights • *Gangs Jail* exhaust • *S-mann* rear valance and stainless vents • *Hi-Spec* 4 pot brake calipers and 2 piece ventilated disks • *Bilstein* Streetline suspension • *BBS* wheels with *Dunlop* SP9000 Tyres • *Philips* Blue Vision Light Bulbs

Interior

• Custom made *Evil Twin* Interior with black Leather, grey *Alcantara* and yellow Piping • *Sony* Head Unit with a 6 CD changer • *Focal* Speakers with Tweeters in the pillars • *JVC* Sub under passenger seat • *MDC* Alloy Fuel Intake

Drageron

Drageron (or *Snozy* as he is also known as), must be one of the most humorous **smart** owners there is. He attends all the big meets and has become very good friends of both *s2trash* and *Miss Polkadot*. Full of hysterically funny jokes and anecdotes, this man can have your sides splitting for hours on end. As only one of only five cars in the country right now with a Clever End fitted (basically a single storey extension so you can carry more **smart** stuff), this car is a real head turner and a real passion wagon; as that is what its owner has in abundance for this car, passion. It is full to the brim with gadgets and gismos but all with the aim of those special words – comfort and speed. Compared to a standard **smart**, driving this vehicle is like floating on marshmallows, a real comfy ride. However, despite the laid back attitude, this beautifully modified car was recently verified doing 0-60mph in a top time of 5.2 seconds!

Model: smart fortwo Passion – September 2003 – Mk 7

Colour: Star blue

Engine

- 698cc Roadster Engine • Roadster Turbo • **Red Dot** Custom Re-Map • *Viper* Induction Kit • **Brabus** TIK Pipe • **Magnecor** Competition Silicon Ignition Leads • **Janspeed** Intercooler Pipes • Oil Cooler • Spin-On Oil Filter • **Bonalume** Performance Clutch

Exterior

- **Clever End** Storage Extension • **Janspeed** Stealth Exhaust • **Red Dot** Personalised Brake Disks (with name engraved) • **Red Dot** Brake Pads • Braided and covered Brake Pipes • **RS** Springs 40mm drop • **Bilstein** Street Line Shocks • **smart** 3 Spoke strikeline 15" Alloy Wheels • **Bridgestone** 175 55 R15 Tyres on Front • **Yokohama** 195 50 R15 Tyres on Rear • 10mm Spacers on Front Wheels • Switched Fog/Brake lights in Chassis Tube Ends • **Oriace** Valance with Red LED Lighting • 14" **Loco** Air Horns • **S-Mann** scoop with de-lipped Air Intake • Silver colour-coded Fuel Filler Flap • Silver Eyebrows • Stainless Steel Valve Caps • **Bosche** Wipers • Polished Stainless Dummy Rear Disks • Chrome Mirror Covers • Chrome **S-Mann** Grille • Chrome Indicator Light Surrounds • Chrome Door Handles • Chrome Door Handle Surrounds • **S-mann** Front Spoiler • **S-mann** Side Skirts • Front Indicator Diffusers Removed • Blue **Enigma** Indicator Bulbs Front and Rear

Interior

- Polished and Dimpled Silver Speedo, Pod and Air Vent Rings • Polished and Dimpled Heater, Fan and Ventilation Buttons • Polished and Dimpled Indicator and Wiper Stalk End Caps • Chrome Window Button and Door Catch Covers • Polished and Slotted Air Vent Balls • Chrome Hexagonal Tax Disk Holder

Kym1959

As a lover of stunning jewellery *Kym1959* has transferred her passion with bling onto her beloved roadster, which is called the *Chameleon*. With an incredibly beautiful full body re-spray (over the original glance grey panels) using Rage Illusion Flip paint, both inside and out, Lamborghini style doors and fabulous wheels, this car is a fantasy come true. With her fine attention to detail *Kym1959* has recently had the roadster's seats re-upholstered in purple and green leather with a customised chameleon embroidered into the backs.

Model: smart roadster 2003
Colour: Green, purple, gold

Engine

• 698cc • *Smarts R us Evil Twin* Re-Map • *Bailey* Dump Valve • *Blindschleiche* Twin Pipe Exhaust

Exterior

• *LSD* Lambo Doors • *Smarts R us* Complete Body Re-spray inside and out with Green to Purple *Rage* Illusion Flip Paint with *Spectra-Flair* Rainbow Fleck Lacquer • 17" *BK* Racing High Power Wheels • 3 to 5 Wheel Stud Converters • *Tarox* Brake Discs • Black *EBC* Brake Pads • *Eibach* Lowering Springs • Front and Side Chrome Bars • *MDC* Chrome Petrol Filler Cap • *Michalak* Chrome Wing Mirror Covers • Chrome Lettering To Rear • Fog Lights • Light Sensor • Rain Sensing Wipers • *Evil Twin* Rear Spoiler • *S-mann* Custom Air Vent

Interior

• Full Custom Interior in Green & Purple Leather including Dashboard and Doors • Cruise Control • Trip Computer • Front and Side Airbags • Electric/Heated Mirrors • Leather Sports Steering Wheel • Paddle Change Gearshift • ABS • Electric Windows and Roof • Air Conditioning • Heated Leather Seats • CD/Cup Holder • *Pioneer* Head Unit • *Pioneer* 150w Amp/Sub Woofer • *Infinity* Speakers

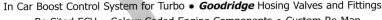
This has to be the most extreme version of a **smart** you will ever see! A fully qualified engineer and sports photographer, formally working in the world of Superbike racing, *s2Eagleye*, more recently becoming the manager of Smartarse Design, Watford; has taken the rule book on modifying **smarts** and used it as loo paper! There is not a millimetre of this car that he probably hasn't tweaked, tuned or transformed. The engine is a sight to behold, protected behind a Perspex cover so that it may be admired as the work of art that it is. Meticulously painted in red and blue with shiny metal pipes, there is not a micron of dirt anywhere to be seen. It is astounding, as is the whole car full stop! At best this highly modified **smart** will only manage 20 mpg. Want to see a **smart** do a wheelie? This one can, along with removing the tarmac off the road at the same time! We once drove behind this car on way to an event; to see it pull away just leaves you breathless, as it quickly becomes a dot on the distant horizon. Talk to *s2Eagleye* and you will soon discover what a really nice guy he is and the passion he has for the car, but at the same time he will never make you feel uncomfortable for having a standard car, always giving advice freely with a smile. The **smart** scene has certainly become part of his life; he even spent the day after his wedding at an event! This man is truly dedicated and a legend in his own oil sump!

Model: smart fortwo passion 2001 – LHD
Colour: Phat red and metallic black tridion

Engine

• 599cc • **BMC** Carbon Fibre Cold Air Induction • Hybrid **Mitsubishi** Turbo on Race Tuned 3 Branch Manifold • **Samco** Silicon and Aluminium Intake and Intercooler Pipes • **Baileys** Dump Valve (to be replaced with **HKS** Re-circulating type) • Modified Throttle Body • Modified Injector Rail • Different Injectors • Modified Fuel Pressure Regulator • **Kent** Race Cam • Later Valves and Springs • **Magnecor** Silicon Race Leads • **Denso** Iridium Spark Plugs (2 Heat Ranges) • One Off Exhaust Down Pipe from Turbo • Titanium **Akrapovic** Exhaust • Add on Oil Cooler and Spin On Filter • Add on Oil Catch Tank (from Nissan Skyline) for Turbo • **TFI** Techlusion System to add an extra 10% of fuel through Injectors •

In Car Boost Control System for Turbo • **Goodridge** Hosing Valves and Fittings • Re-Sited ECU • Colour Coded Engine Components • Custom Re-Map • Was tested on Dyno machine at 110BHP at 1.5 Bar

Exterior

• **Schmidt** 16" Wheels • **Toyo** Proxy T1R Tyres 195/50/16 Front 215/45/16 Rear • One off Adjustable Aluminium Dampers • Lowering Springs and Modified Front Suspension • Adjustable Aluminium Rear Strut Braces • Strengthening Interior Chassis Stainless Strut • Rear 30mm Spacers • **Red Dot Racing** Machined Discs • **Red Dot Racing** Race Compound Pads • **Goodridge** Brake Hosing • Modified **Konigseder** Front Spoiler • **Michalak** Quad Headlights • Carbon Fibre Front Grille • Painted Front Vents • Front Arches with Carbon Fibre Flame Inlay and Back Lit with Fibre Optics • Side Skirts • Racing Side Skirt Wings • Modified Rear Wide Arch Kit • Modified Rear Centre Section with Extra Venting • Carbon Fibre Adjustable Top Wing • LED Rear Light Clusters • Stainless Rear Valance Surround • Quick Fill Petrol Cap Mounted in Carbon Fibre • Aluminium 60mm Intake System • All Windows Tinted • All Panels where possible Colour Matched • Under Car Million Colour LED System

Interior

• Red **Corbeau** Carbon Fibre GRP Seats • 3 Point **Luke** Harnesses • All Interior Colour Coded to Match Outside • Black Cloth Dash and Inner Door Panels • Leather Steering Wheel • **Michalak** Alloy Clock and Vent Surrounds • **Michalak** Alloy Knobs on Switch Gear • Perspex Transparent Engine Cover • Aluminium Floor Plates • **HKS** Turbo Timer and Rev Counter • **Turbosmart** Boost Control System • **SPA** Electronic Boost Gauge and Temperature Gauge in Carbon Fibre Pod • Gear Shift Lights • 3 Electronic Temperature Gauges for Engine Bay, Oil Cooler and Intercooler • **Simoni** Racing Pedals • **Simoni** Racing Hand Brake Lever • In Car/Under Car LED Control Unit • Master Override Switch • Blue Back Lit Dials • Blue Interior Lighting • **Kenwood** Graphic Head Unit • Carbon Fibre Speakers with Directional Tweeters • Under Dash Bass Boxes

T1NY W

How on earth *T1NY W* has fitted so much into this car is beyond us and most others that look at it. He has owned this car for the past five years and cheerfully admits to shelling out a staggering £20k plus during that time on his incredible and unique modifications! Another of our longstanding **smart** friends, *T1NY W* is an extremely experienced modifier, and every time we see this car something new pops up, lights up, or lifts up, and we just stand there and marvel at what he has achieved. Following the route *T1NY W* has taken we can honestly say that there isn't another **smart** in the UK to match it with its mixture of light show, fairground ride and entertainment centre on wheels. Just read this specification list and your jaw will drop at how much work has gone into it. *T1NY W* once said that the only reason he had a re-map was to get the car to move under all the weight he had added, including the two batteries required to run the thing! We are sure that at some stage a jet engine will appear strapped on the back with retractable wings and have the ability to sail the high seas! This is certainly a car that every **smart** owner should make the effort to see in the dark; it really is a mesmerising work of fantasy!

Model: smart fortwo passion cabrio 2001

Colour: Silver

Engine

• 599cc • Air Scoop • Modified Air Intake • Performance Air Filter • Development Re-map – 96.3 bhp • Performance Plugs • Delimited & Traction Control Removed • Aftermarket exhaust removed (too noisy, removed to enjoy the stereo) • Dump valve removed (as above)

Exterior

• 17" x 8" Alloy Wheels • Full Air Suspension • Custom Painted Bodywork • Colour Keyed Plastic Parts • Modified Front Spoiler, Side Skirts and Rear Valance • Nickel Carbon Air Intake and Fuel Cap • Wheel Arches and Body work stretched and modified to suit 17" wheels • **Brabus** grille • Totally rebuilt Head Lights, including: Hand cut Angel Eyes, Custom Neon Side Light Bars, 2 Million Colour LED's, Emergency 360w Strobe Lights Strobe Lights also fitted to the rear lights Chrome Mirror Bulbs and modified housings front and rear • Total under body LED lighting, digitally remote controlled with 2 million colours and computer-controlled sound activated patterns including wheel arches, grille and engine area totally lit and digitally linked together • Billet Alloy Chassis Caps • Aperiodic Membrane venting under car • LED Strobe Lights mounted under boot lip and in lower front panel • Fog Lights replaced with 2 Million Colour LED's • Personalised Number Plate **T1NY W**

Interior

• Full multimedia installation with two 15" widescreen TV's

– **TV1** motorises out of the dash, which required cutting, moving and relocating of blower and air conditioning components, rerouting of wiring etc.

- **TV2** is a 15" screen in a custom amplifier rack, which can slide to allow full access to the engine for servicing • Amp Rack includes 2 modified amplifiers and with the 15" screen in between them, clip hinged to allow quick access to circuit breakers and IASCA competition standard wiring • Totally Modified, Hand Built Dashboard including: a) 7" Focal Utopia Mid Bass Speakers, floating in custom thick tinted (glass look) Perspex and stainless steel movable enclosures b) 17" Horn Speakers mounted vertically into the lead edge of the custom dash c) 10" Sub Bass Speaker mounted through the passenger floor, with the floor metal work cut out and replaced with an under floor speaker enclosure, with a hand built fibreglass & steel, moulded Aperiodic membrane enclosure • Two Gel Batteries relocated under the car, in hand crafted steel cradles with all the cars wiring replaced to suit • Quick disconnect plug to allow power at indoor car shows • 2000w **Dolby Digital** 5.1 DTS Surround Stereo • **Alpine** Head Unit • **Alpine** DVD Player • **Alpine** 31 band Digital EQ, crossover & time alignment • Fibre Optic interconnecting cables • Totally Digital Dash – All clocks and displays replaced with a 7" touch screen monitor, controlling a custom built computer system, which includes: **1** - GPS Tracking, Voice guided satellite navigation, WIFI networking, 3G GPRS Mobile Internet Access, Wireless Keyboard & Gyroscopic Mouse, Bluetooth, DVD cdrw slot loading drive fitted into the central air vent and LCD Dash Readout Display including speed, RPM, boost etc. **2** - Centre Channel Speaker also fitted into central air vent and custom hidden switch panel • All lit up with 2 million colour changing, digital, remote controlled LED lights, including headrest lights, under dash, floor mounted and front scanner • **Brabus** steering wheel • Custom Steering Wheel Mounted Button Shift • Large amounts of sound deadening • **Brabus** Alloy Pedals • **Ipod** connection

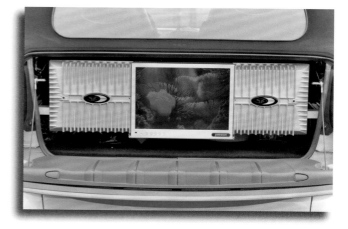

Security

• 3 Alarms - including Microwave Proximity Sensors, Smart Windows, remote activation of lights, strobe's, windows etc and anti hijack • Tracking System • Custom modified and plated – locks removed • Additional Sirens • Alarm Status Displays fitted into headlights • Hand built Strobe Light Interface (360w strobe lights fire when alarm is triggered)

8 Interesting smart Stuff

The smart world of Advertising

Over the past few years, **smarts** have come into their own as a highly effective method of advertising. All manner of businesses have blazoned their corporate images upon this distinctive vehicle and all have said how invaluable it has proved. This eye catching car just on its own attracts recognition even before the graphics are applied, so no wonder it has become a winner for advertising gurus. As contributors to Smartimes magazine we have produced many articles and photographs of such cars under the heading of *'Working smarts'*. The companies that use this form of advertising are so diverse, from yacht sales, air conditioning, shoe shops and insurance. Their design themes too have to be admired for their style, and, in a lot of cases their tongue-in-cheek humour. One presumes that goes with the territory of **smart** ownership; well it does with all the owners we know anyway! On a more serious side the **smart** has become a tool for the people, with local government bodies and public services such as the AA, Paramedics, Fire Brigade, and even the London Metropolitan Police getting in on the act and purchasing **smarts** 'for-the-use-of'. People will no doubt laugh at this tiny car in its public duty robes of office, (seeing a **smart** dressed up in Met livery with a flashing light on top does tend to make one smile), but it certainly provides a big service, which the following article will just go to prove.

Essex Police 'Crimestoppers' Smart Cars

The Central Division of Essex Police currently has 9 **smart** cars, the majority of which have been purchased with the aid of funding from the local councils when it becomes available. The first of these vehicles was purchased in 2004. The newest additions are two vehicles that have been sponsored by Braintree District Council. The whole fleet of Essex smarts are un-modified Pulse models, in either black, white or Stream Green colourways. Helen Jerrold, Communications & Media Officer from the Planning & Performance Unit Central Division said that the Police thought that the cars were very "green", and this was an important consideration when deciding to purchase vehicles. 'Like any responsible fleet we are constantly looking to reduce our impact on the environment, although suitability for the role will always be the deciding factor. The other unique advantage of these cars is that all the panels are interchangeable. This allows us to have different colour schemes or liveried messages, just by changing the body panels. Because we have different body kits, there is also a perception that we have more of the cars than we actually do. As the **smart** cars are a unique shape they are eye catching and quickly identifiable too, and, if you pardon the pun, the smart car certainly fits the bill!' Heather Owen and Mick Joslin are the Police Community Support Officers from the Maldon Community Policing Team that drive the **smarts** around *Miss Polkadot's* local area, which covers the six villages of: Tollesbury, Tolleshunt D'Arcy, Tolleshunt Knights, Tolleshunt Major, Goldhanger and Mayland. *Miss Polkadot* first met PCSO Heather Owen in 2005 when she was organizing a mobile traffic speed check in a village near to where *Miss Polkadot* lives. Before you gasp, you can rest assured that it

Ocean Yachts

House to house call

Checking all is well

wasn't at the end of a speed gun that they first interacted! Heather was parked up in a lay-by observing the data recorder when *Miss P* decided to pull up and say hello to a fellow *smart* driver. Having such a highly visible car as hers, it pays to keep on the right side of the law! *Miss Polkadot* had already been giving the two *smart* police cars the odd 'flash' of her headlights now and then when she saw them and so she thought she had better say hello and try and prove to them that she wasn't totally round the bend.

PCSO Heather Owen did a degree in Psychology and Criminology at Lincoln University before joining Chelmsford town police as a constable 2 years ago. Heather decided that she was more 'community' minded and decided to make the shift to Police Community Support Officer just over a year ago. Little did she know she would be driving a nifty **smart** for a living! Thoroughly enjoying the community contact, she spends the majority of each shift patrolling the streets, talking to and reassuring people, preventing and deterring any possible crime rather than responding to incidents. Heather explained that in the role of PCSC, she is able to take a more pro-active approach to policing, whilst the PC's will more often have to deal with the results of crimes that have already been committed. Heather and her fellow colleagues all work within specific areas of the local community. They put the cars to good use when conducting area searches and house-to-house enquiries, and they get to know the individuals that often cause problems. As they largely deal with antisocial behavior incidents and often know the youths involved, their local knowledge acts as a huge deterrent with any future interactions with the local kids! 'Local trouble-makers cannot provide false details to a PCSO and sometimes it scares them into thinking twice about committing an offence, as they are well aware that we know their personal details! It is vital to be approachable, noticeable and visible whilst on the beat – and nothing fills those criteria better than a **smart**. It is certainly a great talking point'. In this local area there are two **smarts** on the beat, a lite white and a stream green Pulse. Both carry eye-catching livery with the 'Crimestoppers' theme and sometimes with additional local council decals.

'My PCSO partner Mick Joslin drives the white **smart**, but everyone knows that I drive the green and black one', says Heather, 'and I have been tragically bestowed the unfortunate nickname of the "Wheelie-bin" cop, which seems to have really stuck with the locals. I sometimes wish I had the white one!'

Heather is often asked to bring the 'Crimestoppers' **smart** along to local village fêtes and fairs because it is now a recognisable tool for the local police.

"Sometimes my inferiority complex gets fed when people ask more questions about the car than they do about local policing issues! There is one small negative issue that I have on being asked to village fêtes, and that is I'm often asked to help with traffic control at these events - which inevitably means providing signs or cones. The boot space just never seems big enough. My current record is being able to get 2 large signs and 12 Traffic cones in the boot space, plus the odd pair of handcuffs! So, as far as providing a tool for showing that I'm out and about, the **smart** obviously works as a fantastic talking point and advert for Crimestoppers. As to instilling fear and dread into the local community when I arrive at the scene of an incident – hardly! But sometimes kids have been so shocked when we turn up that it helps to break the ice and get positive results from an incident!" Now that is **smart**! Heather has one last comment to make about **smarts** and their drivers, and it is something that we will not relish hearing. Apparently, it is actually an offence under the 'Construction and Use Regulations Act', to flash one's headlights at another driver in acknowledgement or greeting!

smart owners – You have been warned – Frantic waving and not flashing should now be compulsory!

Kinder Egg Smarts

"Over the next two years, the number of smart fortwo coupé, forfour, roadster-coupé and crossblade models in circulation will increase by no less than 40 million!"

This would have been a headline from heaven if it had come from the financial department at **smart** head office. Instead it refers to the staggering number of petite model **smart** cars that were put inside 40 million chocolate Kinder Surprise eggs produced by the confectionery manufacturer Ferrero in August 2004.

In a very **smart** collaboration with Ferrero, **smart** GmbH agreed to the production of faithful miniature reproductions of their full-size cars, which came complete with interiors and accurate wheels. All of the models had painted **smart** logos and tail lights and transparent headlight inserts, except of course the crossblade, which doesn't come with those in real life.

The fortwo and crossblade models which were produced to approximately 1:70 scale, were small enough to fit into the Kinder Egg's plastic yellow capsule in their entirety. The roadster coupé and forfour, produced for some reason at approximately 1:74 scale were just a tad too large, and so they came in little bits that the finder could have fun putting together themselves. Although it is obvious that the procedure isn't rocket science, the roadster coupé which came in two sections and the forfour that came in four pieces, both required the finder to read a set of instructions on how to snap together the assembled parts along with some adult supervision.

One tends to forget that these chocolate eggs were initially aimed at children and not at grown ups. But grown ups tended to be the ones that bought them this time round, they weren't interested in the chocolate either, just in getting the **smarts**!

Having said that, despite 40 million of them being churned out over a period of two years, they seemed to be remarkably thin on the ground here in the UK, despite some frenetic searching by obsessive car owners. Unless you purchased a Kinder Surprise egg that was sitting in a special **smart** promotional display box, it was impossible to tell if the egg being bought stood any chance of containing a much-in-demand model. Many a disappointed adult with tell-tale crumbs of two layered chocolate on their faces, could be seen sulking along Britain's high streets. Many **smart** owners in search of these eggs often resorted to gluttony and perilous overspending in a desperate attempt to find one. There were whole topics on the website forums devoted to where the best places to buy the eggs were, and of course there were always the few gloating that they did indeed have the whole set!

Indeed, such was the demand for these tiny toys it was amazing that no-one had been mugged for their haul. In their infinite wisdom, **smart** GmbH sent some UK **smart** dealers whole boxes of the eggs to distribute as they saw fit. When word got out and addresses of dealers with eggs were posted on the forums, some named dealers were suddenly overcome by 'over-interested potential car buyers', who had just turned up to swipe the eggs!

"We are initiating long-term cooperation with Ferrero because it supports our goal of using unusual and innovative marketing channels for Smart," said Philipp Schiemer, vice president of marketing and sales at Smart. He went on to say, *"Ferrero is an ideal partner for us because the products of this brand have an extremely positive image and express a great deal of joie de vivre, just like the cars we have at Smart."*

Ferrero and **smart** surely had no inkling, when they started this promotion, of the lengths folks would go to, to acquire their products. Still, Ferrero did well to sell 40 million chocolate eggs; pity **smart** didn't sell 40 million cars!

Photo courtesy of DCUK Media Archive

Kinder Egg smarts

The C7 Kit Car

What you see here is a fantastic kit car based on the **smart** fortwo coupé. More than 50 years after the invention of the Lotus Super Seven, Shelby Cobra and the three-wheeler Morgan, Bernd Michalak, of Michalak Design has awoken the senses for sports car enthusiasts and **smart** car lovers with this amazing kit car design for a two seater roadster. Using the carcass of a worn out **smart** fortwo, you can turn your conventional production automobile into an exclusive and unique sports car with relative ease, that offers more driving pleasure than other many factory models do. As you might have guessed it, both *Miss Polkadot* and *s2trash* have had a drive in both the first and second C7 prototypes and for *s2trash*, the extra leg room that it provided made the car a pure comfort zone compared to the original **smart** roadster. The C7 felt much lighter than the **smart** roadster, but then it was a full open top version and it wasn't sporting a hard top roof. It felt very tight to drive with nice direct steering, reacting instantly to the turn of the wheel, and despite the very small windscreen didn't feel too exposed. It certainly makes for a fun drive and definitely has the smiley factor just like the rest of the **smart** family of cars, which is what driving something like this is all about. At the end of the summer in 2006 the first production version of the C7 was completed. It was a steep learning curve building the two prototypes and several detailed modifications were made to enhance the new model. New lights front and rear, a new one piece grille, a modified rear panel, side air intakes, new mirrors, new door handles, a re-styled dash and a full windscreen were amongst the changes. The C7 now has weather gear too. Bernd Michalak has created an innovative roof system which incorporates a removable windscreen and an ingenious buttress fitment system. November 2006 saw the first customer's car built and registered in the UK by Smarts R us in Nottingham. With the demise of the **smart** roadster this could be a good alternative for anyone wanting a **smart** powered car built to their specification. With the choice of engines and new gear box in the new G3 fortwo launched in November 2006, there is greater scope for this car and no reason not to have a diesel version.

Every C7 kit consists of a robust fibreglass body that is stretched over a computer-designed and crash tested tube chassis frame that includes the floorboards.

The entire body is virtually produced in one whole piece. Only at a much later stage are the doors and bonnet finally fitted. Initially, the C7 will be available either as a classic two seater roadster or as the one seater open-wheeled Clubsport version. After that, hard and soft-top models are planned as well as the Shooting-Break model, a two-door estate car. Michalak Design has developed instrument panels and door skins unique to every model. Above and beyond that, the C7 can be had with special Recaro seats, aluminium wheels from 6x15 to 9x17 and Xenon headlights.

Under the stainless and fibre reinforced plastic body, Michalak Design incorporates trusted production technology from the **smart** fortwo. Parts such as axles, engine and transmission, seats and instruments; all are used without any modifications. "This way a used or even crashed micro-car can turn into a new sports car with a few twists of the wrench", says developer Bernd Michalak. The actual assembly of the C7 is quite easy and not a problem even for beginners. This is due to the fact that no special tools are required nor are a vehicle hoist or welding skills necessary. All the parts either snap together or are screwed together and can be assembled in a few hours after work within about a week. 'If you can put together a bedroom dresser from a Swedish furniture store, you'll have no problem assembling the C7', the developer promises. Nevertheless, Michalak Design, together with *Smarts R us* in the UK and several other partner companies in Germany, Canada and Australia, will offer professional support during assembly to those requiring expert advice or who just can't be bothered with the DIY. Customers that don't have the space in their own garage can even have their C7 assembled at a workshop. Here, the manufacturer will carry out a final inspection. In addition, the company will support customer's on location with registration and certification of the vehicles. For instance, in Germany co-operation is planned with the AvD Automobile Club. They will accompany completed C7's along with their owners to Michalak headquarters in Mainz or to one of the other locations, so that TÜV (Association for Technical Inspection) can give its seal of approval.

The C7 is not just easy to assemble; it is also easy to drive. The fibre reinforced plastic bodywork drops the kerb weight by 23 percent to 620 kilograms. Even conventional **smart** engines starting with the 30 kW/41 hp Diesel right up to the Brabus power plant with 74 kW/101 hp literally have only a light load to push when powering the C7. Michalak also offers a tuning kit similar to that available for other **smart** models. This will increase the power output of the C7 to up to 80 kW/110 hp, with maximum torque peaking at 130 Nm. This kind of power would translate into sub-nine second acceleration times to 100 km/h, and allow for a theoretical top speed of 190 km/h. All of this performance is achieved while maintaining exemplary fuel consumption of just 5.2 litres per 100 kilometres and the emissions output remains distinctly on the clean side of the Euro4-Norm. More information on this and the main C7 Kit Car package are available from the UK agents Smarts R us www.thec7.co.uk

TRIKEtec Trikes

Back in 2002, at a show in Dusseldorf, Stuart Dunne saw these amazing vehicles manufactured by TRIKEtec GmbH, and they made a lasting impression on his memory. In 2005, when the opportunity arose for him to search for a business opportunity, he was amazed to see that TRIKEtec GmbH had not secured a dealer or importer in the UK. Here was his chance, and later that year he became Managing Director and founder of TRIKEtec UK, who are now the sole importers of TRIKEtec vehicles into the UK. TRIKEtec vehicles actually began life in 2000. The revolutionary designed Trike with its anti-lock brakes and traction control has already dramatically squeezed the marketplace of its competitor's vehicles in countries such as Germany, Switzerland, USA, South Africa and France.

For years, three wheeled vehicles and high performance capabilities never went hand in hand. TRIKEtec has managed to bring the power to weight ratio of a Porsche Boxster to their three wheels, but more importantly they have done it in such a way as to be able to harness that power in a totally safe way. Electronic Bosch Traction

The first complete C7 driven by Liam 2005

The gorgeous blue C7

The latest handsome version, photo courtesy of Michalak Design

Control on all TRIKEtec roadsters prevents the vehicle losing stability and traction when powering through the hairpin bends on that serious adrenalin seeking run. What's more, the Power and Traction control are just the start of the innovations at TRIKEtec. Every vehicle is equipped with Anti-Lock Braking as standard, so if you use the power and agility of the patented chassis and the Brabus engine, then you know you are going to stop safely in an emergency situation. With the higher powered vehicles the Racing Brake system is a must. Used by Rossi and Gibernau, this braking system is proven in tests to be more than twice as effective to comparable products. TRIKEtec UK will be supplying the latest state of the art, three wheeled roadsters. The imported TRIKEtec Motorcycle Trikes will come into the Chester headquarters and distribution points placed around the UK. These Motorcycle Trikes are fully compliant with all the European legislation to make them a complete road legal vehicle without the need for SVA testing. The only Trike around with anti lock brakes, electronic traction control and stability program and automatic Tiptronic transmission as standard; TRIKEtec Roadsters are the first three wheeled vehicles to include such sophisticated electronics, and are about to change the face of three wheeled vehicles forever. Built in Eschbach, South West Germany, they use both **smart** engines and electronics, so all the parts like ABS, stability and traction control and the **smarts** 6 speed gear box will be a familiar sight on the Trike. The engines fitted are 61 bhp, 82 bhp and a 41bhp diesel, all of which are turbo charged.

Besides the Trikes using **smart** technology they are relevant to this book because Smarts R us are one of the designated point of sales, and it was here on one of their photo shoots that *s2trash* and *Miss Polkadot* first saw a C2 in the flesh. At Newark in 2006 they were both lucky enough to try out two of them for size. Size being the operative word – they are massive!

If, like *Miss Polkadot* you have only been a pillion passenger before, straddling this vast work of art in chrome is a somewhat daunting experience, but one that had to be overcome for the shear thrill of the drive! The most daunting part of driving the C2 was actually having *s2trash* as a passenger, and despite having a tripod thrust into the back of her head several times, the test drive was sensational. From *s2trash's* point of view as a passenger, it was very odd; the rear seat is higher than the drivers and so one has the illusion of greater height than is actually real. Combine that with the speed and the wind in your hair and you could be the 'Hells Angel King' on a three wheeled throne! *Miss Polkadot* seems to think that the term 'Hells Passenger' might be more appropriate in *s2trash's* case! As for comfort and safety they are both excellent, the Trike soak the bumps up so well, unlike the fortwo or the roadster. The rear seat is very comfy, rather like a high quality arm chair, but at the speed this Trike can go, nodding off isn't an option despite the safety bar. Riding this Trike is just pure, unadulterated fun. It is simplicity itself as all controls are the same as the **smart**. The exception to this is that the gear selectors are on the handle bars, but they work to the same principle as the **smart** with a button for up and one for down. A two minute lesson in how to use it was all that was required, even for a novice motorcyclist like *Miss P*. The narrow front and very wide rear takes a few minutes to adjust to when going round corners, but getting to grips with the size doesn't take long.

The much larger three seater C3 was the next trike waiting to be tried out. With a member of the TRIKEtec UK staff as chauffeur, *Miss P* and *s2trash* were subjected to a ride on this vehicle at speeds they had not dared to attempt on the C2! Haring round corners, over gravel, grass and potholes, this three wheeled trike left the pair speechless in the amazingly stable way it handled. No tipping, no nasty jolts, even after driving over a large trench across the road that would have ripped the rims off a normal car, it was as if they were floating on a cushion of air. If the chance ever arises to have a test drive; grab it with both hands. The **smart** has the ability to out a smile on your face; these Trikes take that experience to a whole new level of fun! There are four models in the range, the C2 Roadster 2 seat Tourer with a choice of 61bhp petrol, 41 bhp diesel and 82 bhp petrol variants and the C3 Roadster 3 seat Tourer. All models come with an endless options list! One word of caution though, they are meant for dry weather use, so they may not be an every day mode of transport for the UK. At time of going to print there are only ten in the UK. Any of these vehicles can also be customised for riders with disabilities.

For more information call TRIKEtec UK office - 0151 357 4101 or visit www.3wr.co.uk

The C2 Trike

A groovy custom C2

The C3 Trike

9 Independent UK smart Businesses

Not long after the first **smarts** were made the UK saw the start of independent **smart** businesses forming. All of the companies either began importing cars to sell, servicing and modifying them and or selling bling and parts for folks to do self modification. Eight years down the line, the UK is fairly well served by such companies and for many people on tight budgets they have been a godsend, particularly on the car servicing front as the prices at DCUK **smart** dealerships tend to be a lot higher. If an owner wants to take the modifying route, these independent companies can do the work DCUK **smart** centres just do not do and they have developed many specialist parts that we now take for granted.

Smartechnique

It is fair to say that they are the oldest UK independents, having first formed in early 1999, that are still up and running. Smartechnique do everything from modifying, servicing to second hand **smart** sales. This was the first independent company *s2trash* ever looked round, and what an eye opener it was with so many different custom wheels and parts to choose from. As a company, they appear mainly at the larger **smart** events and many of you reading this might not have heard of them, but some of their cars have been the best modified cars, in terms of quality.

Smartechnique - Chiswick Office - 91 Wellesley Road, London W4 3AT. Tel: 020 8995 3837

Smartechnique - Swiss Cottage Office - 59-65 Belsize Road, London NW6 4BE. Tel: 020 7604 3456

www.smartechnique.co.uk

Southeast Smart Centre

The Southeast Smart Centre, founded in 2001, is the place where *s2trash* ordered and bought his beloved car. Very much a family affair, the Southeast Smart Centre was one of the very first businesses to offer the **smart** fortwo for sale in the UK. The centre has a bright and cheery bijou showroom, sells new and used **smarts** and is fully equipped to provide the reassurance of total after-sales support, including servicing, the supply and fitting of any of the extensive range of optional accessories, plus any warranty work that may be required. The main office is a 19th century building that has a charm all of its own. *S2trash* has bought several **smart** parts from them and found them very accommodating. Their one claim to fame is that they were probably the first garage in the UK to re-build a car using a new tridion safety cell, after a customers car had rolled down a bank after the owner left the hand brake off.

Southeast Smart Centre - Rye Garage, Rye Lane, Dunton Green, Sevenoaks, Kent TN14 5HD. Tel: 01732 450890

www.thesmartcar.com

Two of Smartechnique's cars at Billing 2004

Southeast Smart Centre

Sussex Cars

They call themselves the company with the cuddle factor, but having been on the Smartball Charity Run with both Andrew Shipp and Gary Stevens in 2005 to Blackpool and back, *s2trash* reckons its best to give the cuddle a miss! Only joking! Sussex Cars were the back up guys if there were mechanical problems with cars on the run, providing their van, trailer and facilities free of charge. They are actually great people and very helpful. As a company, they offer parts, accessories, styling, performance and tuning, servicing, along with terrific custom built cars. They are very friendly and go out of their way with help and advice. They are stockists for such companies as Ms Design Body Kits, Michalak Design, EBC, Eibach and Blindschleiche Exhausts to name but a few and also stock new and second hand **smarts**.

Sussex Cars - 3 North Lane, East Preston, West Sussex BN16 1BN. Tel: 01903 784784

www.sussexcars.com

Smartarse Design Ltd

Smartarse Design have saved both our hides on several occasions; from ruined water pumps to blown turbos, in fact, if it wasn't for Sasho and Dave Murphy the spotty duo would never have made their trip to Hambach. Smartarse Design was set up by Paul and David Murphy during the latter part of 2000, in Romsey, Hampshire. Growing from strength to strength, they opened a second workshop in Somerset with Paul Woolley in 2005. As sometimes happens with new ventures the overall situation didn't gel, and they parted company and closed the Somerset branch. However, in early 2006, Paul and David Murphy opened another branch in Watford, London, which is run by Rob Baker (*s2Eagleye*), passionate owner of the 'Red **Smart** with Wings'. Both premises have full workshops with diagnostic equipment and have been known to help out **smart** dealerships when they have been landed with troublesome cars. They offer a wide range of services from all types of performance enhancement and engine re-builds, vinyl customising, engine diagnostics, to MOT's and general servicing, which is acknowledged by **smart** so allowing them to carry out warranty work. They also sell pre-owned **smarts** and offer a finding and selling service from their database. They work closely with Janspeed and together have produced some amazing exhaust systems and collaborated with Pipercross to develop a **smart** specific performance air filter. They also retail a wider range of nice shiny bling along with goods from such companies as S-mann, SW Exclusive, Kahn, Millennium, Eibach and Michalak. Whilst the car is being serviced each premises offers facilities to while away the time. As with all the other independents they never talk down to the girls and everyone is treated the same; with all aspects of the work being shown and talked through as it is carried out.

Smartarse Design Ltd - Unit 6, Wynford Farm Industrial Estate, Belbins, Romsey,

Hants SO51 0PW

Tel: 01794 367878

Smartarse Design Ltd - Unit 2b, Blueprint Commercial Centre, Imperial Way,

Watford WD24 4JP. Tel: 01923 288199

www.smartarsedesign.com

Andrew Shipp of Sussex Cars

Smartarse Design

Wellsmart

After parting with Smartarse Design, Paul Woolley re-opened as Wellsmart in 2005, at the same location in Wells, Somerset. Not long after opening he was joined by Kate (*lil.smartie*) and Gav, (the mechanic with the lovely lilting voice and a glint in his eye), who had come from a newly opened and recently defunct, second premises belonging to Smarts R us.

As the youngest of the big three companies in the UK, they too grow from strength to strength and now own the Digitec ECU re-mapping system, allowing them to offer re-maps for all **smart** models. They work closely with David Webber from Smart-Suits who has produced some completely stunning custom re-sprays on **smart** cars, and was probably singularly responsible for the rise in popularity of **smarts** being sprayed with glittery paint!

They sell custom made steel and aluminium heater vents, paddles for the paddle-shift wheel, other internal shiny bits and custom rear valances, including various makes of alloy wheels and tyres, have full diagnostic and servicing facilities, recondition engines, sell pre-owned **smarts** with warranties, and specialise in accident repairs. They are a super group of people whose permanent smiles always put you at your ease, and nothing is ever too much trouble. They also made the first right hand diesel fortwo ever to be produced, many of whom have said that this could never be done. This was certainly a world's first for Wellsmart and the UK **smart** scene!

Wellsmart - Units 14-15, Lodge Hill Industrial Estate, Station Road, Westbury-sub-Mendip
Wells, Somerset BA5 1EY. Tel: 01749 871178
www.wellsmart.co.uk

Smarts R us

Paul Holmes and Liam Wilkinson, both with a family background in the motor trade and life-long car fanatics, met each other 15 years ago through mutual friends and became very good buddies. They formed the company in 2002, after a chance viewing of a **smart** in a German tuning magazine, which blew them away and they realised it was something the Brits would love. From humble beginnings Smarts R us has become a nine strong team with a super showroom and garage and a forecourt full of cars. They both have a great sense of humour and immediately put their customers at their ease. They do a lot of mail order, not just to the UK, but Canada and the Middle East. Their web site has up to 7000 hits a week from all over the world! They are the UK stockist for the amazing Michalak C7 Kit Car and are able to supply the customer the C7 in kit form or a full build if requested. They have invested heavily in a top spec paint booth, allowing them to produce some of the most fantastic **smart** car re-sprays around, several of which can be seen in this book. They also stockists for the Clever End extension (as seen on *Drageron's* and the Smartimes car), TRIKEtec Trikes and many other products such as their own brand Evil Twin, Konigseder, Lester, Lorinser, Michalak Design, Mister Dot Com, RS-Parts, and S-mann. You get the idea, the range of accessories is vast. Again, as with the other independents they have full diagnostic equipment and offer servicing, repairs, MOT's, re-sprays and re-builds.

Smarts R us - Unit 12, Easter Park, Lenton Lane, Nottingham NG7 2PX Tel: 0115 9567896
www.smartsrus.com email - sales@smartsrus.com

Kate and Paul from Wellsmart

Smarts R us showroom at Nottingham

SmartSport Ltd

Formally known as **Blindschleiche** exhausts - this company, producing some of the most beautifully designed and high quality stainless steel **smart** exhausts around, was started by Andy Peace back in 2002. Amusingly renowned as the company with the brand name that nobody could ever pronounce, we can now reveal just how the linguistic tongue twister initially came about. We only got to the bottom of this at when we met up with Andy at the Newark 'smartbeat' camping weekend in 2006. With a bit of arm twisting we persuaded Andy to come clean with that unpronounceable name. Apparently, while over in Germany with friends and feeling slightly the worse for wear after visiting a beer festival, Andy got chatting to some of his German friends about his new venture producing performance enhancing exhausts and that he needed to think up for a name for his new company. With brains cells fuelled with alcohol the word 'Blindschleiche' was muttered. It sounded good, but not speaking German he asked what on earth it meant. With his companions rolling around on the floor in howls of laughter they told him it actually meant 'Slow Worm'. Immediately seeing the funny side of this, as his exhausts were supposed to increase speed and a slow worm is, well, slow; he thought it was a perfect name, and decided to adopt it with immediate effect, but with the German spelling. Although Andy sold the company at the start of 2006, to Richard Hickman, a well known manufacturer of metal parts, he is still around on the **smart** scene and Richard continues to carry on the top quality work set by its original owner. As with any product there are always discussions over who makes the best, but slow worms definitely have a loyal fan base here in the UK. Smartsport make stainless steel exhausts and rear valances for all models of **smart**; fortwo, roadster and forfour.

SmartSport Ltd - 7 Wise Street, Leamington Spa, CV31 3AP . Tel: 07921 398736

www.smartsport.co.uk

C.H.A.L.K.Y Engineering

This little cottage industry all came about when Dave White did not like the solid door pockets on his **smart** pure. Dave was originally going to replace them with the standard net pockets but then thought he would try and design one himself, working along the lines of the solid one, but with a much flatter shape. The design was taken to a company that made stainless steel sinks and they produced his design using waste material from their sink production. As with anything different that appears on the **smart** scene, they were soon spotted on his car and he had several orders from those who wanted some too. This gave him the idea of setting up a small business making **smart** parts with slightly more unusual design appeal. Custom rear valances were soon added to his list of re-designed parts, and like all of his products they are made as limited runs. His list of parts includes Alloy heater knob covers, stainless steel gear shift discs; stainless steel fascia cover, **smart** fortwo and roadster dump valve medication inserts (a very clever gadget to make the dump valve work more efficiently and save damage). Dave produces all of the aluminium parts himself on his own lathes, so even if you want a one-off item, Dave is the man who can do it for you. He has many more products available which can be found on the E-Bay auction site, where he sells his products under the User name C_H_A_L_K_Y.

Tel: 07738 099604 for details.

Mr Blindschleiche himself – Andy Peace

CHALKY heat shield and bull bars

Flying the flag

Stephen Goddard – Mr Smartimes

SW Exclusive

Although this company has its base in Germany, its extensive range of performance parts, re-maps and tuning have become so popular in the UK, that they are now available here via their new on-line store, and utilise fitting centres such as Smartarse Design Ltd, Smarts R us and Cambridge Smarts to carry out their work. You only have to glance through the list of modifications on cars in our Customised chapter to see what we mean. Since 1998, SW Exclusive has been developing its own brand of tuning and performance parts. These include springs, sports clutch, turbos, filters, exhausts, wheels, tuning and re-maps, which are professionally tested at the Nurburgring and Hockenheim race circuits which are local to their development headquarters in Wiesbaden, Germany.
For more information e-mail info@sw-exclusive.co.uk or check out their website: www.sw-exclusive.co.uk and www.sw-exclusive.de

There are many other companies out in the **smart** world and we have only just touched the tip of the iceberg, concentrating on companies we have used or ones we will feel have some historical interest. The following company, although not selling **smart** products, has been fundamental to the rise in the **smart's** popularity in this country. It has not only provided **smart** owners with abundant information about the cars, it has brought together a tight knit community of wonderful like minded people willing to divulge their innovations, modifications, thrills and spills, mammoth journeys, charity do's, diaries and 'Get together's' for all to share; in a way that inspires new owners to want to join this mad **smart** scene. If it wasn't for Steve Goddard and the tireless effort he puts into this publication, *Miss P* would never have trodden the rocky road of writing and supplying him with articles; and likewise *s2trash* would not have been Smartimes official photographer.
So praise be for Smartimes, for without it this book just wouldn't exist!

Smartimes Magazine

Founded by Steve Goddard (*Massive*) with the support of a few like minded **smart** enthusiasts, the first printed issue hit the streets in spring 2003. It was then and still is, the UK's *only* **smart** car magazine. The initial plan was to publish three issues a year and to involve all the **smart** club members by getting them to submit written articles, photos, stories and' How to' information regarding anything **smart** related. The first issue had a 'How to: De-lip your Air intake and replace your air filter'. *Miss Polkadot* and *s2trash* have contributed something to every publication to date except the very first issue. The first ten issues were in print form but with rising costs and being non profit making, the spring 2006 issue was released as a 'view online' or downloadable magazine via the internet. Out of the two, *s2trash* was the first to get involved with the magazine after meeting Steve at the 'Badgers Mount' meet in Kent and offering to help with some of the photography. *Miss Polkadot* first submitted a photo of her car accompanied with a poem about her spotty **smart** in the second issue. The third issue, winter 2003, saw *s2trash's* first pictures go into print and another poem by *Miss Polkadot* about the London to Brighton run. Always beavering away in the background is Steve's wife Karen, often standing out in the wind and rain at meets selling or promoting the magazine with a smile, even when Steve wanders off on his little chats with owners, leaving her alone to deal with enquires. One of Steve's trusty right hand men is Roger Broome, the long suffering proof reader and all round nice guy. Today Smartimes is a truly global magazine with contributors from all parts of the worldwide **smart** community including; Canada, South Africa, Europe, Australia, Hong Kong and now the USA, covering every thing **smart** you could wish to read about. Unfortunately, just as this book is going to print we have learned that Steve is no longer able to carry on his sterling work of producing Smartimes, however the website will be kept running and all the back issues will be available to download.
www.smartimes.co.uk

...and finally

Spotty Badger Productions
Well, we wouldn't be here if it wasn't for **smarts**.
Mix one off beat Photographer from the land of the Norman conquests and a Graphic Designer who lives in the middle of a marsh, (who oddly has the surname Saltmarsh), and you have the producers of the **smart** car calendar and authors of this collection of **smart** stuff!
This book only has a finite number of pages and so the **smart** scene and all that it entails has had to be condensed to fit within these few pages. This has enabled us to only give you just a taster of our personal **smart** experiences but we hope that it has wet your appetite enough to entice you to join a local club, visit a **smart** rally and experience the enjoyment of meeting other enthusiastic owners and maybe persuade you to make a few modifications to your own **smart**. Like we said at the beginning of this book, **smarts** have a lot to answer for as far as we are concerned; they really have changed our lives and we love and will continue to love every minute we spend with them and their fabulous owners.
Miss Polkadot and s2trash

133

10 Monthly Meets

Go on any **smart** car website forum and under the Meetings and Events section you will see that there are many meets held across the UK every month. They can vary greatly in the attendance numbers from just a few to the high thirties. The first one *s2trash* went to was the original Kent Meet when it was held at The Badgers Mount pub, near Halstead in Kent. Badgers Mount is quite an apt name all things considered. His first trip up there from Battle was in August 2002 and true to form he got lost; so lost in fact that he ended up going to four other pubs and driving around for fifty minutes before finally spotting a pub with over 30 **smarts** in the car park. Pulling in was rather a rather daunting experience, especially parking up close to so many obviously modified cars with a totally standard one. Worrying about what to do next and who to talk to, he thought about turning round and driving home. He thought about getting out having a fag then driving home; or alternatively getting out going to bar having a drink and fag and then going home. Decisions, decisions. Finally plucking up some courage from heaven knows where, *s2trash* decided to at least look round at some of the other cars and maybe say hello to somebody. Standing in the car park with his drink he was approached by a lovely lady called Debbie Moss, who sadly is no longer with us, and was immediately made to feel welcome. Having turned up with a new Mk 6 pure, people soon started to stop and have a look round his car, as the new right hand drive **smart** was a bit of a novelty and at that time not many had yet been seen. It didn't take many minutes before *s2trash* was chatting nineteen to the dozen, and inflicting himself on many more of their meets. The Kent Meet is still going but is now held in two different locations. The moral of this little tale is not to be afraid to go along to a local meet, as you will find everyone very friendly and welcoming. So what happens at meets? Well, for starters, the poor pub that has been chosen as the venue for the meet will get invaded once a month by a bunch of looney **smart** car owners, often craving food all at the same time. Most monthly meets are held on a weekday evening, but will often organise other social activities at the weekends so that those unable to attend the weekday gatherings get an opportunity to go along too. It is a great way to meet new friends and fellow owners and learn a wealth of information about the **smart** car. You can find out where to get a service, how to fix some problems, (often with people fixing then for you in the car park); we have seen anything from panel changes to dump valves being fitted in car parks, as well as re-maps. Car clubs are not everybody's cup of tea and what they get up to varies from club to club, but none of them are stuffy occasions with minute taking you can be rest assured. If you have a partner who isn't really into cars but just tagging along, they probably wouldn't get bored because unlike many other car clubs the ratio of female to male owners is often on an equal footing. The conversation can run from lip gloss to spark plugs with folks from all walks of life, there is never a dull moment. The best thing is to go to one and see what you think; you will be pleasantly surprised just how much fun it can be. Not long after getting his own **smart,** *s2trash* started his own meet at The Mermaid Pub on the seafront at Bexhill-on-Sea. This, until very recently, had become a bit of a one man event, due to the cock-ups, too numerous to mention, regarding the organising of said Mermaid Meet. Lack of attendees could be put down to apathy along the coast, but *Miss Polkadot* would like to let you in on the fact that most of the time *s2trash* turned up at the right time on the wrong day, or the wrong time on the right day and going home and missing everyone! On one occasion in the middle of winter, and this time the day and time were correct, he sat all alone in his car with a thick sea fog rolling in; very much like a scene from the Steven King film 'The Fog', waiting for people to turn up. They didn't, and he went home with the hump thinking...'is it me?' The Mermaid Meet lasted until *s2trash* had to stop driving, whereupon he conveniently moved it to Battle for a few months, and which was within walking distance for him. In November 2006 he reformed the old Bexhill/Battle Meet at a new location. It is now held at a hotel in Whatlington, East Sussex which dates back to the 15th century, but luckily the beer doesn't! Hopefully this will be take off and be frequented by East Sussex and Kent owners too.

Miss Polkadot helps run the Essex Smarties Meet, held at The Six Bells pub in Boreham, Essex. Originally started up by *Bulldog* in 2002 at a different location, it failed to attract many owners and fizzled out. When *Miss P* bought her car in early 2003 she looked around for a local meet to her and finally contacted *Bulldog* and persuaded him to resurrect the meet again. The Essex Smarties have now gone from strength to strength and members can always be found attending and supporting the more national **smart** events, particularly the Billing, Beach Party and London to Brighton gatherings. Infamous Essex Smarties include *Sally Sweet Pea* (she owned the S6 Pea **smart** covered in green peas...don't ask why she had peas, she doesn't really know herself!), *Funkymonkey* who has owned every variant of **smart** you can possibly get, *Magnet* who owns a roadster with the wonderful number pate S44 4RT, *Junglebunnies* who have a numeric blue fortwo full of stuffed animals and make their journey to the meet all the way from Tunbridge Wells, *Mr.T* who now owns two fortwos (one for each foot), and *Amber* who was one of the first people in the country to have their car sprayed with holographic glitter; to name but a few.

When we started to write this book we both thought it would be a good idea to take in a long standing large meet that we had never been to. So, off we went to the Donni Meet held at the Donnington Park Race Track at Castle Donnington. Although it was a nippy Sunday in May, there was a good turnout of cars and a chance to catch up with people that we usually only get to see once a year at other annual **smart** events. People such as: *Smartie, Batman, Otisb, Mad Max* and *Vladaria*.

As luck would have it, the café wasn't serving food that day so gannet face (*s2trash*) got the hump and seriously contemplated cannibalism. It is a great location for a meet and as it is held a Sunday afternoon it attracts good numbers.

Here is a small selection of more regular meets that occur around the country. Do check on the website forums for other clubs that may be more local to you, because venues and times can vary.

The Battle Meet (s2trash)

Second Monday in the month from 8pm

Leeford Place Hotel, Leeford Place, Whatlington Road, Battle, East Sussex TN33 0ND

Essex Smarties Smart Car Club (Miss Polkadot)

Second Tuesday in every month around 8pm - without fail

www.essexsmarties.co.uk

The Six Bells, Main Road (B1137), Boreham, Essex CM3 3JE

E.A.S.T East Anglian Smart Tribe

Cambridge Meet variable meet times – Check website for meeting venues and times

www.eastsmart.co.uk

Donni Meet

Meet on a Sunday – check www.smartmaniacs.co.uk for up to date details

Hoggs Lodge Bi-Monthly Meet

Check www.smartmaniacs.co.uk for up to date details

1 Second Tuesday in the month at:

The Old Forge, Main Rd, Otterbourne, Winchester, Hampshire, SO21 2EE

2 Last Tuesday in the month atThe Hoggs Lodge, London Road, Clanfield, Waterlooville PO8 0QD

Kent — Bi-Monthly Meet

Check www.smartmaniacs.co.uk for up to date details

1 First Tuesday in the month - The Wharf Galleon Boulevard, Dartford, Kent DA2 6SL

2 Last Tuesday in the month - The Woodman, Goathurst Common, Ide Hill, Sevenoaks, Kent TN14 6BU

The Essex Smarties Meet at The Six Bells

The Kent meet at Badger's Mount

The Donni Meet at Donnington Park race track

Essex Smarties

We are the Essex Smarties
Together or apart
We are a happy bunch of folk
And we all love our Smarts.

There are yellow ones and silver ones
Red, green, purple, blue
There's scratchy, dotty, pea-green ones
And aqua orange too!

The colours, they are all sorts
And the insides just the same
And every little Smartie has
It's own exclusive name!

We really love our Smarties
We're a happy little club
We meet one Tuesday every month
At 'The 6 Bells', Boreham, pub!

ESSEX SMARTIES SMART CAR CLUB

THE One to be seen at!

© Miss Polkadot 2004

137

11 Smart Website Clubs

'People who do not drive blancmange shaped Euro boxes have a tendency to be natural born anarchists or extraverts', a quote once made by *Vladaria* of Smartmaniacs, and which could be a good general description of **smart** car owners and website forums users. There are many websites around on the internet now, but back in the day when both *s2trash* and *Miss P* became owners, around 2002-2003, they were very few and far between, the main two being Funkysmart and thesmartclub. All the website based clubs differ from one another in both graphic presentation and personal style of running. Some are very strict on advertising and will not allow it unless you are a site sponsor, while others have a free section to self promote. What they all share in common is that they are free to join, they welcome new owners, (or 'Newbies' as they are affectionately called throughout all of the website clubs), allowing all who visit the sites access to a wealth of **smart** information. If, for instance you were to post up a question on a forum as to what size tyre was required for the rear of a fortwo, you could guarantee an answer within five minutes, whether it came from a site official, moderator or from another **smart** owner who happened to be perusing the forums. Technical information that some **smart** dealers cannot always divulge for one reason or another, can also be guaranteed to be answered on the forums within time. It is not uncommon for details of car changes, including spy shots or new models to be announced on website clubs first, as there are users out there with a knack of getting their grubby hands on this information even before its official release! It has been hinted at that **smart** themselves keep an eye on the websites forums to get up to date with what is going on! If you want to know what is going on, all of the websites have a Meetings section; covering topics from local meets to international gatherings, and charity events too, where you can have a great drive out and do some good at the same time. There are always general and 'how-to-fix-this' sections, along with non-**smart** areas where folks are allowed to discuss all sorts of topics, have a good rant and get the chance to put the world to rights. Some debates can and often get over-heated, and are normally about subjects that have nothing to do with **smart** cars at all. Luckily, website clubs have poor, unpaid moderators, who give up their free time to police the forums and try to keep love, peace and harmony amongst the masses. Most amusingly, *s2trash* was a moderator for a short time, but he ended up being the most moderated user on the site he helped on and so he thought it best to step down from his position before he got deleted! Chat rooms have been added to some websites and these are a free for all; they remain un-moderated and can be very funny places to be and have a laugh. Needless to say *s2trash* has been known to lurk in there from time to time...

Yahoo had the first website forum in the UK called The Smart Club UK, (not to be confused with thesmartclub), which started back on the April 26th 1999 and it is still going. Many other sites have come and gone; come back again and then vanished, whilst others have grown to such a size they are now limited companies.

thesmartclub

Without doubt, thesmartclub is the biggest website **smart** club in the UK and maybe the world, with their membership hovering around 23,000. However, most clubs do not remove users who no longer visit the sites and so actual regular user figures could be significantly reduced. Founded by Al Young in July 2000, it was the first website club to become a limited company in 2004. It was founded to provide UK owners of **smart** cars with an internet based source of totally independent advice and information about their car. This premise quickly expanded to provide members with the ability to 'share experiences, knowledge and co-ordinate local meetings, and to provide the best, impartial, central sources of information, parts, help and advice on 'all things **smart**'. Within a matter of months of going online, thesmartclub had dozens of members in countries within continental Europe and now has members in 51 countries around the world. Their club secretary continues to receive new membership applications at the rate of 14 per day; seven days a week and, according to their statistics, over 69% of all UK **smart** car owners are already members of thesmartclub. It is the only independent club for **smart** cars to be formally recognized by, and affiliated with DaimlerChryslerUK. Administered in Edinburgh, UK, thesmartclub is 100% independent and supported by a team of dedicated individuals around the world. Over 99% of their members around the world communicate 'online' via thesmartclub web site; 4.8% of the membership do not yet own a **smart** and thesmartclub's statistics indicate that 7.1% of members purchased a **smart** as a direct result of the information provided via their website. Their website currently attracts over 12,200 unique visitors each day (approximately 50,000 daily hits) to share their knowledge and view the latest topics in a variety of forums.

Because the site has got so large, it costs a fair amount of money to run efficiently, which it receives through company sponsorship, advertising their Privilege card scheme and the sale of club merchandise. This in turn tends to give the site a more corporate feel. Having spoken to other large website clubs, the situation is a catch 22 thing. As more folks join, the bandwidth increases and costs rise. To keep the sites free to join and prevent those running it from footing the bills, as most were initially started and run from a home environment, this obviously has to be the way forward.

www.thesmartclub.com - Email - admin@thesmartclub.com

Smartmaniacs

This website was originally known as Funkysmart. It has since undergone some major changes but was primarily set up by **smart** owner Dave Kaye (*Mr Funkysmart*) in 2002, after he decided that he wanted to join a site that was a little more light-hearted than some around at the time, but couldn't find one. Membership wise it had lower numbers than thesmartclub, but nether the less it had a very dedicated following. As the amount of visitors to the site and the actual membership grew, Funkysmart's size, just like thesmartclub, started to become an issue. A form of revenue was needed to pay for the extra bandwidth required to continue running the site as the high volume of users was now overloading the system. Companies paid for advertising banners and later on an Aviators discount card was introduced for a small fee, giving members' discounts from certain **smart** related companies.

Sadly, after the Billing Aquadrome camping rally in 2005 Dave had to step down from his involvement with Funkysmart. Other business ventures were playing a more prominent role in his life and as Dave couldn't commit to the website as much as he wanted too, he decided to fold Funkysmart. There were many upset and shocked members at this news, particularly as it all happened in such a short space of time. However, all was not lost, as like the phoenix from the flames; the site arose bearing a new name and a new leader. *Vladaria*, who had been an early member of Funkysmart, persuaded Dave to give her access to the website itself, along with all forums and membership data, so that she could carry on with the site where he had left off. In September 2005 Smartmaniacs was born. For anyone who had been away, it all looked and worked the same way as before, just a different name. As with all take-overs, there were a few teething problems, but within time it all settled down, and is still as popular as it ever was. These days, Smartmaniacs is a very busy site, often outdoing thesmartclub with the number of site visitors.
www.smartmaniacs.co.uk - Email - mail@smartmaniacs.co.uk

Smart Mania & Smartz

Both of these sites are very active but not on the scale as some of the others. SmartzPlanet Smart Car Club was the first to be formed in October 2004 and Smart Mania September 2005. There is nothing wrong with smaller sites, in fact they can often be quicker to use if you need to look something up in a hurry and some people find their size less daunting and will post on them rather than the bigger ones. What you may notice is that the same user names crop up on different sites, as some people will register on every site that there is going. One down side to this is that the same posts can appear on all the sites. For those who flit from site to site this can be annoying, but for the ones who stay on their one favourite site all the time they benefit due to not having to surf the web so much, so it swings and roundabouts. Another anomaly is that some people registered with a different user name on each site, making things a tad confusing when you actually get to meet them as you think they are one person and they turn out to be another!

S2crew

If you read the members names on many of the sites you may see some user names starting with s2, i.e. *s2trash*. These are old members from the s2crew. This was an exclusive little club for those with modified cars only and which ran from 2001 to 2006. Joining was by invitation only and everyone was given a special s2 user name. There were a few members who didn't use their special user name such as *Miss Polkadot*, who would have been s2Dot, as she wanted to remain using her same name throughout all of the website clubs. Several of the members managed to find personalised number plates with the S2 prefix and letters to match their user name, such as S2 SYT, belonging to Stephen White, nicknamed YT.

The s2crew was one of the forums that came and went, came back and went again due to different personalities within the club, but in it's hey day it had the members with the most radical cars and quite often radical views, and is now sadly missed. They have kindly left a lasting momento of their existence with an internet message for all to read. If you type http://p068.ezboard.com/bs2crew into an internet search engine you will get the message 'so long and thanks for all the fish - s2crew woz ere 2001-2006'.

Evilution

We are going to finish off with one of the best individually owned sites - www.evilution.co.uk

A man of strong mind and strong views *Evilution* wanted a site that was sponsor free and aimed more at car related topics rather than reading about the goings on from the previous night's television or news about whose gold fish had just died. The Evilution site originally went live in March 2004 and the updated PHP based site followed on in Feb 2006. With the expert IT help of Mrs Evilution (*Kat*) and contributions from other owners and online users, they have put together one very good site indeed. This fantastic website, full of technical help, tips, parts guide and how-to topics complete with photographs, emerged at the right moment, filling a gap that needed to be plugged. He even has the technical know how to be able to design and manufacture his own modified components. Evilution has been offered sponsorship for his site, but to keep it in the manner he set it up in, he has kindly refused, preferring to foot the bills himself and keep his true faith.

www.evilution.co.uk

With the largest sites taken care of, there are many more we could talk about next, but with many county **smart** club meets starting their own website forums this could be another book in itself; so we have decided to list as many as we can for you to explore on your own.

Smart Car Clubs/Websites

Listed below are some of the **smart** car websites from the UK and around the world. They do vary greatly, but all make interesting viewing, so when you get a spare moment on your PC or laptop have a look around.

www.thesmartclub.com www.smartmaniacs.co.uk www.smartmania.co.uk www.smartz.co.uk www.evilution.co.uk www.sussexsmarts.co.uk www.fq101.co.uk www.nwsmarties.co.uk www.essexsmarties.co.uk www.t1ny.com www.theroadster.net www.talksmartcar.com www.clubsmartcar.ca www.smartcarforums.com www.aussiesmarts.com www.smart-roadster-board.de www.smartcarofamerica.com www.smartmania.gr www.smartforum.nl www.smart-club-niedersachsen.de www.setbb.com www.smartupfrance.com www.mysmart.ru www.smarter.pl

Dave Kaye – Mr Funkysmart

Funkysmart moderators

Smartmaniacs web mistress Vladaria

Evilution and Kat

IN EVERLASTING
REMEMBRANCE OF
MARION
THE BELOVED WIFE OF
HORACE HEDLEY GATES
CALLED TO THE HIGHER LIFE
24TH JUNE 1928

THE MEMORY OF THE JUST
IS BLESSED

SO OF HORACE HEDLEY GATES
WHO FOLLOWED 23RD NOV

12 The New Generation smart

This new G3 **smart**, photo courtesy of the Daimler Chrysler Media Archive (and enhanced by *s2trash*), shows the new face of the **smart** car, and gives serious modifiers a brand new toy to play with!

Acknowledgements

We have had a lot of help along the way with this book and would personally like to thank all of the following and every **smart** owner who took the time out to allow us to photograph their cars – particularly those who turned up for the Lindisfarne shoot

Al Young - thesmartclub

All of the old s2crew

Andy Peace - Mr Blindschleiche

Bat - for modelling for the front cover

Bigperformance

Brabus

Brabusmatt

Bubski

Campbell McCutcheon - Messerschmitt Owner

Clementine Wells RBLI

Coolfart

DaimlerChrysler Media Archive

Dave Webber

David Robinson

Debbie Hull and Sheena Hamilton (DCUK)

Drageron

Essex Police

Essex Smarties

Evilution

Fq101

Fudge – Cambridge Smart Cars

Hogster

Importedsam_123

Jamie Beveridge

Kym1959

Leeford Place Hotel Battle, East Sussex

Lil.smartie

Mccsmartarse

Meknoy - for loan of his Kinder Egg smarts

Michalak Design – C7

Miss Polkadot's Cappuccino maker

Miss Radley and Besty

NeilOs

Nicola Callow - Smartmaniacs

Ocean Yachts, Battle

Paul Sedgewick

Racingsnake

RichG

s2Eagleye

s2gtmracing

s2stealth

Sally Sweet Pea

S-mann

Smart Centre – Saarbrücken, Germany

Smart GmbH for the use of the smart logo

Smart of Lakeside

Smart of Milton Keynes

Smart owners everywhere

Smartarse Design

Smartechnique

Smartimes

Smartmania

Smarts R us

Smartypartfast – Smart of Hertford

Smartzplanet

Southeast Smart Centre

Stuart Dunne –TRIKEtec UK

Sussex Branch

Sussex Cars

The Ace Café, London

The Crawford family

The De La Warr Pavilion, Bexhill-on-Sea

The Saltmarsh family

TracyB

Ulrike Bianchi from Smartville, Hambach, France

Vermaak

Warbird

Wellsmart

Wikipedia

Ye Olde Café, Battle